THE BEHAVIORALLY INFORMED ORGANIZATION

Behaviourally Informed
Organizations

BEHAVIOURALLY INFORMED
ORGANIZATIONS

To date, there has been a lack of practical advice for organizations based on behavioural research. The Behaviourally Informed Organizations series fills this knowledge gap with a strategic perspective on how governments, businesses, and other organizations have embedded behavioural insights into their operations. The series is rooted in work by academics and practitioners co-creating knowledge via the Behaviourally Informed Organizations Partnership (www.biorgpartnership.com), and is written in a highly accessible style to highlight key ideas, pragmatic frameworks, and prescriptive outcomes based on illustrative case studies.

The Behaviorally Informed Organization

EDITED BY DILIP SOMAN AND
CATHERINE YEUNG

WITH A FOREWORD BY CASS R. SUNSTEIN

UNIVERSITY OF TORONTO PRESS
Toronto Buffalo London

Rotman-UTP Publishing
An imprint of University of Toronto Press
Toronto Buffalo London
utorontopress.com

Library and Archives Canada Cataloguing in Publication

Title: The behaviorally informed organization / edited by Dilip Soman and Catherine Yeung ; with a foreword by Cass Sunstein.
Names: Soman, Dilip, editor. | Yeung, Catherine, 1976– editor.
Description: Series statement: Behaviourally informed organizations | Includes bibliographical references.
Identifiers: Canadiana (print) 20200344285 | Canadiana (ebook) 20200344439 | ISBN 9781487507893 (cloth) | ISBN 9781487537173 (EPUB) | ISBN 9781487537166 (PDF)
Subjects: LCSH: Organizational behavior – Case studies. | LCSH: Organizational change – Case studies. | LCSH: Human behavior – Case studies. | LCSH: Psychology, Industrial – Case studies.
Classification: LCC HD58.7 .B456 2021 | DDC 302.3/5 – dc23

ISBN 978-1-4875-0789-3 (cloth)
ISBN 978-1-4875-3717-3 (EPUB)
ISBN 978-1-4875-3716-6 (PDF)

We acknowledge the financial support of the Government of Canada, the Canada Council for the Arts, and the Ontario Arts Council, an agency of the Government of Ontario, for our publishing activities.

**Canada Council   Conseil des Arts
for the Arts   du Canada**

ONTARIO ARTS COUNCIL
CONSEIL DES ARTS DE L'ONTARIO
an Ontario government agency
un organisme du gouvernement de l'Ontario

Funded by the   Financé par le
Government   gouvernement
of Canada   du Canada

Contents

Acknowledgments

The co-editors thank all the members of the Behaviourally Informed Organizations partnership (biorgpartnership.com) housed at the Behavioural Economics in Action at Rotman (BEAR) research center for their many comments and suggestions on the manuscript. Special thanks are given to the founding project manager, Melanie Kim, and to BEAR team members Bing Feng, Matthew Hilchey, Liz Kang, Aki Kim, Cindy Luo, and Renante Rondina for assisting with project coordination and preparation of the manuscript. This book project is funded by BEAR, and by a grant from the Social Sciences and Humanities Research Council of Canada (SSHRC), and we are grateful for their support.

The Foreword draws upon a brief essay: Sunstein, C.R. (2014). Nudging: A Very Short Guide. *Journal of Consumer Policy, 37*, 583–8. Available at https://doi.org/10.1007/s10603-014-9273-1. The material is used with permission of the publisher.

The material in chapter 2 is an expanded and revised version of an earlier report: Feng, B., Oyunsuren, J., Tymko, M., Kim, M., and Soman, D. (2018). *How Should Organizations Best Embed and Harness Behavioural Insights? A Playbook*. Toronto: Behavioural Economics in Action at Rotman (BEAR) Report Series. Available at http://www.rotman.utoronto.ca/bear. The authors thank BEAR for permission to use materials from the report in this chapter.

The material in chapter 5 is based on a report: Soman, D., Cowen, D., Kannan, N., and Feng, B. (2019). *Seeing Sludge: Towards a Dashboard to Help Organizations Recognize Impedance to End-User Decisions and Action*. Toronto: Behavioural Economics in Action at Rotman (BEAR) Report Series. Available at http://www.rotman.utoronto .ca/bear. The authors thank BEAR for permission to use materials from the report in this chapter.

The author of chapter 7 thanks Ken Whitehurst, executive director, Consumers Council of Canada (CCC), for his excellent comments on earlier drafts of this chapter; and Jay Jackson, also of CCC, for his encouragement and assistance with the research on the boundedly rational consumer over the past twelve years.

The material in chapter 13 is an expanded and revised version of an earlier report: Kim, M., Ly, K., and Soman, D. (2015). *A Behavioural Lens on Consumer Privacy*. Toronto: Behavioural Economics in Action at Rotman (BEAR) Report Series. Available at http://www.rotman .utoronto.ca/bear. The authors thank BEAR for permission to use materials from the report in this chapter.

Foreword: A Very Short Guide to Nudging

Cass R. Sunstein

Some policies take the form of *mandates* and *bans*. For example, the criminal law forbids theft and assault. Other policies take the form of *economic incentives* (including disincentives), such as subsidies for renewable fuels, fees for engaging in certain activities, or taxes on gasoline and tobacco products. Still other policies take the form of *nudges* – liberty-preserving approaches that steer people in particular directions but that also allow them to go their own way. In recent years, both private and public institutions have shown mounting interest in the use of nudges, because they generally cost little and have the potential to promote economic and other goals (including public health).

In daily life, a GPS is an example of a nudge; so is an "app" that tells people how many calories they ate during the previous day; so is a text message, informing customers that a bill is due or that a doctor's appointment is scheduled for the next day; so is an alarm clock; so is automatic enrollment in a pension plan; so are the default settings on computers and cell phones; so is a system for automatic payment of credit-card bills and mortgages. In government, nudges include graphic warnings for cigarettes; labels for energy efficiency or fuel economy; "nutrition facts" panels on food; the "Food Plate," which provides a simple guide for healthy eating (see choosemy plate.gov); default rules for public-assistance programs (as in "direct certification" of the eligibility of poor children for free school meals);

a website like data.gov or data.gov.uk, which makes a large number of data sets available to the public; and even the design of government websites, which list certain items first and in large fonts.

NUDGES MAINTAIN FREEDOM OF CHOICE

It is important to see that the goal of many nudges is to make life simpler, safer, or easier for people to navigate. Consider road signs, speed bumps, disclosure of health-related or finance-related information, educational campaigns, paperwork reduction, and public warnings. When officials reduce or eliminate paperwork requirements, and when they promote simplicity and transparency, they are reducing people's burdens. Some products (such as cell phones and tablets) are intuitive and straightforward to use. Similarly, many nudges are intended to ensure that people do not struggle when they seek to interact with government or to achieve their goals.

It is true that some nudges are properly described as a form of "soft paternalism," because they steer people in a certain direction. But even when this is so, nudges are specifically designed to preserve full freedom of choice.

TRANSPARENCY AND EFFECTIVENESS

Any official nudging should be transparent and open rather than hidden and covert. Indeed, transparency should be built into the basic practice. Suppose that a government (or a private employer) adopts a program that automatically enrolls people in a pension program, or suppose that a large institution (say, a chain of private stores, or those who run cafeterias in government buildings) decides to make healthy foods more visible and accessible. In either case, the relevant action should not be hidden in any way. Government decisions in particular should be subject to public scrutiny and review. Nudges should never take the form of manipulation or trickery. The public should be able to review and scrutinize nudges no less than government actions of any other kind.

All over the world, nations have become keenly interested in nudges. The growing interest in nudges stems from the fact that they usually impose low (or no) costs, because they sometimes deliver prompt results (including significant economic savings), because they maintain freedom, and because they can be highly effective. In some cases, nudges have a larger impact than more expensive and more coercive tools. For example, default rules, simplification, and uses of social norms have sometimes been found to have even larger impacts than significant economic incentives.

In the context of retirement planning, automatic enrollment has proved exceedingly effective in promoting and increasing savings. In the context of consumer behavior, disclosure requirements and default rules have protected consumers against serious economic harm, saving many millions of dollars. Simplification of financial-aid forms can have the same beneficial effect in increasing college attendance by making it easier to access thousands of dollars in additional aid (per student). Informing people about their electricity use, and how it compares to that of their neighbors, can produce the same increases in conservation as a significant spike in the cost of electricity. If properly devised, disclosure of information can save both money and lives. Openness in government, disclosing both data and performance, can combat inefficiency and even corruption.

THE NEED FOR EVIDENCE AND TESTING

For all policies, including nudges, it is exceedingly important to rely on evidence rather than intuitions, anecdotes, wishful thinking, or dogmas. The most effective nudges tend to draw on the most valuable work in behavioral science (including behavioral economics), and hence reflect a realistic understanding of how people will respond to government initiatives. Some policies, including some nudges, seem promising in the abstract but turn out to fail in practice. Empirical tests, including randomized controlled trials, are indispensable. Bad surprises certainly are possible, including unintended adverse consequences, and sensible policymakers must try to anticipate such surprises in advance (and to fix them if they arise). Sometimes empirical tests reveal that the planned reform will indeed work – but that some variation on it, or some alternative, will work even better.

Experimentation, with careful controls, is a primary goal of the nudge enterprise. Fortunately, many nudge-type experiments can be run rapidly and at low cost, and in a fashion that allows for continuous measurement and improvement. The reason is that such experiments sometimes involve small changes to existing programs, and those changes can be incorporated into current initiatives with relatively little expense or effort. If, for example, officials currently send out a letter to encourage people to pay delinquent taxes, they might send out variations on the current letter and test whether the variations are more effective.

TEN IMPORTANT NUDGES

Nudges span an exceedingly wide range, and their number and variety are constantly growing. Here is a catalogue of ten important nudges:

1. **Default rules** (e.g., automatic enrollment in programs, including education, health, savings)
2. **Simplification** (in part to promote take-up of existing programs)
3. **Uses of social norms** (emphasizing what most people do, e.g., "Most people plan to vote," or "Most people pay their taxes on time," or "Nine out of ten hotel guests reuse their towels.")
4. **Increases in ease and convenience** (e.g., making low-cost options or healthy foods visible)
5. **Disclosure** (for example, of the economic or environmental costs associated with energy use, or the full cost of certain credit cards – or large amounts of data, as in the cases of data.gov and the Open Government Partnership, see opengovernmentpartnership.org)
6. **Warnings, graphic or otherwise** (as for cigarettes)
7. **Precommitment strategies** (by which people commit to a certain course of action)

8. **Reminders** (for example, by e-mail or text message, as for overdue bills and coming obligations or appointments)
9. **Eliciting implementation intentions** ("Do you plan to vote?")
10. **Informing people of the nature and consequences of their own past choices** ("smart disclosure" in the United States and the "midata project" in the United Kingdom)

INSTITUTIONALIZING NUDGES: TWO APPROACHES

What is the best method for implementing nudges? It is certainly possible to rely entirely on existing institutions. We could imagine a system in which an understanding of nudges is used by current officials and institutions, including leaders at the highest levels. For example, the relevant research could be enlisted by those involved in promoting competitiveness, environmental protection, public safety, consumer protection, and economic growth – or in reducing private and public corruption and combating poverty, infectious diseases, and obesity. Focusing on concrete problems rather than abstract theories, officials with well-established positions might be expected to use that research, at least on occasion.

If the relevant officials have both knowledge and genuine authority, they might be able to produce significant reforms, simply because they are not akin to a mere research arm or a think-tank. (Even a single person, if given the appropriate authority and mission, could have a large impact.) On one model, the relevant officials would not engage in new research, or at least not in a great deal of it. They would build on what is already known (and perhaps have formal or informal partnerships with those in the private sector who work on these issues). In an important sense, this approach is the simplest, because it does not require new offices or significant additional funding but only attention to the relevant issues and a focus on the right appointments. In the United States, this kind of approach has proved highly successful, with the adoption of numerous nudges.

A quite different approach would be to create a new institution – such as a behavioral-insights team or a "nudge unit" of some sort. Such an institution could be organized in different ways, and it could have many different forms and sizes. On a minimalist model, it would have a small group of knowledgeable people (say, five), bringing relevant findings to bear and perhaps engaging in, or spurring, research on their own. On a more ambitious model, the team could be larger (say, thirty or more), engaging in a wide range of relevant research. A behavioral-insights team could be created as a formal part of government (the preferred model, to ensure real impact) or could have a purely advisory role.

Whatever the precise form of this approach, its advantage is that it would involve a dedicated and specialized team, highly informed and specifically devoted to the relevant work, and with expertise in the design of experiments. If the team could work with others to conduct its own research, including randomized controlled trials, it might be able to produce important findings (as has in fact been done in the United Kingdom and the United States, and with similar efforts that are occurring elsewhere). The risk is that such a team would be akin to an academic adjunct, a kind of outsider, without the ability or power to initiate real reform. Authority greatly matters. The United Kingdom has had the most experience with this kind of approach, and it has succeeded in part because it has enjoyed high-level support and access.

In this domain, one size does not fit all, but it is noteworthy that a growing number of nations have concluded that it is worthwhile to have a dedicated team. Of course, the two approaches might prove complementary.

THE WAY FORWARD

This book offers an exceedingly valuable exploration of what it means for both private and public organizations to be behaviorally informed. It is full of both findings and ideas. It is based in large part on the inspiring work of the BI.Org partnership, which includes many of the best researchers, working at the frontiers of theory and practice. These include the Behavioural Insights Team from the United Kingdom (now working in dozens of nations), the World Bank, ideas42, and BEAR, along with prominent academic researchers.

For all the progress, a great deal remains to be done. Nudging, and behaviorally informed approaches in general, are out of their infancy – but still in their early teenage years. There is so much more to be done, to save money, to improve health, to prevent premature death, and to increase well-being in general. The nudgers themselves need to be nudged. This book helps point the way.

Preface: The Behaviorally Informed Organization

In the year 2008, Richard Thaler and Cass Sunstein published a book, *Nudge,* which has revolutionized the way in which organizations all over the world think about using behavioral science in their operations, and in particular in designing their last-mile interfaces. The field of behavioral science had been around for decades. In the years before *Nudge* was published, an academic discipline that had come to be known as behavioral economics had begun to capture the imagination of policymakers, governments, and the lay public alike. This interest was fueled by a Nobel Prize in 2002 to Daniel Kahneman, and the publication of books such as *Predictably Irrational* by Dan Ariely. *Nudge* harnessed all of this growing interest in the field and made it practical and real for organizations. The book provided a large number of examples of how organizations could steer the behavior of end-users without the use of restrictions, incentives, or even traditional communication-based persuasion techniques. The word "nudge" started becoming part of the organizational lexicon. Shortly after the book was published, the UK government launched their first ever Behavioral Insights Team within the Cabinet Office. Since then, a large number of governments – and eventually businesses – have begun to appreciate the importance of behavioral insights (BI) in their operations. In the foreword to this book, Cass Sunstein introduces nudging, and provides examples of its use.

In academia, researchers in behavioral science have long been studying human behaviors. A more recent movement within academic economics – behavioral economics – seeks to apply behavioral science to economic decision making. Practitioners often refer to the learning from these fields as behavioral insights (BI). We will use the term "BI" as the catchall term that represents both the science and the findings and insights that arise from it. However, authors of individual chapters might use the word "science" or "economics" to reflect which part of the collective their material draws from, as well as their own philosophy.

Despite this growing surge in interest in BI, it is our contention that the potential of behavioral insights to fundamentally change the way in which organizations operate and interact with their stakeholders is nowhere near to being fully harnessed. Given that organizations are fundamentally in the business of changing the behavior of their internal and external stakeholders, and given that we have a rich science of how behavior change is brought about, this gap is a bit of an enigma. We see two major challenges for our field in the next decade. First, we have had a lot of success with pilot projects but have not yet developed a framework for how these pilots can be scaled. Second, we need to understand how organizations can become better behaviorally informed. We believe that overcoming the second challenge will allow us to tackle the first. We – along with several other behavioral scientists and partner organizations – have put together an international partnership of scientists and practitioners with the goal of understanding how organizations can better harness behavioral insights (see biorgpartnership.com). Our partnership is housed in the Behavioural Economics in Action Research at Rotman (BEAR) research center at the University of Toronto.

We believe that the gap between the promise of behavioral science and the actual adoption of BI arises from three fundamental factors. First, there is a mismatch between the expertise of an academic researcher and the needs of a practitioner. In particular, behavioral scientists tend to make careers by developing expertise in a particular phenomenon – a researcher who studies how social forces influence behaviors would recommend overweight consumers to sign a public weight-loss petition, whereas another researcher who studies incentives would suggest using money to reward weight loss. The practitioner, on the other hand, is interested in the outcome without a specific preference for any one phenomenon. Further, researchers are typically not keen on mixing up interventions, because the scientific value of academic research comes from its preciseness in testing how a particular intervention drives a behavioral change. If a researcher were to choose between using an intervention to achieve a moderate outcome and a cocktail of interventions to achieve a better overall outcome, the researcher will likely choose the former. The practitioner, on the other hand, needs a cocktail of interventions that yields significant behavioral change, but this need is unmet because behavioral scientists rarely research the formula for such a cocktail mix. Second, much behavioral science is done in a laboratory, and participants make static (i.e., at that point in time) choices in relatively sterile environments. In contrast, behaviors in the real world are often complex (i.e., multiple determined) and dynamic (i.e., liable to change as a function of past decisions). Furthermore, the practitioner is often interested in behaviors that are guided by habit (as part of a routine); these behaviors lose their flavors once they are isolated from their routines and studied as "single-shot" behaviors in the lab. Therefore, such lab-based findings may not be particularly insightful for practitioners who are interested in understanding habitual behaviors. These divergences limit the adoption of BI in practice. Finally, academic research is conducted in environments with an academic culture that encourages experimentations and testing, while the realities in organizations often require the practitioner to make quick decisions and to look decisive, constraints that might preclude experimentation and testing.

Compounding these fundamental reasons is a misunderstanding of how the process of behavior-change interventions actually works. A reading of past BI successes can easily lead to the misunderstanding that the application of BI is linear and therefore straightforward. However, each success is only the tip of a proverbial iceberg that contains a lot of groundwork, iterations, and experimental failures. Indeed, while the field needs to share its successes, it also needs to highlight the fact that BI is not a simple off-the-shelf solution that is guaranteed to work.

Our partnership was set up with the objective of helping every organization become behaviorally informed. In particular, it seeks to develop a science for using behavioral science by addressing some of the reasons underlying the gap between the promise of behavioral science and its adoption in organizations. What is a behaviorally informed organization (BIOrg)? It is an organization that (a) recognizes that its external and internal stakeholders are human (and not "econs" – agents that comply with the assumptions of utility maximization); (b) understands the importance of context; (c) designs for humans; (d) believes in testing, learning, and adapting; and (e) has the agility to update products, processes, and programs in response to learning from experiments. In general, a BIOrg is deeply committed to being human compliant in every possible way!

This edited volume represents the first output from this international partnership. The book is designed to reflect our conceptual thinking, outline some early results from the partnership and an agenda for research and practice, and provide roadmaps to help both practitioners and academics converge in the common quest of developing behaviorally informed organizations. The book is divided into four parts. In *Part 1, "The Behaviorally Informed Organization,"* four chapters lay out an agenda for what such an organization should be and could be. In chapter 1, Soman talks about the science of using behavioral science by developing a brief history of the field of behavioral science, outlining organizational realities, and generating a research agenda to help develop BIOrgs. In chapter 2, Feng and colleagues further develop an understanding of organizational realities and outline what resources and capabilities organizations need to develop in order to be truly behaviorally informed. In particular, they develop the notion of the cost of experimentation and make the point that driving down the cost of experimentation is key in developing behaviorally informed organizations. In chapter 3, Vinski asks and answers the question, "Why should organizations even want to be behaviorally informed?"; and in chapter 4, O'Malley and Peters add to that question by further addressing why organizations might actively resist the need to be behaviorally informed.

Organizational settings provide existing tools and also additional complexities, and in *Part 2, "Overarching Insights and Tools,"* four chapters address some of these organizational realities. Chapter 5 talks about "sludge" – small aspects of an organizationally created context that create impedance for end-users. If sludge is not cleared, the effectiveness of behavioral interventions will be constrained, and hence this chapter makes a case for identifying and eliminating sludge. In chapter 6, Duncan and colleagues provide a guide to writing guidelines, an important tool for most policymakers and businesses as they attempt to provide helpful information to their citizens and customers. Given that organizations have multiple interactions for multiple products and services with their end-users, a binary classification into econs and humans is not feasible or helpful. Therefore, in chapter 7, Ireland talks about the boundedly rational complex consumer continuum, a nuanced framework for segmenting recipients of behavioral interventions. Given that end-users are inundated with information and other types of stimulus from organizations, it is unclear that they will attend to it all. In chapter 8, Hilchey and Taylor write about the psychology of attention and its implications for helping end-users make better decisions.

Part 3, "Examples of Behavioral Initiatives from Business and Policy," captures results from case studies in several domains of both welfare and business. In chapter 9, Murray and Chen discuss the science of habits and how to change them. In chapter 10, Howe and colleagues describe applications of behavioral science to financial decision making, while in chapter 11, Hardy and colleagues describe a series of projects applying choice-architecture interventions to program development and policy in the Canadian federal government. In chapter 12, Robson discusses how we can use insights to help low-income Canadians file taxes and hence help them obtain many income-tested benefits that are tied to tax returns. In chapter 13, Kim and colleagues present a behavioral approach for studying and tackling issues related to online privacy. In chapter 14, Dalton and colleagues from the World Bank present several cases illustrating the application of BI to international development efforts.

Part 4, "Making It Work," presents two chapters that start identifying key elements and provide guidelines to the practitioner for developing behavioral interventions. In chapter 15, Audet and colleagues discuss the importance of building partnerships and using

BI in practice. Finally, in chapter 16, Yeung and Tham leverage their experience in working together on several policy issues in the Singapore government, and present a roadmap to help both academics and practitioners navigate the challenges of being scientific in solving practical problems.

For our partnership, this book is merely the beginning of a long, complex, yet important journey. We are confident that the reader will finish this book feeling that they have added an idea or two to their understanding of how to make BI relevant. It will help academics think differently about how to create knowledge that can have an impact in the real world, and it will help practitioners better understand how to read, internalize, and embed science in order to make organizations as behaviorally informed as they could be.

Happy reading.

Dilip Soman, Toronto
Catherine Yeung, Hong Kong

PART ONE

The Behaviorally Informed Organization: An Agenda

CHAPTER ONE

The Science of Using Behavioral Science

Dilip Soman

Organizations come in many shapes, sizes, and flavors. A government is a complex entity comprising a number of different units with the goal of enhancing the welfare of its citizens. Each of its many ministries, bureaus, and offices handles a precise subset of this large and complex goal. For instance, a financial-services regulator might care about ensuring that financial markets are fair and transparent; the Ministry of the Environment might want to make sure that enterprises comply with laws on pollution and emissions; and a Transportation Ministry would like to encourage a safe and efficient transportation network while ensuring that citizens are motivated to utilize public transit.

On the other end of the spectrum, the typical industry organization is also a complex entity but with a different objective of maximizing value to its multiple stakeholders (investors, consumers, and employees). Profit and long-term relationships with their customers have been primary goals of these organizations, with customer experience and loyalty being intermediate goals. Like governments, industrial entities are organized into departments and units, each tasked with a specific aspect of creating value.

There are numerous other types of organizations on this spectrum. Not-for-profit social organizations are typically looking to influence and improve the welfare of citizens in specific domains; consumer advocacy groups are looking to influence governments and industry appropriately to enhance citizen welfare; think tanks and universities are in the business of educating and changing the behavior of young citizens; small start-up organizations are in the business of successfully launching their first product; and lawyers, doctors, fitness consultants, dieticians, wealth managers, and coaches are all looking to help their clients make better, welfare-enhancing choices.

THE BUSINESS OF BEHAVIOR CHANGE

While organizations differ significantly in terms of their goals, size, organizational structure, resource bases, and operating principles and procedures, there is one surprising similarity across all forms of organizations. That is the fact that most organizations are fundamentally in the business of behavior change. Behavior-change challenges faced by governments, industry, and not-for-profits alike can be categorized into four types: *compliance* (i.e., getting people to behave per prescribed standards), *switching* (i.e., getting people to choose A instead of B), *consumption* (of information, medication), and *acceleration* of decisions (i.e., minimizing procrastination).[1] We also have a rich literature in the area of behavioral insights (BI) that studies behavior change. Findings from decades of research in BI suggest that a cocktail of four approaches can tackle all these behavior-change challenges. *Restrictions* prevent access to certain options by passing laws against them, or otherwise curtailing supply. *Incentives* take the form of carrots (subsidies, bonuses, discounts, rewards, or recognition) to reward desired behavior, or sticks (penalties, taxes, lower priorities) to dis-incentivize undesired behaviors. *Information* or persuasion relies on the belief that raising awareness of the benefits of good behavior and making compelling arguments in its favor will drive that behavior. And *choice architecture* relies on a deep understanding of human nature to create contexts and circumstances that will steer people toward the desirable behavior.[2]

These challenges are compounded by the fact that decision makers in these organizations are also human, and therefore susceptible to human tendencies such as being overconfident, or making unrealistic forecasts, or using heuristics in making decisions, or ignoring large data in favor of a smaller number of compelling and vivid stories. Therefore, an important part of an organization's behavioral strategy should include the use of BI to recast and improve its own decision-making process.

THE SCIENCE OF BI

The field that we collectively call behavioral insights (BI) today has its roots in many theoretical disciplines that date back to a couple of hundred years ago. The field of judgment and decision making (JDM) studies how human agents make choices and reach judgments about options and is arguably the central pillar of today's BI. Elsewhere, models of marketplace behavior often did not predict actual marketplaces; and hence a group of economists started to enrich these models by including behavioral variables. JDM starts with the psychology of the individual, while the behavioral-economics approach often starts with marketplace behavior and infers the underlying psychology. Collectively, these two streams of work have merged with social and cognitive psychology and form the bulk of what we know as BI today. While some of the key developments in the history of JDM are summarized below, the interested reader should definitely consult an excellent and more comprehensive account (*Research on Judgment and Decision Making*) written by William Goldstein and Robin Hogarth.[3] Perhaps the earliest dominant paradigm in the field of judgment and decision making was the so-called expected-utility model of decision making. The overall utility of a particular option is the weighted utility of its attributes/components, weighted by either the importance of those components or the probability of the occurrence of each component. The simplest form of these expected-utility models took the form of what is known as an Expected Monetary Value (EMV) model.[4]

To understand the basic idea of this model, imagine that a decision maker is confronted with the choice of either receiving $100 with absolute certainty (Option A) or entering a lottery with two possible outcomes: $200 with a probability of 60 percent and $0 with a probability of 40 percent (Option B). In its simplest form, the

Expected Monetary Value model would assign an overall value of $100 to the first option (100 percent multiplied by $100) and a value of $120 to the second option (60 percent multiplied by $200 plus 40 percent multiplied by zero). Given that the Expected Monetary Value of B is great than that of A, the decision maker would end up choosing the second option.

Over a 200-year period beginning from the mid-1700s to the mid-1900s, this approach to decision making was formalized in a series of models that increased in complexity over time. For example, the EMV model simply multiplied the probability with the outcome to arrive at the Expected Monetary Value. However, in 1738 a mathematician called Bernoulli recognized that the happiness associated with increasing dollar amounts might not be linearly related to the amount, and hence developed the notion of utility. Further developments of the model acknowledged that the value of increases in probability are not linear with probability (as described by prospect theory,[5] a change from 0 percent likelihood to 10 percent likelihood had a significantly greater impact than a change from, say, 60 percent to 70 percent), and added technical sophistication by making a distinction between utility (which can only be inferred through choices) and value (which could be measured in dollar equivalents).[6]

By the mid-1950s, utility theory had now been accepted as the theoretical basis for understanding human decision making by most economists. In order to make the mathematics work, utility theory had to be founded on a series of assumptions (or axioms).[7] These axioms seem completely reasonable at first blush. For instance, *transitivity* assumed that if people chose A over B, and B over C, then they should choose A over C. Similarly, the axiom of *substitution* (or *cancellation*) says that a person's preferences between two options should not change if an identical attribute is added to (or subtracted from) both options.

In the mid-1950s, several scholars started critiquing the assumptions and the approach of utility theory. The French physicist and economist Maurice Allais conducted a famous experiment in which he was able to demonstrate the violation of the cancellation principle.[8] Suppose people choose between $100 for sure (Option A) and $160 with a 30 percent probability, $100 with a 45 percent probability, or $0 with a 25 percent probability (Option B). It is easy to see that the majority would choose A; after all a (proverbial) bird in the hand is worth two in the bush! Now suppose people choose between $100 with a 55 percent probability (Option A*) and $160 with a 30 percent probability (Option B*). Here, we might tend to see a greater preference for B* – 30 percent and 55 percent both seem to come from the same risk category, but $160 seems much larger than $100. While both choices make sense independently, the trouble is that both A* differs from A and B* differs from B in removing a 45 percent chance of winning $100. The axiom of cancellation would say that if you chose A over B, you should choose A* over B*. This preference reversal posed a problem for utility theory.

A few years later in 1961, American economist Daniel Ellsberg (who later became known as a hero for being a whistle-blower for releasing the "Pentagon Papers" about the Vietnam War) demonstrated ambiguity aversion. In particular, Ellsberg showed that people are more willing to take risks if the probability is precisely known (say 60 percent), than if it is ambiguous (say, 50 percent to 70 percent).[9]

Much of the research in this era commenting on utility theory followed the same general narrative. It first presented a prediction of utility theory (e.g., the cancellation principle). It then provided empirical support to show that the said prediction was violated (e.g., Allais paradox experiments). It then concluded with concerns about utility theory as a descriptive model of behavior, and called for a new theory. In the context of many such papers, the broader narrative of "economics describes rational behavior" but "people are irrational" was born. This narrative is unfortunate; it signals that people make mistakes and are poor at decision making. As I wrote elsewhere, people are simply being human, and utility theory was perhaps simply the wrong model to benchmark human behavior![10]

Three categories of responses to the experimental criticisms of utility theory started developing in the 1970s and 1980s. The *first* tried to generalize the utility model. For example, researchers tried to incorporate the utility function to include contextual variables. The *second* was to introduce new models that drew from cognitive psychology to try to enrich our understanding of decision making.

David Bell showed that regret – wishing you had made a different choice – influences decision making.[11] The heuristics-and-biases research program by Kahneman and Tversky[12] and the mental-accounting research by Richard Thaler[13] were further examples of research that introduced additional psychological processes to decision making. Kahneman and Tversky argued that heuristics are simple rules of thumb or relatively straightforward decision-making procedures that allow the decision maker to bypass the complexities associated with a more comprehensive analysis. These simple rules of thumb usually work in many conditions but could sometimes lead the decision maker astray. Richard Thaler first started writing about mental accounting in the 1980s by making the simple yet profound observation that the economic assumption of fungibility (the idea that a dollar is always a dollar, irrespective of where it comes from) is not always true. People treat money differently as a function of how it is earned, how it is budgeted, and how it is earmarked. Since money is so central to economic behavior, Thaler's ideas and the resulting research that came out of it posed a substantial challenge to the way in which we think about economics.

A third category of responses postulated that consumers followed other (non-utility-maximizing) approaches or procedures in making decisions. For example, Amos Tversky showed that people often use an approximation procedure that results in systematic violation of the simple property of transitivity.[14] Tversky also showed that features of similarity between different options tend to influence the decision-making process.[15] Elsewhere, John Payne and his colleagues developed the theory of contingent decision making.[16] In particular, they argued that there exist several strategies for decision making ranging from the simple to the most complex. An example of a simple decision-making strategy is the so-called lexicographic decision rule by which the decision maker only considers the most important attribute and chooses the option that is the best on that attribute. A most complex approach to decision making would be a comprehensive expected utility – an approach in which all of the probabilities/weights associated with all outcomes are used in arriving at a decision. Payne and his colleagues argued that people make decisions using a two-stage process. First, they decide on how to decide, and then they use the selected procedure to make a choice. For example, making a purchase of chewing gum at a local convenience store might use a simple choose-the-cheapest decision-making strategy. On the other hand, purchasing a house or investing in a retirement fund might be a more complex decision where one might expect the decision maker to do a comprehensive analysis of all available information. Payne and colleagues also introduced the notion of constructed preferences – the notion that people do not have inherent preferences, and that preferences are manufactured only when a decision needs to be made.[17]

By the 1990s, researchers in economics and finance had begun to acknowledge the importance of considering human behavior. However, organizations were still far from paying serious attention to behavioral economics.

Organizations were typically founded by the work of inventors, engineers, scientists, or policy experts. In the early years of industry, their focus was on trying to improve processes and increase throughput. The beginning of the industrial era was marked by the desire to streamline processes to maximize production and to increase efficiencies of scale as much as possible.[18] That mindset continued to pervade organizations. As we now know, efficient processes are not necessarily the most human-centric. Some scholars and a handful of organizations began to appreciate the importance of customer experiences for maximizing profitability.[19] However, these organizations were blissfully detached from the academic storm that was gathering in the field of behavioral economics.

THE PRACTICE OF BEHAVIOR CHANGE AND THE SEEDS OF RELEVANCE

Despite the growing interest in the field, BI has not made inroads into industry and government to the degree that we would like. After all, if all organizations are fundamentally in the business of changing behavior, and the field of BI helps us understand behavior change, it should be deeply ingrained into all processes and operations of an organization. For organizations to be truly behaviorally informed, they should behave like scientists not only in designing products, processes, and interfaces for customers but also in designing internal processes for their employees and other stakeholders. However, even today, in meeting rooms of organizations, one often hears about disconnects between the academic approach to making decisions and business priorities. Policymakers lament that they do not have the time or the resources to be completely scientific. Businesses often do not understand the need for testing. Even the homes of academia, educational institutions and behavioral teams, are not as behaviorally informed in their decision making as we might expect.

Why are the science and the practice so disconnected? The worlds of academia and practitioners are vastly different (see also chapter 16 for a related discussion). Academics publish in scholarly journals, and their articles are highly technical, therefore relatively inaccessible to practitioners. Academics work on problems for a long time; practitioners want answers immediately. Academics make their careers by understanding phenomena in depth; practitioners make their careers by solving problems, with relatively less concern for why the solution was effective in the first place.[20]

Consider a scientist studying the effects of information framing (e.g., whether a food is called "75 percent lean" versus "25 percent fat") on healthy-eating / preventive-health behaviors.[21] Given the goal of testing theory, the scientist runs a series of studies in which all factors that could possibly affect choice (other than framing) are held constant. They also test their theory across a number of different versions of framing (e.g., whether a price is framed as "$80" or "$100 with a 20 percent discount") and across multiple decision types (e.g., healthy eating, financial well-being). At the end of this exercise, the scientist has a comprehensive understanding of framing, but only in a world where everything else is held constant. An organization, on the other hand, is less interested in framing per se than in trying to get the end-user to engage in, say, making healthy choices or opening retirement accounts. A practitioner might learn from a literature review that framing is one approach to influencing choice, an incentive is another, and presenting information visually is a third. However, they would learn nothing about the relative strengths of these approaches, or about when one should be used over another, or in what sequence.

The acceptance of the science in practice was catalyzed by the book *Nudge* written by Richard Thaler and Cass Sunstein.[22] Their thesis is crystallized into one simple observation – if we know that human decisions are influenced by the context in which they are made, could we somehow create a context to steer people toward the decision we (or they) would like them to make? They referred to this process as choice architecture. They made a distinction between "econs," hypothetical creatures that existed only in the pages of economics textbooks and were oblivious to elements of context because they focused solely on the utility of the chosen option, versus humans, agents that used heuristics and therefore sometimes incorrectly used elements of context in decision making.

Their book was full of anecdotes of how behavioral science could be relevant to a practitioner. For example, they wrote about the manner in which framing price differences as either gains or losses has an effect on consumer decision making. They wrote about the notion of social proof – the fact that if you told people what the majority of others were doing in the context of policy and welfare decisions, they would be more likely to do the same.[23] They also wrote about small frictions in the environment that might discourage certain behaviors. For example, making healthy snacks easier to access and unhealthy snacks slightly more difficult to access would increase the likelihood that people would choose healthy alternatives. They also wrote about the fact that making retirement accounts easy to open – for example, by auto-enrolling people in them – increases the likelihood that people will engage with their retirement and save more for the future. They presented examples such as Save More Tomorrow, a savings program built on behavioral insights in which participating employees pre-committed to directing a portion of their future salary increases into a separate savings account.[24]

The book suddenly brought the field of behavioral science to the forefront. Its many examples made practitioners see the relevance of the science. It was not the fact that the book sold a large number of copies or that it attracted attention for the science. Other books had done that in the past. Dan Ariely had written a bestseller called

Predictably Irrational.[25] Daniel Kahneman had previously won the Nobel Prize in Economic Sciences (and Thaler won it in 2017). It was really *Nudge* that showed practitioners that the science had utility, and gave them a vocabulary to talk about it. Many years later, Sunstein would write a book entitled *How Change Happens,* in which he would argue that some events, in hindsight, end up being tipping points for significant changes in society.[26] Perhaps *Nudge* was the tipping point for behaviorally informed organizations. Perhaps it might not have become a tipping point if the authors had entitled the book "Libertarian Paternalism" (the original working title[27]).

Within two years of the publication of *Nudge,* UK Prime Minister David Cameron committed to the use of behavioral science in government by opening the first-ever Behavioural Insights Team (BIT), also known as "the Nudge unit." BIT still remains a large player in the field of applied behavioral economics. Governments elsewhere started following suit. Canada, Singapore, Australia, the OECD, France, and several others started developing Nudge units that all embraced behavioral science in order to develop solutions to last-mile problems.[28] Experimentation, design innovation, the use of randomized controlled trials, and rigorous testing and piloting before launching programs and policies became the hallmarks of the activities of these various behavioral teams. In the business world, many in marketing and customer-facing parts of organizations felt that they were already using behavioral science. In reality, they were using creative ideas whose success could be explained by science after the fact. However, the systematic practice of theorizing, testing, piloting, and running randomized controlled trials was not part of "business as usual." It was in the post-*Nudge* era that industry began to open its eyes to the benefits of behavioral science. For instance, consulting firms such as ideas42 (a not-for-profit firm that had operated long before *Nudge* was published) and BEworks in Toronto now had more support to make businesses aware of the potential of behavioral science.

Despite this encouraging start, there is still a lot of unfulfilled potential in organizations. One big reason for this relatively low rate of adoption of BI by organizations is the absence of a science of using science.[29] We need a better understanding of organizational variables that can affect adoption, a model of how BI could be infused into organizations, and – above all – additional research that makes our science more relevant to a practitioner.

THE SCIENCE OF USING BEHAVIORAL SCIENCE

The science of using science has been defined as an understanding of "what approaches work in enabling the use of research by policymakers, practitioners and members of the public."[30] I have eight proposals for research that could form the foundation of the science of using behavioral science.

Proposal 1: Conduct Practitioner-Relevant Research

Because academics tend to work in silos of domain-specific expertise, there is little research that presents a landscape analysis of everything we know in the field of behavioral science.[31] Academic journals typically do not reward such effort. The field needs integrative research that would help practitioners answer questions like the following: "If I need to change behavior, should I rely on incentives or on choice architecture?" "What is the best sequence in which I could use incentives, restrictions, choice architecture, and information in engineering long-term behavior change?" "How big are the effects of incentives vis-à-vis other forms of behavior change?" "What is the stability of choice-architecture interventions?" This research can be conducted by using systematic literature reviews and meta-analyses with emphasis on organizational variables or policy-relevant variables and on understanding the relative effect sizes of different types of interventions.

Proposal 2: Use Human-Centric Versions of Basic Variables

In an attempt to make problems tractable and solvable, academics tend to use simple approaches to measuring complex variables like risk and time. These impoverished measures have found their way into government and industry applications. Risk has often been conceptualized in the academic literature as a function of the probability of an outcome, the actual dollar value of the outcome, and – in finance – the volatility over time. However, most humans think about risk very differently. For some, risk is an emotion while for others it simply refers to the chance of negative outcomes.[32] It is also possible that humans use a causal-chain heuristic for assessing risk – the easier it is to construct a causal chain of events leading to an outcome, the more likely the outcome is. Likewise, most models of intertemporal choice and most approaches in industry treat time as a continuous and simply scaled variable. In particular, organizations tend to design keeping objective time durations in mind, while humans experience time subjectively.[33] We also know that frustration associated with waiting for products and services is not only a function of the actual time but also of whether the time is empty or filled, what the duration is relative to expectations, the nature of the physical location in which the wait is held, the geography and structure of the queuing arrangement, and a whole host of other contextual factors.[34] Research also seems to suggest that people might be categorizing time, rather than treating it as a continuous variable.[35] Indeed, it now seems likely that what we see as hyperbolic discounting might actually be an artifact of the way in which humans perceive future-time durations.[36] Both "risk" and "time" have their book definitions, and these definitions are adopted in academic research for the sake of clarity. However, we must now acknowledge that these are pure concepts that do not reflect the reality of how they take part in human decisions. In general, we call for ongoing research to take concepts like risk and time and develop more human-centric models for understanding the effects of these in important policy and organizational contexts.

Proposal 3: Research the Cost of Experimentation

Experiments conducted in organizations can be on a spectrum from quasi experiments based on surveys, to laboratory experiments based on hypothetical choices, all the way to randomized controlled trials and field experiments. It is our contention that, in addition to defining precisely what the nature of an experiment is and what needs to be done to conduct a successful experiment, organizations need to invest to bring down the cost of experimentation. If experimentation were cheap, organizations would naturally tend to rely more on experiments to generate evidence. The cost of experimentation can include both the direct costs of collecting and analyzing data and the indirect costs associated with organizational and personal issues of the managers who are tasked with running the experiment. We discuss this proposition in greater depth in chapter 2.

Proposal 4: Use Multiple Tools and Avoid a Fixation on Randomized Controlled Trials

As the field of applied BI gained traction, practitioners from all over the world were suddenly asked to move from a time in which experimentation was not the norm (was not even done by many organizations) to an era in which randomized controlled trials (RCT) became the gold standard for collecting evidence. Many find this transition hard to make; it is simply a big conceptual, psychological, and pragmatic leap to make for many organizations. In some cases, as we saw recently during the COVID-19 pandemic, when the world is changing very rapidly, organizations might not have the time to conduct experiments. If the field is to gain traction within organizations, ongoing research needs to study how the experimental approach to collecting evidence can best be integrated with other approaches like machine learning / artificial intelligence, design thinking, customer-experience (CX) and user-experience (UX) methods, and even traditional research techniques such as surveys or interviews.

Easy access and lower costs of generating data mean that most organizations have more data than they have ever had access to in the past. Machine-learning techniques (e.g., causal forest and causal tree) or clustering techniques can be used for segmenting behavioral patterns of different stakeholders. In some ongoing research, we have used machine-learning techniques to study the heterogeneity in responses to behavioral interventions or nudges in large-scale experiments.[37] Similarly, design thinking can be combined with behavioral sciences to yield methodologies that might not only provide rich insights conceptually but also be more acceptable to existing organizational structures.[38] Finally, redesigning surveys and interviews such that they are based on choices that respondents make (much like an experiment) rather than on opinions will improve the value of those techniques.

Proposal 5: Develop a Better Understanding of How Practitioners Consume Research

Imagine that a practitioner has received two published papers that study the effect of some variable A on another variable B. One paper finds that increasing A increases B. The second paper finds the opposite effect, that increasing A actually decreases B. How should the manager reconcile these findings?

When a behavioral scientist is presented with two seemingly conflicting findings, their natural instinct is to search for a hidden moderator that might explain why A increases B in one context but decreases B in the other (the moderator hypothesis). What else might a practitioner do? One possibility is that they might simply conclude that there is no relationship between A and B (the averaging hypothesis). A second possibility is that they simply lose trust in the research because there is no consistency across multiple papers (the trust hypothesis). A third possibility is that they anchor on one of the findings and update beliefs based on the second result (the Bayesian hypothesis). The Bayesian hypothesis further raises the question of which result is chosen as the anchor – the first result they saw, the result with the larger sample size, the result with a similar context to their own context – and of how well known the authors are and/or the prestige associated with the journal or the authors' universities.

Understanding the answer to questions like this is critical for applied behavioral scientists as they attempt to embed their results into an organizational context. Without knowing how practitioners consume the results of research, it will be difficult to anticipate how a series of findings will be interpreted.

Proposal 6: Identify the Value of Being Evidence Based

At first blush, it seems obvious that having evidence as the basis for decision making is better than not having evidence at all. Indeed, if the cost of experimentation were actually zero, then it would make perfect sense for organizations to run experiments routinely before making decisions, rather than relying on the results of prior experiments or on what has worked best previously. However, the harsh reality is that the cost of experimentation is not zero. The question then is, "Can we prescribe when organizations should rely on experimentation and when they should not?"

Ongoing experimentation is clearly valuable in dynamic environments where the results of past experiments may no longer be true.[39] In particular, we would expect continual experimentation to play a critical role when we expect heterogeneity in consumer responses or the responses of citizens; when the environment changes significantly in response to the introduction of new products, processes, ideas, or insights; or when there are large geographic or time variations in people's tastes and preferences. Likewise, experiments will be invaluable when there are a large number of elements of contexts that might vary and therefore change the possible results of an intervention. However, there are obvious limitations to this proposition, as the recent COVID-19 pandemic has shown. While experimentation would have been very helpful in designing interventions to help people change behavior, the situation changed so rapidly that there was no time to experiment. On the other hand, if environments are less dynamic and not much changes with time, location, or the type of end-user, then perhaps less frequent experimentation would be sufficient. This adjustment would allow organizations to conserve resources for other, more dynamic environments.

This suggests an inverted U-shape function of the value of experimentation as a function of how dynamic the environment is. More research needs to be done to understand when organizations should be encouraged to pursue continual experimentation and when it would be okay for them not to do so.

Proposal 7: Develop an Understanding of the Scaling Challenge

If we have interventions that are tested in the laboratory and in small-scale pilots and they consistently turn out to be effective, will they always scale well? Recent research suggests that there are a number of challenges in scaling interventions.[40] First, it is likely that there are contextual differences in the fully scaled-up version of the launch as compared to the experiments, and that these contextual differences might change the result.[41] Second, there might be heterogeneity in responses to the intervention, which might weaken the overall effect in a scaled-up environment. More generally, there might be a voltage drop.[42] "Voltage drop" is a term used to describe the lower treatment-effect sizes of a scaled-up intervention as compared to the effect in the lab or pilot test. More research needs to be done to identify what scaling challenges exist, what the antecedents of voltage drop are, and how they can best be mitigated.

Proposal 8: Identify the Value of Failure and Groundwork

It is tempting to read case studies and books on "BI successes" and believe that the application of BI is relatively straightforward. For instance, chapters 6 and 11 might make the reader believe that the process of developing and applying behavioral interventions is linear and formulaic. In reality, the process of developing and testing interventions for many of those examples was iterative and marked by earlier failures (or lack-of-successes). Additionally, this process also requires extensive groundwork, including a landscape analysis, identification of key stakeholders, and an audit of decision-making processes and environments.[43] Further research on the value of early failures and the necessary groundwork will help organizations develop better processes for using BI effectively.

BEHAVIORALLY INFORMED ORGANIZATIONS

Humans are humans, and they always will be. Rather than try and get humans to be econs (which in my opinion is a very difficult exercise), it would be productive to create a more human-compliant world. Organizations therefore need to be behaviorally informed in dealing with all of their human stakeholders. This involves an understanding of the motivations, emotions, perceptions, and cognitions that underlie human behavior, with the understanding that "one size does not fit all." It further involves the ability to relentlessly experiment and test products, programs, processes, and interventions to make sure they are human-compliant. As markets mature, competition for attention becomes more intense, and tastes become more sophisticated, it is all the more important for organizations to master this science and embed it in their organizational processes.

NOTES

1 Soman, D. (2015). *The last mile: Creating social and economic value from behavioral insights*. Toronto: Rotman-UTP Publishing.
2 See ibid. for a discussion on the four types of behavior-change challenges and the four approaches to behavior change.
3 See chapter 1 of Goldstein, W.M., & Hogarth, R.M. (1997). *Research on judgment and decision making: Currents, connections and controversies*. Cambridge: Cambridge University Press, for an excellent history of the JDM research; and Thaler, R.H. (2015). *Misbehaving: The story of behavioral economics*. New York: W.W. Norton & Company, for an account of the development of behavioral economics.
4 See Schoemaker, P.J.H. (1982). The expected utility model: Its variants, purposes, evidence and limitations. *Journal of Economic Literature, 20*(2), 529–63, for an excellent discussion on the variants of the expected utility model.
5 Kahneman, D., & Tversky, A. (1979). Prospect theory: An analysis of decision under risk. *Econometrica, 47*(2), 263–91.
6 See Barberis, N.C. (2013). Thirty years of prospect theory in economics: A review and assessment. *Journal of Economic Perspectives, 27*(1), 173–96, and Kahneman, D., & Tversky, A. (2000). *Choices, values, and frames*. Cambridge: Cambridge University Press.
7 Von Neumann, J., & Morgenstern, O. (1953). *Theory of games and economic behavior* (3rd ed.). Princeton, NJ: Princeton University Press.
8 Allais, M. (1953). Le comportement de l'homme rationnel devant le risque: Critique des postulats et axiomes de l'école Américaine. *Econometrica, 21*(4), 503–46, as described in Oliver, A. (2003). A quantitative and qualitative test of the Allais paradox using health outcomes. *Journal of Economic Psychology, 24*(1), 35–48.

9 Ellsberg, D. (1961). Risk, ambiguity, and the savage axioms. *Quarterly Journal of Economics, 75*(4), 643–69.

10 Soman, D. (2015). *The last mile: Creating social and economic value from behavioral insights.* Toronto: Rotman-UTP Publishing.

11 Bell, D.E. (1982). Regret in decision making under uncertainty. *Operations Research, 30*(5), 961–81.

12 Tversky, A., & Kahneman, D. (1974). Judgments under uncertainty: Heuristics and biases. *Science, 185*(4157), 1124–31.

13 See Thaler, R.H. (1999). Mental accounting matters. *Journal of Behavioral Decision Making, 12,* 183–206, for a review.

14 Tversky, A. (1969). Intransitivity of preferences. *Psychological Review, 76,* 31–48.

15 Tversky, A. (1977). Features of similarity. *Psychological Review, 84*(4), 327–52.

16 See Payne, J.W., Bettman, J.R., & Johnson, E.J. (1993). *The adaptive decision maker.* Cambridge: Cambridge University Press, for a comprehensive account for this research program.

17 See Bettman, J.R., Luce, M.F., & Payne, J.W. (1998). Constructive consumer choice processes. *Journal of Consumer Research, 25,* 187–217; and Slovic, P. (1995). The construction of preference. *American Psychologist, 50,* 364–71. Also, see Simonson, I. (2008). Will I like a "medium pillow"? Another look at constructed and inherent preferences. *Journal of Consumer Psychology, 18,* 155–69, for a nice discussion on inherent versus constructed preferences.

18 See, for instance, Allen, R.C. (2017). *The Industrial Revolution: A very short introduction.* Oxford: Oxford University Press.

19 Verhoef, P.C., Lemon, K.N., Parasuraman, A., Roggeveen, A., Tsiros, M., & Schlesinger, L.A. (2009). Customer experience creation: Determinants, dynamics and management strategies. *Journal of Retailing. Enhancing the Retail Customer Experience, 85*(1), 31–41.

20 Von Winterfeldt, D. (2013). Bridging the gap between science and decision making. *Proceedings of the National Academy of Sciences, 110*(Supplement 3), 14055–61.

21 Levin, I.P., & Gaeth, G.J. (1988). How consumers are affected by the framing of attribute information before and after consuming the product. *Journal of Consumer Research, 15*(3), 374–8.

22 Thaler, R.H., & Sunstein, C.R. (2008). *Nudge: Improving decisions about health, wealth, and happiness.* New York: Penguin Books.

23 See also Halpern, D. (2015). *Inside the nudge unit: How small changes can make a big difference.* London: Ebury Publishing.

24 Thaler, R.H., & Benartzi, S. (2004). Save more tomorrow: Using behavioral economics to increase employee saving. *Journal of Political Economy, 112*(S1), S164–S187.

25 Ariely, D. (2010). *Predictably irrational: The hidden forces that shape our decisions.* New York: Harper.

26 Sunstein, C.R. (2019). *How change happens*. Cambridge, MA: MIT Press.

27 Sunstein, C.R., & Thaler, R.H. (2003). Libertarian paternalism is not an oxymoron. *University of Chicago Law Review, 70*(4), 1159–1202.

28 See Soman, D., Chen, K., & Bendle, N. (2017, Spring). Policy by design: The dawn of behaviourally-informed government. *Rotman Magazine*, 7–12; and OECD. (2017). *Behavioural insights and public policy: Lessons from around the world*. Paris: OECD Publishing, for details on the evolution of nudge units worldwide.

29 See also *BETA podcast: Interview with Professor John A. List*. (2018, 31 August). Podcast transcript from the Behavioural Economics Team of Australia. Retrieved from http://behaviouraleconomics.pmc.gov.au /podcasts/interview-professor-john-list.

30 Breckon, J., & Dodson, J. (2016). *Using evidence: What works?* Alliance for useful evidence. Retrieved from https://www.alliance4usefulevidence .org/publication/using-evidence-what-works-april-2016.

31 For an exception, see Kwon, H.R., & Silva, E.A. (2019). Mapping the landscape of behavioral theories: Systematic literature review. *Journal of Planning Literature*, 1–19. doi:10.1177/0885412219881135.

32 See, for example, Loewenstein, G.F., Weber, E.U., Hsee, C.K., & Welch, N. (2001). Risk as feelings. *Psychological Bulletin, 127*(2), 267–86; Gardner, D. (2015). *Risk: Why we fear the things we shouldn't – and put ourselves in greater danger*. Toronto: Emblem Editions; and Slovic, P. (2010). *The feeling of risk: New perspectives on risk perception*. Oxford: Routledge.

33 Ahn, H.K., Liu, M., & Soman, D. (2009). Memory markers: How consumers remember experiences. *Journal of Consumer Psychology, 19*(3), 508–16.

34 See Soman, D. (2013, Spring). The waiting game: The psychology of time and its effects on service design. *Rotman Magazine*, 41–5, for a review.

35 Tu, Y., & Soman, D. (2014). The categorization of time and its impact on task initiation. *Journal of Consumer Research, 41*(3), 810–22.

36 Zauberman, G., Kim, B.K., Malkoc, S.A., & Bettman, J.R. (2008). Discounting time and time discounting: Subjective time perception and intertemporal preferences. *Journal of Marketing Research, 46*(4), 543–55.

37 Shah, A., Osborne, M., Lefkowitz, J., Fishbane, A., & Soman, D. (2019, 25 September). Can making family salient increase financial savings? Quantifying heterogeneous treatment effects in voluntary retirement contributions using a field experiment in Mexico. Available at SSRN: https://ssrn.com/abstract=3460722, or http://dx. doi:10.2139/ssrn.3460722.

38 See Hampton, D., Leung, M., & Soman, D. (2016, Spring). The empathic mindset. *Rotman Magazine*, 94–6; and Barrows, A., Dabney, N., Hayes, J., & Rosenberg, R. (2018). *Behavioral design teams: A model for integrating behavioral design in city government*. ideas42. Retrieved from https://www .ideas42.org/wp-content/uploads/2018/04/BDT_Playbook_FINAL -digital.pdf.

39 See Hoch, S.J., & Schkade, D.A. (1996). A psychological approach to decision support systems. *Management Science*, 42(1), 51–64, for a discussion of the value of decision support systems.

40 See also Soman, D., Kumar, V., Metcalfe, M., & Wong, J. (2012, Fall). Beyond great ideas: A framework for going global with local innovation. *Rotman Magazine*, 50–5.

41 Kim, J., Yoon, Y., Choi, J., & Soman, D. (2019). Do text reminders about credit card spending help reduce spending? A quasi-experimental evaluation. Working paper.

42 Al-Ubaydli, O., List, J.A., & Suskind, D. (2019). The science of using science: Towards an understanding of the threats to scaling experiments. Working paper no. 2019-73. Retrieved from https://bfi.uchicago.edu/wp-content/uploads/BFI_WP_201973-1.pdf.

43 See Soman, D. (2015). *The last mile: Creating social and economic value from behavioral insights*. Toronto: Rotman-UTP Publishing.

CHAPTER TWO

Embedding Behavioral Insights in Organizations

Bing Feng, Melanie Kim, and Dilip Soman

The claim that every organization is in the business of changing the behavior of its external stakeholders is now not controversial.[1] Governments are often faced with the task of getting citizens and businesses to comply with regulations, to file taxes on time, or to comply with environmental-protection legislation. Businesses are looking to try to get consumers to purchase their products rather than those of their competitors. Financial institutions are looking to encourage their consumers to make better financial decisions by seeking and following the advice of their financial adviser. A dietitian or a doctor is trying to encourage healthy behaviors rather than non-healthy activities such as eating fatty foods or having a sedentary lifestyle. A privacy commissioner wants to get users of online games and apps to spend more time reading the privacy policy and understanding the implications of posting personal data online. These are all examples of organizations' efforts to influence the behavior of external stakeholders.

Every organization is also in the business of influencing behavior internally. For example, a manufacturing facility might be hoping to increase the productivity and morale of its workforce by providing them with suitable incentives. Likewise, an organization might want to encourage the creativity and innovation of its employees by structuring processes differently. Furthermore, departments within organizations routinely interact with one another. These interactions essentially involve elements of human behavior. We suspect that every reader, with a few minutes at their disposal, will be able to generate a large list of internal behavior-change challenges that organizations – small and large – routinely face.

How do organizations go about solving these outward- and inward-facing behavior-change problems? One approach – a rather academic one – is to think about a theoretical understanding of human behavior and identify implications of those theories for the desired behavior change. There are a number of theories – such as prospect theory,[2] construal-level theory,[3] multiple-attribute decision-making theory,[4] or utility theory[5] – that make predictions about how external or internal stakeholders might react to specific decision tasks. A second approach to influencing behavior is to rely on experience. In particular, seasoned and experienced managers often engage implicitly in a process called pattern matching[6] whereby they compare the features of an existing behavior-change challenge to previous similar situations and extrapolate from successes in the past to come up with solutions for the present. In organizations, pattern matching often takes the form of relying on a similar past experience (either past successes within the organization), or on shared success stories (often called "best practices").

Our contention, backed by research conducted in the 1980s and 1990s, is that theory-based and pattern-matching-based approaches work well in stable environments.[7] Stable environments are characterized by simple, easy-to-define problem structures that do not change with time. However, the business and policy environment today is characterized by dynamism (problem structures change rapidly), complexity (multiple causes might be simultaneously responsible for outcomes), as well as an abundance of data and information. Indeed, it has been argued that we live in an era of information overload, and that the policy and business environment is in a state of continuous flux.[8] This complexity in the decision-making environment, therefore, limits the effectiveness of both theory-based and pattern-matching-based approaches to solving behavior-change challenges. The success of behavior-change strategies is conditional on the context, including the timing of the intervention, the physical location, the manner in which the intervention is structured and delivered, the culture, and the language of communication.[9] Interventions that worked well yesterday might not work well today, and interventions that worked well in one country might not work well in another. When many things in the context influence the success of interventions, the predictability of success based solely on theory or pattern matching is limited.

Relying primarily on theory or past experience ("best practices") to create behavior-change interventions results in a number of scaling challenges.[10] This is best illustrated by some recent work done in the area of helping South Korean credit-card consumers make better credit-card choices. It has been established in research in both the laboratory and field studies that consumers spend more when they use a credit card as opposed to using cash or checks.[11] Furthermore, this increase in spending occurs because consumers have a weaker memory for past expenses. In making a purchase, people seem to ask themselves the question, "How much have I spent on similar items in the recent past?" If they can recollect many similar items, then they are less likely to spend on the next opportunity. If recall is poor, then they are more likely to spend. Credit cards weaken the memory trace for the past expense, and hence increase the likelihood of purchase. Lab research also shows that one successful intervention to reduce this so-called credit-card overspending is to provide people with feedback that could take the form of reminders or running totals of prior spending.[12]

The South Korean government introduced a requirement for all credit-card companies to offer a text-alert system that would send an SMS reminder to all consumers after they had made a credit-card purchase. In addition to helping prevent fraud, this system was meant to help people make responsible spending decisions. Results showed that for the vast majority of citizens, the intervention backfired – it actually system increased credit-card spending overall.[13]

This backfiring can be explained by the differences in the context of the experimental studies and the real world. In the lab experiments, attention was not an issue because the reminders and running totals were provided within the context of the experiment, and participants were solely focused on the experimental task. In the real world, there was potential for distraction. In particular, it appears that people fell prey to a phenomenon called *digital dependency*[14] – knowing that their mobile phones had a record of their transactions, the motivation to even try to remember past expenses declined. Recent work in applied behavioral insights shows increasing evidence for such backfiring effects via the failure to replicate the success of interventions that worked elsewhere. Therefore, behaviorally informed organizations must couple their understanding of theory with (a) a broader understanding of the context – of contextual variables that can either facilitate or impede decision making and action – and, most importantly, (b) the ability to rigorously test their ideas in the context in which they will be implemented. We believe that it is important for truly behaviorally informed organizations to conduct in-situ testing of the intervention to ensure its efficacy in the current context, rather than simply borrowing off-the-shelf interventions that have been successful elsewhere.[15]

BUILDING A BEHAVIORALLY INFORMED ORGANIZATION

What should an organization do to embed behavioral insights into its operations and create behavior change at scale? In this chapter, we start by introducing the four roles that behavioral insights (BI) can play within an organization to create value. We then talk about two strategic decisions that organizations need to make as they think about how best to embed BI into their capabilities. We discuss the concept of the cost of experimentation and propose that reducing the cost of experimentation is critical to ongoing success with using BI effectively in engineering behavior change.

FOUR ROLES BI COULD PLAY IN AN ORGANIZATION

The optimal role of BI – and hence the resources needed – will vary depending on the needs of every organization. We identify four roles that BI can play, spanning various points in the organization's value-creation chain (figure 2.1).

Figure 2.1 Four roles for behavioral insights

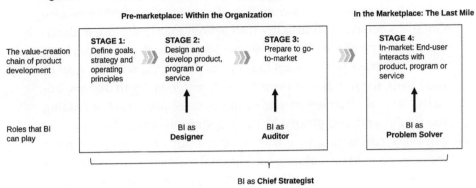

Role 1: BI as Problem Solver

One of the key tools that enables problem solving is the concept of choice architecture – the idea that organizations can proactively design the choice context in such a way as to steer or nudge users in a particular direction. Choice architects can influence four types of choices:[16]

1. *Compliance.* Getting people to act in accordance with a regulation set by a government or agency – for example, nudging citizens to file their tax return on time or to comply with regulatory paperwork requirements.
2. *Switching.* Getting people to convert from one option to another. For instance, businesses try to get customers to switch from purchasing from their competitor, and health organizations encourage consumers to replace soda with water at meals.
3. *Following through and acceleration.* Getting people to follow through on a commitment that they themselves have made, be it completing a weight-loss regimen or acting on their good intentions to be healthy and active. More generally, these involve nudges that get people to accelerate decisions – planning for retirement or leading a healthy lifestyle – before it is too late.
4. *Active choosing.* Getting people to break undesired habits by converting passive, mindless decisions into active choices.

It is fair to say that the biggest successes for BI to date have come in the domain of choice architecture. For example, a few years ago, Ontario's Behavioural Insights Unit set out to increase organ donations in the province. The unit worked closely with project partners Service Ontario and Trillium Gift of Life Network, with the goal of increasing the number of people who register as organ donors. Initially, several "barriers to registration" were identified, including the length and complexity of the registration form, the failure to ask every customer if they wanted to register, and the requirement for customers to undertake an additional transaction after they had waited in line and completed other paperwork. Removing these barriers – and thereby enhancing the choice architecture – increased registration rates by 143 percent.[17]

The problem-solving role for BI is particularly helpful at the "last mile" in product or program delivery – the place where end-users directly interact with the organization.[18] Last-mile issues often arise when the delivery mechanism or the supply chain hasn't fully anticipated and planned for behaviors of the end-user. For instance, a financial literacy agency might offer the most interesting game for teaching financial decision making, or the most user-friendly application for tracking expenditures, but it still needs a good "last-mile" strategy to bring consumers to these resources. Whether the last-mile issue is a low take-up rate, poor sales, or low conversion rates, BI can be harnessed to make subtle changes to better align the product or service with the desired behavior.

Role 2: BI as Auditor

At the end of every design process for products, services, or processes, a behavioral scientist can be tasked with auditing the outcome and evaluating it for human-centricity. In this role, behavioral insights are used to evaluate and provide suggestions for further "humanizing" organizational outputs.

The federal government's Impact and Innovation Unit (now called Impact Canada), along with Behavioural Economics in Action at Rotman (BEAR), recently worked with the Canadian Armed Forces (CAF) on its goal of increasing the percentage of women in its ranks from 15 to 25 percent by the year 2026.[19] The team used a BI lens to audit the application process, marketing effort, and policy design of the recruitment process.

In the application process, BI-informed changes were made to the Armed Forces' application form to increase clarity and understanding. Furthermore, the Department of National Defense (DND) made improvements to the appointment-booking and recruitment follow-ups to minimize pain points in the application process. During the marketing campaign, the unit conducted a social-media marketing trial aimed at understanding "what works" in attracting Canadian women to a career in the armed forces so that the campaign would target the right audiences at the right channel. Last but not least, behavioral insights were used to audit CAF's current policy and guidelines to identify areas for improvement. A number of policy areas, including deployments and relocation, leave without pay, childcare support, and long-term commitments were identified for consideration and BI-inspired improvements.

The auditor role of BI can also be applied in identifying sludge in an organization. Behaviorally speaking, sludge is any component of the context that makes it difficult for people to make decisions or accomplish a task, leading to decreases in consumer welfare.[20] Examples of sludge abound, from companies that make it difficult to cancel subscriptions or to return products, to online businesses that do not disclose relevant information in a timely manner to end-users. Sludge may unintentionally exclude some populations (e.g., an organization that accepts applications only electronically may exclude people who have no access to a computer or the Internet). BI can be used to audit sludge and identify areas that need improvements in process, communication, or inclusivity (see chapter 5).

Role 3: BI as Designer

In this role, a behavioral scientist builds a behavioral solution for a business need using the "behaviorally informed design" approach, which combines the principles of BI with those of design thinking.[21] The design process begins with the question of what is the human need behind a product or service. The behavioral scientist, as a designer, is involved from the very start, observes the actual users in a natural setting, and empathizes with them to understand their motivations and experiences.

Another example of this role is the growing realm of self-control products.[22] Products and services are being created to enable customers to close the intention-action gap[23] whereby people intend to do something positive but fail to act on it. Examples include Clocky, an alarm clock that runs away when the sleepy user hits the snooze button – propelling itself off the bedside table and across the floor, out of reach of the dozing user; and StickK, a website that uses incentives and peer effects to encourage people to stick to their goals.

The BI-as-designer approach was also used by an agency that set out to raise awareness of consumer-protection issues in the domain of financial markets. The website for this agency was improved by using language that was more "human" in nature to maximize website viewers' engagement. For instance, making sure that the anxiety associated with words such as "hazards," "risk," or "unhealthy" is not too strong to drive the viewer away; and testing the balance between visual and text information to minimize the risk of information overload. The results were impressive and included increased traffic to the website, an increase in public debate and discussion on the site, and greater public reporting of marketplace frictions.

Role 4: BI as Chief Strategist

In these cases, every process that touches an internal or external stakeholder is run from a behavioral perspective. The organization is human-centric and behaviorally informed in everything that it does, with behavioral science as its operating principle.

All members of such an organization, including management, content designers, and engineers, are trained to understand the basic principles and applications of behavioral science. The objective is for the entire team to resolve problems using a scientific method and to approach daily operating roles with a BI lens. Behavioral science is seen as the business foundation, rather than just a tool for a designer or a problem solver.

FOUR APPROACHES TO EMBED BI IN AN ORGANIZATION

In addition to deciding which of the four roles of BI makes the most sense for the organization, there are two further key decisions to be made, regarding

(1) the locus of expertise – whether to set up a concentrated team/unit within the organization[24] or to diffuse expertise throughout the enterprise; and
(2) the locus of applications – whether to use BI in a narrow application where they are applied to a specific geographic location or department or to use BI in broad applications where they are applied across domains, geographies, and departments.

These two decisions create four main approaches to embedding BI in an organization (figure 2.2).

1. The Focused Approach

With the *focused approach* an organization decides to develop concentrated expertise within the unit or department to apply BI in specific projects. For example, Employment and Social Development Canada (ESDC) has its own Innovation Lab comprising behavioral scientists, data analysts, designers, and policy analysts. The lab works on projects with internal partners to tackle problems using a combination of human-centric design and BI methods. Its full-scale design project for 2017 was the Canada Learning Bond,[25] with a focus on finding ways to increase uptake of the program and improve understanding of education and financial decision making among low-income families.

2. The Capacity-Building Approach

In the *capacity-building approach* an organization diffuses expertise across the organization – for instance, by stationing personnel in specific departments. In Canada, the Impact Innovation Unit at the Privy Council Office of the federal government houses expertise in four areas: innovative finance, partnerships and capacity

Figure 2.2 Embedding BI in organizations: Four approaches

	Concentrated Expertise	Diffused Expertise
Narrow Application	**FOCUSED**	**CAPACITY BUILDING**
Broad Application	**INTERNAL CONSULTING**	**BEHAVIORALLY INFORMED ORGANIZATION**

building, impact measurement, and behavioral insights. Through the unit's fellowship model, behavioral scientists are deployed to other Government of Canada departments and agencies to provide behavioral-science expertise and run behavioral-insights trials. At the time of writing, it had deployed five behavioral scientists across the Government of Canada.

3. The Internal Consulting Approach

When a concentrated team or unit is set up to apply BI in broad applications across the organization, we call it the *internal consulting approach*. For example, the World Bank's Mind, Behavior, and Development Unit (eMBeD) is a behavioral-science team housed within the World Bank's Poverty and Equity Global Practice. The team works closely with World Bank project teams, governments, and other partners to diagnose, design, and evaluate behaviorally informed interventions. The eMBeD unit currently has sixteen employees working on forty-nine projects across nine thematic areas in sixty-five countries.

4. The Behaviorally Informed Organization Approach

The organization using a *behaviorally informed organization approach* applies BI in broad applications when interacting with external and internal stakeholders, including in project management, human resources, product and service design, customer services, and sales and marketing. The BI expertise is diffused across the organization from the CEO to managers to engineers. The BI approach becomes foundational to the entire organization and to all streams of its work, making it a behaviorally informed organization.

As mentioned earlier, the key to a behaviorally informed organization is use of the scientific method to test solutions and resolve problems. Regardless of which role of BI is most appropriate for the organization, and which approach it chooses to embed BI, experimentation is a crucial component of success. In that sense, critical to using BI effectively is reducing the cost of experimentation.

REDUCING THE COST OF EXPERIMENTATION

Earlier in this chapter, we made the point that human decision making is influenced by almost everything in the context. As a result, a theory that would help us predict exactly how people would behave would be almost impossible to create, given the complexity of all the factors involved. Elements of contexts might interact in unpredictable and complex ways to change the effectiveness of any intervention that was successful elsewhere.

Consider the simplest example of a communications specialist trying to determine which of two messages is most likely to get people to upgrade to an energy-efficient appliance. In one case, the message promises end-users a reward if they upgrade. In the other (functionally identical) message, end-users are told that they would lose the reward if they fail to upgrade. Prospect theory and the principle of loss aversion would predict that the second (loss) frame is more likely to elicit action. Will a loss framing always work?

It is possible that people are more likely to respond to a loss frame in a monetary domain, but are less likely to be influenced in other domains (for example, organ donations). It is also possible that people from certain cultures or past experiences might react positively to losses, while others might react more positively to gains. The competitive context will also matter – in particular, if everyone else in the marketplace is adopting a loss frame, then perhaps a gain frame might possibly be more successful because of the sheer novelty of the messaging.

Given that this is really an empirical question, the obvious answer is to test. The manager could simply create an experiment in which some people are exposed to the first version and others to the second version, and then compare the success rates across the two versions. This experiment could be done in the laboratory, on an online panel, or, indeed, in the real marketplace, taking the form of what is called a randomized controlled trial.[26] This same principle of relying on empirical evidence to decide which of two or more options should be chosen could be similarly used in the domains of marketing, product design, program design, incentive structure, human resource policies, retirement planning, and many, many others. Rather than having expert panels, armchair theorizing, external consultants, or a legacy approach dictate which of two options is better, the manager could simply test and use the results to make decisions. Why do we often not see this happening?

We contend that the biggest barrier to the use of this scientific approach of experimentation, learning, adaptation, and scaling is that experimentation is expensive. Indeed, we contend that the first thing that organizations need to do in instilling a culture of behavioral science is to reduce the cost of experimentation.[27]

The cost of experimentation isn't limited to the direct cost of collecting and analyzing data. We propose that the following costs are central to the costs of experimentation:

1. Costs of data collection

    In order to run perfect experiments, organizations need to test interventions in relevant contexts and with the appropriate populations. In the perfect experiment, whether the experiment is conducted in the lab or in the field, participants need to be randomly assigned to different versions of interventions (treatments). To analyze whether the intervention works from an experiment, organizations will need at least two groups, the control group and the treatment group. The cost associated with data collection and analysis is not just having access to representative sample data but, more importantly, having the right platform for randomization.

2. Cost of creating an experimental mindset

    For a lot of organizations, the process of creating an experimental mindset might be very costly. Changing the theory- and experience-driven mindset to an experimental mindset takes time and effort. In fact, many organizations note that getting partners or senior managers comfortable with experimentation is initially most challenging when embedding BI. Organizations also need to be alert to resistance during the process. Setting up a baseline for experiments might help in the initial stage, but a commitment to try on a few concrete projects without expecting immediate success will help cultivate an experimental mindset.

3. Cost of institutional impatience

    Organizations or managers might expect immediate success from one experiment. However, we know that experimentation is not always successful, and that a series of experiments over time is needed to converge to solutions. Leaders might therefore pull the plug on experimentation too soon, increasing the pressure on units to "get it right" quickly.

4. Cost of building agility – so that organizations can easily adapt to learnings

    Building agility in an organization can be costly, but it is essential for a behaviorally informed organization. A flexible organizational structure or process allows for quick feedback loops to be incorporated and a test-learn-adapt strategy to be put in place.[28] Agile organizations also tend to have an appreciation for the complete canvas of BI applications.

We know from the law of demand – and it makes perfect intuitive sense – that as things become cheaper, the demand for those things increases, the demand for substitutes decreases, and the demand for complements increases. In particular, as the cost of experimentation goes down, the demand for experimentation will go up. Therefore, the demand for well-trained behavioral-insights expertise that will create the appropriate experiments will go up. The demand for armchair theorizing and relying on legacy to make decisions will go down. We contend that the cost of experimentation is a critical factor in enabling the diffusion of BI and, therefore, the creation of behaviorally informed organizations.

What can organizations do to drive down the costs of experimentation? We believe there are five key sets of solutions:[29]

1. Investing in hard and soft infrastructure. This includes (a) building or adopting an online experimental platform to collect data and being able to randomly assign participants to treatments, (b) building participant pools that recruit from the appropriate populations, (c) setting up laboratory space and facilities to collect behavioral data and run experiments, and (d) recruiting researchers with expertise in experimental methods. The marginal cost of running experiments will diminish as organizations get proficient at testing and researchers become more familiar with the experimentation process.[30]

2. Developing expertise in appropriate problem selection with increasing complexity over time. Organizations or managers can be tempted to solve broad and aggregated outcomes at the beginning – for example, by using BI to improve satisfaction, or to change consumers' attitudes. Experimentation may be ineffective in addressing a challenge that is too broad in scope. To reduce the cost of experimentation and help build an experimental mindset in the organization, it is vital to decompose large challenges into precise behaviors and run a few experiments without expecting immediate success. Once

progress is made, the organization can build horizontally scalable behavior-change problems or add more complexity to the challenge over time.[31]

3. Building a what-works database, which will allow organizations to narrow down possible interventions to test. The what-works database will also serve as a proof of concept and internal BI resource for future experimentation.[32]

4. Developing a framework for ethical experimentation. Key individuals within an organization might fear experimentation because they are afraid of being perceived as unethical. Developing and disseminating a framework for ethical experimentation within the organization will help reduce the cost. When designing BI solutions, organizations need to ensure that the interventions (a) are consistent with users' values and interests, (b) are for legitimate ends, (c) do not violate any rights of the users, and (d) are transparent and do not take things away without consent.[33]

5. Changing the mindset about failure and incentivizing experimentation. Realizing and clearly communicating that a null-result is a learning opportunity will minimize the fear of failure.[34] Explicitly rewarding experimentation will further build the test-learn-adapt culture in the organization.

CONCLUSION

The early years of BI as a field were marked by a need to score quick wins and find proof-of-concept for this approach to engineering behavioral change. Now that the field has gained broad acceptance, we expect organizations to start using it to tackle more complex behavioral and policy challenges going forward. BI can and should play a key role in important societal domains such as the environment, business sustainability, preventive health, and diversity and inclusion. The more important question is: Should the organization even try to be scientific? There are two different ways that the science can be helpful. The first one is knowing the result of behavioral science, including the process of generating new BI theories and documenting behavioral phenomena. Organizations do not need to be scientific in addressing this area because academics and consultants are capable of doing it more efficiently. The second way is by testing, learning from, and adapting BI to the development of products, processes, and programs. There is a science of doing, and this is the science we want to highlight for a behaviorally informed organization.

NOTES

1 Soman, D. (2015). *The last mile: Creating social and economic value from behavioral insights*. Toronto: University of Toronto Press.
2 Kahneman, D., & Tversky, A. (1979). Prospect theory: An analysis of decision under risk. *Econometrica, 47*(2), 263–91.
3 Trope, Y., & Liberman, N. (2003). Temporal construal. *Psychological Review, 110*(3), 403–21.
4 Dyer, J.S., Fishburn, P.C., Steuer, R.E., Wallenius, J., & Zionts, S. (1992). Multiple criteria decision making, multiattribute utility theory: The next ten years. *Management Science, 38*(5), 645–54.
5 Schoemaker, P.J.H. (1982). The expected utility model: Its variants, purposes, evidence and limitations. *Journal of Economic Literature, 20*(2), 529–63.
6 See Hogarth, R.M. (2010). *Educating intuition*. Chicago: University of Chicago Press, for an excellent discussion on the use of experience, intuition, and pattern matching.
7 Hoch, S.J., & Schkade, D.A. (1996). A psychological approach to decision support systems. *Management Science, 42*(1), 51–64.
8 Soberman, D., Soman, D., & Martin, R. (2012). *Flux: What marketing managers need to navigate the new environment*. Toronto: University of Toronto Press.
9 Thomadsen, R., Rooderkerk, R.P., Amir, O., Arora, N., Bollinger, B., Hansen, K., et al. (2018). How context affects choice. *Customer Needs and Solutions, 5*(1–2), 3–14.
10 List, J.A., Suskind, D., & Al-Ubaydli, O. (2019). The science of using science: Towards an understanding of the threats to scaling experiments. University of Chicago, Becker Friedman Institute for Economics Working Paper No. 2019-73. doi: 10.2139/ssrn.3391481.
11 See Soman, D. (2001). Effects of payment mechanism on spending behavior: The role of rehearsal and immediacy of payments. *Journal of Consumer Research, 27*(4), 460–74. doi: 10.1086/319621; and Prelec, D., & Simester, D. (2001). Always leave home without it: A further

investigation of the credit-card effect on willingness to pay. *Marketing Letters, 12*(1), 5–12.

12 See Soman, D. (2001). Effects of payment mechanism on spending behavior: The role of rehearsal and immediacy of payments. *Journal of Consumer Research, 27*(4): 460–74, Experiment 1. doi: 10.1086/319621. See also, Raghubir, P., & Srivastava, J. (2008). Monopoly money: The effect of payment coupling and form on spending behavior. *Journal of Experimental Psychology: Applied, 14*(3), 213–25; and Trites, S., Gibneym C., & Lévesque, B. (2013). Mobile payments and consumer protection in Canada. Financial Consumer Agency of Canada. Retrieved from https://www.canada .ca/content/dam/canada/financial-consumer-agency/migration /eng/resources/researchsurveys/documents/fcac_mobile_payments _consumer_protection_accessible_en.pdf.

13 Kim, J., Choi, J., Yoon, Y., & Soman, D. (2019). Do text reminders about credit card spending help reduce spending? A quasi-experimental evaluation. Working Paper, University of Toronto.

14 Sparrow, B., Liu, J., & Wegner, D.M. (2011). Google effects on memory: Cognitive consequences of having information at our fingertips. *Science, 333*(6043), 776–8. doi: 10.1126/science.1207745.

15 Soman, D., & Hossain, T. (2020). Successfully scaled interventions need not be homogeneous. *Behavioural Public Policy*, forthcoming.

16 See also Soman, D. (2015). *The last mile: Creating social and economic value from behavioral insights*. Toronto: University of Toronto Press.

17 Behavioural Insights Unit in Ontario. (2018). Retrieved from https://files .ontario.ca/biu_progress_report_2018.pdf.

18 Soman, D. (2015). *The last mile: Creating social and economic value from behavioral insights*. Toronto: University of Toronto Press.

19 Akin, D. (2018, 16 September). Canada's Armed Forces, struggling to hit diversity goals, turns to new digital recruiting tools. Retrieved from https://globalnews.ca/news/4450927/canada-armed-forces-diversity -goals-digital-recruiting/.

20 Soman, D., Cowen, D., Kannan, N., & Feng, B. (2019). Seeing sludge: Towards a dashboard to help organizations recognize impedance to end-user decisions and action. *SSRN Electronic Journal*. doi: 10.2139 /ssrn.3460734.

21 Hampton, D., Leung, M., & Soman, D. (2016, Spring). The empathic mindset. *Rotman Magazine*, 94–6.

22 Soman, D., & Ly, K. (2018, Fall). The growing market for self-control. *Rotman Magazine*, 123–5.

23 Soman, D., Vinoo, P., & Ly, K. (2015). Self-regulation and spending behaviors. In K. Vohs and R. Baumeister (Eds.), *Handbook of self-regulation*. New York: Guilford Press.

24 See, for example, Sunstein (2019), foreword in this volume.

25 Government of Canada. (2018, 1 August). Increasing take-up of the Canada Learning Bond. Retrieved from https://www.canada.ca/en/innovation -hub/services/reports-resources/behavioural-insights-project.html.

26 Cabinet Office. (2012, 14 June). Test, learn, adapt: Developing public policy with randomized controlled trials. Retrieved from http://www .cabinetoffice.gov.uk/resource-library/test-learn-adapt-developing-public -policy-randomised-controlled-trials.

27 For a similar analysis on the effects of the cost of prediction on organizations, see Agrawal, A., Gans, J., & Goldfarb, A. (2018). *Prediction machines: The simple economics of artificial intelligence.* Boston: Harvard Business Review Press.

28 Haynes, L., Service, O., Goldacre, B., & Torgerson, D. (2013). Test, learn, adapt: Developing public policy with randomized controlled trials. *SSRN Electronic Journal.*

29 Easton, S. (2018, 19 July). Cass Sunstein's bill of rights for nudging. *The Mandarin.* Retrieved 15 November 2019 from https://www.themandarin .com.au/96009-cass-sunsteins-bill-of-rights-for-nudging/.

30 For a discussion on field experiments in policy, see Al-Ubaydli, O., Lee, M.S., List, J.A., Mackevicius, C., & Suskind, D. (2019). How can experiments play a greater role in public policy? 12 proposals from an economic model of scaling. *SSRN Electronic Journal.* doi: 10.2139 /ssrn.3478066.

31 Cabinet Office. (2012, 14 June). Test, learn, adapt: Developing public policy with randomized controlled trials. Retrieved from http://www .cabinetoffice.gov.uk/resource-library/test-learn-adapt-developing-public -policy-randomised-controlled-trials.

32 Halpern, D., & Service, O. (2015). *Inside the nudge unit: How small changes can make a big difference.* London: W.H. Allen.

33 See Sunstein, C.R. (2015). The ethics of nudging. *Yale Journal on Regulation, 32*(2). Retrieved from http://digitalcommons.law.yale.edu/yjreg/vol32 /iss2/6. See also Engelen, B. (2019). Ethical criteria for health-promoting nudges: A case-by-case analysis. *The American Journal of Bioethics, 19*(5), 48–59. doi: 10.1080/15265161.2019.1588411.

34 Cannon, M.D., & Edmondson, A.C. (2005). Failing to learn and learning to fail (intelligently). *Long Range Planning, 38*(3), 299–319. doi: 10.1016 /j.lrp.2005.04.005.

CHAPTER THREE

Why Should Organizations Want to Be Behaviorally Informed?

Melaina Vinski

As we embark on a decade forecasted to be fraught with low growth, rapid disruption to the traditional company archetypes, and geopolitical uncertainty, the urgency with which companies need to evolve their traditional decision-making frameworks cannot be overstated. Behaviorally informed organizations – organizations that have been described in the preface – sit at the forefront of this evolution with an empirically based decision framework situated at the nexus of economic theory and the science of behavior. They use a behavioral lens to identify and uncover hidden behavioral patterns of consumers and stakeholders and, in turn, to create greater confidence in how they make big bets, innovate and transform, and craft their competitive edge.

Decision-making paradigms within business have traditionally been dominated by the central tenets of economic theory. While considered an essential asset to understand and define the parameters in which an organization operates, traditional economic theory sits within a tightly bound world where human actors are rational beings striving for utility and self-preservation independent of time or space.

Behavioral scientists have made us think differently. In their conception of the human world, human actors (or "people" as we prefer to be called) live and breathe within an environment heavily swayed by intangible and difficult-to-capture variables such as cognitive-resource availability, emotional reactivity and resonance, social influence, and personal salience. In this ever-evolving environment, what people strive for is dependent on what they consider relevant at that moment in time. In this human world, rational decision making is more the exception than the rule.

One of the unintended consequences of reliance on traditional economic theory is the foundational belief that intention is a proxy for action. Intention, someone's conscious attitude and commitment toward a goal or behavior, is a pragmatic and authentic measure of the likelihood of behavior in a world defined by rationality. If we intend to pay down our savings balance, we likely will. If employees intend to be more productive at work, they likely will. If executives intend to share their differing opinions at an offsite with colleagues, they likely will.

There is one dilemma with the intention-based thesis, however. As anyone would understand from observations of their own behavior – the failure to stick with a New Year's resolution, to follow through on plans with friends, or to break that bad habit – despite our best intentions, we sometimes fall short. We also notice it in the behaviors of those around us. Our family and our friends sometimes fall short of their (and our) expectations, too.

As any executive or strategic decision maker would understand from observations within the walls of their own organizations – for example, the failure of employees to adopt a new technology or customers to buy a product they said was "perfect for their needs" – colleagues and customers can sometimes also fall short of expectations. The behavioral community has come to label this phenomenon the "intention-action gap."[1] Sometimes wide, sometimes narrow, and sometimes not present at all, the gap is a demonstration of how contextual variance defines how people (as opposed to "rational human actors") make decisions in their day-to-day lives.

In this chapter, I will tell you a story about how this gap covertly creates a chasm between the expectations we have of what the future holds and the reality of what happens. From the way we make big strategic bets on where and how to play in the market to the way we design operating models and transformations, from the way we build our products and services to meet the needs of our customers to the way we design and execute customer and employee experiences – the gap lurks within the assumptions we have when making day-to-day decisions within our organizations. It is in this light that I often refer to the intention-action gap as the expectation-reality gap of strategic decision making. The gap creates challenges for organizations attempting to succeed in an uncertain market, and this is one of the many reasons why organizations should strive to be behaviorally informed.

HOW BIG IS THE GAP REALLY?

A deep and systematic study of the gap between intention and behavior helps illuminate why and when it exists and how wide it may be. Examination of the when, where, what, why, and how is a quintessential rabbit hole for the brave and curious mind. A general Google search of the intention-action gap yields more than 50 million results, with Google Scholar providing a slight reprieve with just 2 million scholarly publications on the topic. The sheer quantity of content and dedicated academic focus testify to the myriad situations in which the gap is observed and the degree to which it holds relevance for understanding the "why" behind outcomes.

We know the gap exists, but exactly how wide is it? Young, DeSarbo, and Morwitz used stochastic modelling and found that customer purchase intentions lead to purchase behavior less than 62 percent of the time,[2] while Rongen and colleagues found that only 21 percent of employees participate in employee health programs despite having a positive intention to do so and an understanding of the benefits of participation.[3] In one of the most comprehensive analyses of the gap – inclusive of over 400 studies and 80,000 participants across an array of behaviors ranging from the daily mundane to the rare and meaningful – Sheeran found that intentions account for a mere 28 percent of variance in actual behavior.[4] This finding means that when we use intention to anticipate the behavior of others, our expectations will be aligned to outcomes less than a third of the time. It also means that two-thirds of the time these same expectations will fall short.

For most of us, it is relatively easy to wrap our minds around the idea that reality can get in the way of our best intentions. We can easily list a few "realistic considerations" when we explain (to ourselves) why we decide not to go to the gym today – too tired, too busy, too late, too early. The difficult and perhaps more nuanced task is to consider the influence of reality in what we can expect of our customers, employees, and executives on the most conscious level possible. Expectations of our own and others' behavior is inherently woven within our mental models of the present and future, of risk and reward, and of potential (and likely) alternative outcomes. These expectations are embedded in the formulation of assumptions that underlie the way we quantify and qualify the operational, financial, or reputational risks we take every day.

HOW DOES THE GAP PLAY INTO MY ORGANIZATION'S DAY-TO-DAY DECISIONS?

To consider the influence of context on probable behavior is no easy task and can be a mind bender for even the most experienced behavioral scientists. The challenge lies in the ability to evaluate potential outcomes and calibrate expectations on the behaviors woven within our assumptions, including the size of the change potential relative to the size of the opportunity, the investment required to achieve change relative to the estimated return on investment for the broader initiative, and, perhaps most importantly, whether the desired change is even achievable.

Take for example how market and customer research is implemented, interpreted, and translated into the design of products and services. Have you kept the gap in mind before investing in the skills, teams, and time required to innovate from ideation through to execution?

Research has shown that sometimes the gap between purchase intention and action can rest primarily in the way a choice is structured. In an evaluation of 7,000 consumers across the United States, the United Kingdom, and Australia, the connection between a customer's intention and actual purchase behavior was 86 percent higher if the presentation of choices and related information was simplified.[5] The *same* products being offered in a *different* way shifted purchase decisions in a meaningful way. According to the 22nd Annual PwC (PricewaterhouseCoopers) CEO survey, two-thirds of Canadian leaders are planning to launch a new product or service within the next year to drive revenue growth.[6] This trend surfaces even though creeping product proliferation can lead to a rise in costs, a decline in quality, and a confusion among top performing sales teams about how best to meet customers' needs.[7] Behaviorally informed organizations are able to extract principles from purchase-decision theory and behavioral economics and weave them into assumptions underlying expected purchase behavior and, in turn, better inform whether changes to the choice architecture or product attributes are likely enough to improve segment penetration or market share.

What about how customer insights and experience analytics are implemented, interpreted, and translated into the design of customer experiences? Have you kept the gap in mind before investing in new service operating models, omnichannel integrations, or shiny digital applications?

Research has shown that a balanced and considered approach to managing consumer touchpoints can have a significant impact on expected purchase behavior. A study that analyzed $3 billion in Canadian media spend identified $1.4 billion in loss of potential sales revenue in 2018 as a result of an overinvestment in digital and an underinvestment in television.[8] The study authors concluded that while companies understood the importance of touchpoint frequency on customer experience, they underestimated the halo effect of television advertising on the performance of adjacent media channels and on consumer decision making about product purchases. The initial insight of frequency was there, but the underlying assumptions favored the stated preference of customers over the cognitive mechanisms that drive how impressions are formed. Behaviorally informed organizations draw insights from cognitive models of attention, memory, and context, and weave them into assumptions underlying expected customer behavior. In turn, these organizations are able to better define the marginal benefit of additional (or alternative) omnichannel spend on the likelihood of shifting consumer behavior and eventual outcomes.

What about how financial and operating models are leveraged to define strategic decisions on small-, medium-, and large-scale transformations? Have you kept the gap in mind before investing in the technology, people, and processes required to create and sustain adoption?

Just as minimal convincing is needed to persuade an average reader that a gap can exist between intention and action, limited coaxing is required to make us believe that changing behavior is hard. In a study conducted by Holweg, Staats, and Upton, an analysis of more than two hundred lean projects launched within a European bank showed that while initial efficiency and productivity gains can be promising they tend to be short-lived. Their analysis revealed that 21 percent of projects failed to yield any improvements, and for the remaining 79 percent that showed initial progress, a third failed to sustain momentum after two years.[9] Taken in conjunction with well-worn anecdotes about how the majority of transformations "fail," this kind of finding prompted predictions that digital transformation would be the biggest business risk in 2019[10] and explains why forecasts of spending on transformations have increased by almost 18 percent.[11]

The issue is not that change-management efforts are flawed or that well-conceived plans are not put in place. Changing behavior is not easy, nor does it happen quickly, and when the stakes are high and the socioeconomic environment is increasingly unpredictable, a behaviorally driven account for the array of contextual influences that drive (or hinder) new behaviors is more of a requirement than a nice-to-have. Behaviorally informed organizations would aim at incorporating the most important variables within individual and group-level theories of change into assumptions underlying expected employee adoption. In turn, these organizations would be better able to define the change potential, necessary program-design elements, and investment likely required to make the change happen, and better able to calibrate their expectations of (and timelines for) outcomes. They would also be better able to determine whether the investment in change is proportionate to or worth the potential benefits for business outcomes and pivot their decision-making energy accordingly. Sometimes, they are even able to say, "What else can we try?"

What about how growth strategies trickle down into incentive and motivational programs for frontline employees? Have you kept the gap in mind before changing employees' performance metrics?

The enormous financial penalties served to institutions for unethical behavior show that the consequences of performance-metric decisions can be costly. In 2015, Lloyds Bank was fined £117 million for employees' mishandling of sales of Payment Protection Insurance on loans and credit cards because they did not inform customers who were self-employed or who had existing medical issues that they would never be able to make a valid claim. In 2016, Wells Fargo was fined $185 million by US regulators for the opening of millions of unauthorized checking and savings accounts as a result of a high-pressure sales culture that encouraged cross-selling. More than 5,000 employees were let go as a result. In 2018, the Commonwealth Bank of Australia was hit with a $1 billion charge because of poor management of operational, compliance, and conduct risks. In all of these high-profile cases, it is likely safe to assume that the strategic goal was to drive productive and high-performing sales cultures rather than to cause unethical practices. Incentives drive both intended and unintended consequences, and decision makers need to evaluate and calibrate both outcomes when determining how to translate growth strategies into frontline change. Behaviorally informed organizations draw on theories of motivations to provide a better understanding of employees' reactions to different incentives and, in turn, can better define the potential benefits and consequences of performance-management strategies on reputational (and in some cases financial) risk.

The goal in this chapter is not to undervalue the insights, research, or models that drive decisions in product innovation, customer experience, transformations, or performance measurement. Each insight is uniquely and additively valuable in pointing organizations in the right direction. These insights can, however, be based on a rigid model of the world that is bound in a closed-loop or rational system – a system where the contextual variation described by behavioral scientists' view of the world is not necessarily woven within assumptions driving decision-making efforts.

WELCOMING THE NEW KID (OR NERD) IN TOWN

Behavioral scientists thrive in a world that is highly variable, dependent on environmental and attitudinal context, and in a constant state of change and adaptation. They spend their time trying to wrap their minds around the seemingly erratic and organic realities of human behavior. They sift through empirical studies to uncover mechanisms driving decisions and dig through the noise to uncover the gap between what people say and what people do. They tinker with experimental conditions in an attempt to figure out the most plausible answer to the question "Why?" – the same method that elevated Michael Kremer, Abhijit Banerjee, and Esther Duflo to win the 2019 Nobel Prize in Economics for their experimental approach to alleviating global poverty.

Behavioral scientists help define in what context someone's intentions are likely to predict behavior, and, for the remaining 72 percent of behaviors for which intention is not a valid predictive measure, they are able to leverage psychological models and principles of behavioral economics to design a pathway forward – from the tiniest and most nuanced nudges to the largest program overhauls – in order to shrink the gap and fine-tune our mental models of the world.

Behavioral scientists help create conditions of confidence for those around the table who are making the tough (or not so tough) decisions, and their efforts have translated into tangible business benefits, too. Companies that apply the principles of behavioral economics have been shown to outperform their peers by 85 percent in sales growth and more than 25 percent in gross margin,[12] and companies that are leveraging analytics to implement targeted interventions have been shown to achieve a 50 percent increase in revenue, 24 percent increase in profitability, and 55 percent increase in share of wallet.[13]

At the beginning of this chapter, I wrote that the intention-action gap demonstrates how variability in behavior can complicate the traditional mental model of the world. While a focus on understanding and closing the gap is not the only blueprint for behavioral scientists to create impact for an organization, it is a valuable place to start. The goal of applied behavioral science is not to push people into making decisions for the betterment of an organization. The goal is to ensure that products, services, programs, and experiences are designed to give people the capability, contextual reinforcement, and social infrastructure needed to support their ability for self-advocacy and intention to follow through. It sets the parameters to ensure that the conversation starts in the right place and keeps efforts on the right side of the ethical line.

In an era of enhanced transparency and great economic, geopolitical, and social uncertainty, behaviorally informed organizations have an opportunity to build decision makers' confidence by evolving their mental model of the world. They have the opportunity to dig deep into the real drivers of human behaviors and close the gap between expectations and outcomes when making strategic decisions. They embrace a world where people are humans and, with that, accept the messiness that can sometimes come with a newly informed understanding.

The behavioral science community is ready. What are you waiting for?

NOTES

The views and opinions expressed in the article are those of the author for which PwC Canada takes no responsibility and disclaims all liability.

1 Sheeran, P. (2002). Intention–behavior relations: A conceptual and empirical review. *European Review of Social Psychology, 12*(1), 1–36.
2 Young, M.R., DeSarbo, W.S., & Morwitz, V.G. (1998). The stochastic modeling of purchase intentions and behavior. *Management Science, 44*(2), 188–202.
3 Rhodes, R.E., & de Bruijn, G.J. (2013). How big is the physical activity intention–behaviour gap? A meta-analysis using the action control framework. *British Journal of Health Psychology, 18*(2), 296–309.
4 Sheeran, P. (2002). Intention–behavior relations: A conceptual and empirical review. *European Review of Social Psychology, 12*(1), 1–36.

5 Spenner, P., & Freeman, K. (2012, May). To keep your customers keep it simple. *Harvard Business Review*. https://hbr.org/2012/05/to-keep-your -customers-keep-it-simple.

6 PricewaterhouseCoopers (PwC). (2019). 22nd Annual Global CEO Survey: CEO's curbed confidence spells caution. https://www.pwc.com/gx/en /ceo-survey/2019/report/pwc-22nd-annual-global-ceo-survey.pdf.

7 Mocker, M., & Ross, J.W. (2017). The problem with product proliferation. *Harvard Business Review, 95*(3), 104–10.

8 Dhar, S., Macdonald, C., Hrebik, J., & Corridore, M. (2019). The moneyball moment for marketing in Canada: Leveraging TV to drive improved media spend performance. Accenture Strategy study commissioned by thinktv. https://thinktv.ca/wp-content/uploads/2019/02/The -Moneyball-Moment-for-Marketing-in-Canada-Whitepaper.pdf.

9 Holweg, M., Staats B., & Upton, B. (2018). Making process improvements stick: Early excitement usually leads to backsliding. *Harvard Business Review, 96*(6), 16–19.

10 N.C. State Poole College of Management. (2019). Executive perspectives on top risks for 2019: Key issues being discussed in the boardroom and C-suite. Protiviti. Retrieved from https://erm.ncsu.edu/az/erm/i/chan /library/2019-erm-execs-top-risks-report.pdf.

11 International Data Corporation (IDC). (2019). Worldwide semiannual digital transformation spending guide. https://www.idc.com/getdoc .jsp?containerId=IDC_P32575.

12 Fleming, J.H., & Harter, J.K. (2010). The next discipline: Applying behavioral economics to drive growth and profitability. Gallup, Inc. https://www.gallup.com/services/178028/next-discipline-pdf.aspx.

13 Grafstein, D., & Nelson, B. (2018, 7 November).Why B2B leaders should get in touch with their customers' feelings. Gallup, Inc. https://www .gallup.com/analytics/244607/why-b2b-leaders-touch-customers-feelings .aspx.

CHAPTER FOUR

Gut Check: Why Organizations That Need to Be Behaviorally Informed Resist It

Shannon O'Malley and Kelly Peters

Over the past ten years, we and our colleagues have worked with numerous organizations to develop, test, and implement strategies that are based on scientifically backed behavioral insights. In that time, we have seen a common pattern in how organizations come to adopt behavioral insights. Let's take the story of Karen, a vice-president of customer service at a large financial institution. One day, a friend sends her a TED talk given by Dan Ariely[1] in which he is talking about how humans are irrational, and how there are forces that we are rarely aware of that drive our decision making. Karen starts thinking about the customers she serves and what might be influencing their decisions. She starts to seek out more resources, devouring books she can find on the topic (e.g., *Nudge, Thinking Fast and Slow, Predictably Irrational*).[2] She feels that there must be some way to implement these insights at work, but she isn't sure how to go about it or how to convince her colleagues that this is a good approach. To us, this is a familiar story; this is the point at which so many of our clients initially reach out to us. We call this person our "maverick"; they are our ally in communicating the value of behavioral insights, behavioral science, and the scientific method to the broader organization.

Behavioral science has largely focused on uncovering behavioral insights about consumer, citizen, and end-user behavior rather than insights regarding organizations. However, organizations are made up of teams of individuals; the biases and barriers influencing consumers are the same ones hindering organizations from becoming behaviorally informed. A practitioner or "maverick" may well be aware of the *reasons* for and *benefits* of becoming a behaviorally informed organization but may not be armed with a *strategy* for addressing those barriers. Consumers may be disposed to do things the way they have always been done, even if a newer, better option is available; but the same holds true for executive teams conducting their operations. After all, we are all predictably irrational.

The goal of this chapter is both to acknowledge the very real barriers to the adoption of behavioral economics (BE) within organizations and to identify ways to overcome these obstacles. Barriers can be subdivided into two categories: psychological and organizational. We will also explore realistic solutions for addressing and challenging these barriers. In the words of Nobel Prize–winning behavioral scientist Richard Thaler, "Decision makers do not make choices in a vacuum. They make them in an environment where many features, noticed and unnoticed, can influence their decisions. The person who creates that environment is, in our terminology, a choice architect."[3] If we as behavioral scientists, enthusiasts, and mavericks see the value of being part of a behaviorally informed organization and want to see a greater awareness and integration of behavioral science in our workplace, we have to recognize the biases and barriers in play to effectively influence our environment.

BARRIERS TO ADOPTION

There are a number of barriers that inhibit organizations from embracing new methods. While these barriers apply to the introduction of any new framework or method into a well-established workplace culture, we will nonetheless explore those obstacles that most profoundly impact the adoption of behavioral science and insights. As mentioned, we will group these barriers into two main categories: (1) psychological barriers – the predictably irrational behaviors and attitudes that impact individuals and groups, and (2) organizational barriers, including elements of knowledge quality and acquisition and workplace culture. Both obstacles can be challenging to confront, although organizational barriers can be particularly tricky because in larger, well-established entities culture and tradition are deeply entrenched. We as scientists, mavericks, and enthusiasts need to be considerate of our workplace cultural milieu and explore its flexibility and complementarity relative to the scientific culture as we move forward.

PSYCHOLOGICAL BARRIERS

A number of common biases and heuristics are held by persons or groups within an organization. These barriers are very well known in the behavioral sciences and are useful for our mavericks and advocates to understand in terms both of addressing customers for an upcoming project or communicating with fellow employees when fostering behaviorally informed organizational transformation. An outline of some of these common biases follows.

Status-Quo Bias: A preference for things to remain as they are is a very common bias. This is generally seen as an outcome of loss aversion, because the disadvantages of change loom larger than the advantages.[4] In the context of organizations looking to become behaviorally informed, the costs of implementing behavioral insights can loom larger than the potential gains, especially if the decision makers are unfamiliar with the field. An individual or group within an organization who proposes the adoption of behavioral science needs buy-in from key players within the organization. If the actors and decision makers do not see or understand the value of adopting behavioral science, it is far too easy for them to fixate on the risk; thus the preference will likely be to remain with current operations as the default option.

System-Justification Theory and Semmelweis Reflex: While the status-quo bias is relatively passive (that is, that the current state is preferred over uncertainty-rich change), system justification is a more active process in which certain individuals are motivated to justify and maintain the current state.[5] Because the current system has well-established relationships, order, and predictability, the agents within it will seek to justify its efficiency, credibility, and sovereignty even if the status quo is neither supremely efficient nor beneficial to all. For agents in this mindset, alternatives to the status quo may be disparaged or dismissed. Furthermore, justification for the current methods may occur even in the face of clear contrary evidence. This may be in part due to the Semmelweis reflex, whereby the evidence presented seriously challenges the schema and working model of the current establishment, and therefore is rejected. To resolve the cognitive dissonance that arises from maintaining the status quo in the face of contrary evidence, individuals might find it *easier to dismiss the evidence* rather than change their paradigm and practices.

Group Think: This term describes the psychological phenomenon that occurs within a group of people in which the desire for harmony or conformity within the group results in an irrational or dysfunctional decision-making outcome.[6] Group members try to minimize conflict and reach a consensus without critical evaluation of alternative viewpoints by actively suppressing dissenting opinions and isolating themselves from outside influences. For anyone in an organization looking to implement new methods, it takes courage and strength to speak up and push for change. This is why we consider these people as mavericks; driving change requires someone to stand out from the crowd.

Risk Aversion: This is one of the foundational concepts in behavioral economics. People generally prefer outcomes that are certain over outcomes that are uncertain, even if the expected utility of the uncertain outcome is larger.[7] When an organization is looking to adopt a new methodology, there is some level of risk involved. The approach may not work; or it may even backfire, leading to hesitation or inactivity. If individuals or a team within an organization push to implement behavioral insights, there may be a risk to their reputation or career if the approach fails.

Ambiguity Aversion: We tend to prefer known risks, in which the probability of a given outcome is known, over unknown risks.[8] When we are making decisions in the real world, we are often faced with ambiguous options – for example, which career to pursue, which insurance to buy, or which partner to marry. For organizations deciding to adopt new methodology, the risks can appear very ambiguous. In the case of behavioral insights, one concern we hear from clients is that they are worried that consumers will find out they are "being nudged," and there will be backlash against being "manipulated" (see the discussion on the costs of experimentation in chapter 2). While there are steps that can be taken to mitigate this risk, the probability of a negative outcome for adopting behavioral insights in their practice is rarely clear to organizations. This introduces an uncomfortable ambiguity with respect to their decision to become behaviourally informed.

Sunk-Cost Fallacy: This term describes behaviour characterized by continuing to pursue an endeavor or a project that is not working, primarily because an organization has already invested time or effort into it. Although behavioral science can be informed by and collaborative with other forms of research (e.g., traditional market research and data analytics can inform both ideation and experimentation), the reality is that it sometimes replaces other research methods. When organizations have invested significant resources in such methods, we may observe a resistance to switch to behavioral insights because of the sunk cost. For organizations, course correction with respect to the sunk-cost fallacy is complicated: the problem first has to be identified across the organization, and a strategic plan to shift course then needs to be developed and implemented. If the old methods are deeply ingrained within the company, the sunk-cost effect can be exacerbated, making it improbable that the company would abandon current methods to adopt new ones.

Law of the Instrument: An over-reliance on a familiar tool or method can lead to ignoring or undervaluing alternative approaches. "If all you have is a hammer, everything looks like a nail."[9] The many different tools used by behavioral scientists (e.g., observed behaviors, self-report, EEG, fMRI) are all designed to address different types of questions. For example, if you want to know what parts of the brain are active in memory recall, functional magnetic resonance imaging (fMRI) would be appropriate; if you want to know the types of errors people make during recall, you would score the types of recalled items and errors. Different scales and scopes of measurement require different tools. While this might seem straightforward, the more entrenched a researcher becomes in a method in which they are skilled, the easier it is to lose sight of this fact. All questions seem like they can be answered with one's favorite research tool. When it comes to understanding consumer behavior, the same is true. For example, focus-group practitioners can provide interpersonal insights derived from small groups regarding what customers claim to like, but this method itself is limited in a variety of ways. While people are generally able to articulate their preferences, they are less able to accurately assess what they will actually do; this has been dubbed the "say-do" gap. In the case of organizations, it can be tempting to believe that the traditional instruments that have served them thus far are sufficient and can be applied to newer challenges and emerging markets, even when new methods might bring both critical insights and solutions unattainable by traditional means.

ORGANIZATIONAL BARRIERS TO BEHAVIORAL ECONOMICS

It is important to recognize that, in addition to the psychological biases that lead individuals within an organization to avoid implementing behavioral insights, there are also practical barriers to implementation. These include structural, organizational, financial, and cultural factors – which can be generically labelled "organizational barriers." Even if the psychological barriers can be overcome, these organizational barriers still need to be resolved. An outline of some of these challenges follows.

Knowledge Gap: Individuals within an organization, particularly those at the executive level with the power to implement change, not only need to be aware of the practice of applying behavioral insights and behavioral science; they also need to recognize the value of applying such an approach to their business and organization. We have seen at least two archetypes of executives that are resistant to behavioral insights and behavioral science. The first archetype is the data-science-savvy executive. This type understands the value of making decisions based on data and is comfortable with the concept of experimentation but doesn't fully appreciate and acknowledge the true difference between big-data analytics and experimentation and behaviorally informed decision making and experimentation. While data give a clear picture of past behaviors and patterns that can be used to forecast future trends if all inputs remain relevant and reliable, they do not give us clarity on what actually drives behavior and how we can effectively influence it. The second archetype is the "creative." This type might have a background in design/marketing and is often aligned to traditional approaches or design thinking. This type is proficient at generating new or novel ideas and solutions about a problem but doesn't see the value of testing these ideas with science and experimentation. Both types (data-analytic and creative) and the methods favored by each have their strengths and scope of practice; but as we mentioned in describing the "Law of the Instrument," using just one tool for all jobs and in all circumstances will lead to maladaptation to a constantly changing market. Analytics and creative thinking are, like behavioral science, among the many tools a modern business needs to stay adaptable. Each tool provides useful but not universally applicable strengths, insights, and prescriptions. The successful behaviorally informed organization possesses *both* the instrument of behavioral science in the form of a science team *and* the ability to understand and integrate scientific thinking into its workplace culture. Scientific journals are a treasure trove of rich ideas and clever experiments; however, they can be difficult to integrate into practice without input from someone who is scientifically literate. For example, choice overload is a phenomenon in which users make a suboptimal decision because of the overwhelming variety of choices presented. However, the research underlying choice overload is complex, and it can be difficult to determine how choice overload might influence a customer's response to the product or service we are providing. We cannot be sure until we check the existing literature or conduct our own tests with a falsifiable hypothesis.

Skills Gap: When an organization is clear on the value of behavioral insights and is ready to invest funds, the next step is to identify what skills they need, whom they need to hire, and if they want/need to engage a third-party vendor. One of the challenges we see at this stage is that executives will hire a single behavioral scientist and expect them to carry out meaningful changes. Given all of the barriers we have outlined here, as well as the complexity of behavioral science, it is unrealistic to expect one person to make this level of widespread change. Some companies build upon and invest in a behavioral-sciences unit to address this gap in their workforce. Alternatively, organizations can work with a third-party team of behavioral scientists that allows for more cross-pollination of specialties and knowledge bases. The choice of approach often depends on other considerations such as the locus of expertise and the locus of application (see the related discussion in chapter 2).

Implementation Costs: Embedding a behaviorally informed approach within an organization is a major undertaking that requires a shift in how people think and in how the organization operates. This can present significant implementation costs. During the early stages of understanding and exploration into how behavioral insights can be implemented within organizations, relatively low-cost projects can be undertaken. The size and scale of a project can be determined by the organization's needs and resources – by trying to find an optimal point between contending factors to invest reasonably, scale appropriately, and reap significant returns. Other chapters in this book (e.g., chapter 2) provide specific suggestions on how to reduce implementation costs (such as the costs of experimentation).

Challenges with Experimentation: We opened this chapter by describing the value of experimentation, but it is important to recognize that experimentation poses a particular set of barriers (see also chapter 2). Firstly, the existing empirical research on topics such as loss aversion, nudging, or defaults makes it tempting to want to apply these strategies without experimentation. Even among behavioral scientists, there is debate as to whether or not organizations looking to implement behavioral insights need to test those insights on a regular basis. Some argue that testing is not necessary for a well-established concept (e.g., loss aversion). While this is understandable, we must bear in mind that businesses and consumers operate in a complex world with many variables that may lessen or amplify the impact of some behavioral insights and not others. We take the position that experimentation is a critical part of the process and should be done within reason.

Second, experimentation requires a degree of humbleness. We all feel a level of satisfaction and pride in brainstorming a solution for a problem, so much so that we may be tempted to roll it out before we've tested it in anything closely resembling a controlled microcosm. No matter how much we like a given hypothesis, if the data obtained from our experiment do not support it, we have to accept that result. We have to be willing to be proven wrong in order to engage meaningfully in experimentation, identify which ideas do not stand up against scrutiny, and avoid investing in ineffective strategies.

Third, effective experimentation requires excellent execution. Execution of experiments requires someone who is skilled and experienced at experiment design to oversee the different but critical stages of experimentation and ensure consistent quality control. It is tempting to run "quick" tests to get results, but if the tests lack the rigor and stringent controls of a true scientific experiment, the results may not be meaningful, or may be open to misinterpretation. Even with the best of intentions, one can unwittingly tilt the elements in favor of a preferred hypothesis and result. We need high-quality experimental design to take the raw material of our ideas and separate the tailings from the valuable ore. Thus, a lack of expertise in conducting experiments can hamper an organization's ability to harness the potential benefits of experimentation.

OUR VIEW ON OVERCOMING THE BARRIERS

Organizations are made up of individuals; the same psychological biases and barriers that influence consumers influence executives in resisting a transition toward becoming behaviorally informed. Furthermore, organizational, financial, and cultural constraints can increase the difficulty of making changes within a well-established organization. How do we overcome these barriers? As with consumers, we know that information/knowledge is necessary but by no means sufficient to drive behavioral change. Thus, we ought to also think about increasing motivation and decreasing friction concerning behavioral change. Furthermore, we need to apply behavioral science in a measured and piecemeal fashion that will complement the present needs and resources of the organization. Some of the ideas we develop here are also echoed further in chapter 16 in the context of government organizations.

Addressing Psychological Barriers

Barriers like the status-quo bias, the system-justification bias, risk aversion, and the sunk-cost fallacy are challenging to overcome, whether we are dealing with customers, citizens, or coworkers within an organization. As a starting point it is important to consider where and at what levels resistance may be experienced. We know it is easier to flow with the familiar, the status quo, and that the risks of an unfamiliar approach are perceived to be more profound than they may actually be. Making the insights and culture of behavioral science approachable and familiar begins to address these biases, as does the launch of pilot projects alongside enculturation (covered in more detail below). Getting influential agents and executives curious, knowledgeable, and excited about behavioral science and not confused by or afraid of it is our hope and our goal. This is why we commend our mavericks and allies for their boldness and courage in presenting behavioral science against the backdrop of group think and status-quo bias. Often, the most effective way to bring about change in an organization is not through external pressure, which may elicit reaction and defensiveness, a doubling down on tradition and the old ways, but through internal initiatives. In working with large organizations, it is important to be sensitive to and identify the individuals who are most likely to hold these biases as well as those who feel threatened by the introduction of behavioral science, particularly in cases where experimentation is poised to question the success and efficacy of touted concepts or traditional tactics. In our experience it is critical to identify these people early on and get their buy-in from the start to reduce future friction.

Addressing Organizational Barriers

Although psychological barriers are by themselves challenging to overcome, there may be additional structural, financial, and cultural factors within well-established organizations that compound the problem. If an organization is ready to proceed with becoming behaviorally informed, it must now become familiar with and integrate the scientific language and culture within the organization, recognize what resources it has available to engage in scientific work, and minimize the gap between existing resources and what is required to facilitate needed change. It then needs to launch pilot projects that help it realize the value of experimentation, and avoid the temptation to blindly and faithfully apply behavioral insights without testing them first.

Education

A lot of knowledge, training, and experience is necessary to make a behavioral economics scientist. The knowledge required to be a practitioner of BE is more intensive than what is required to be a leader of a behaviorally informed organization. For example, the BEworks team's practitioners enter the firm with the minimum requirement of a PhD in a behavioral science field. As other training programs (notably master's degrees) dedicated to developing practitioners of behavioral science become more common, this requirement may change. However, being a practitioner requires specialized training and skills. This is not to say that the knowledge and understanding required to speak about and comprehend behavioral science necessitate years of additional schooling or are beyond the reach of mavericks or business people. Nor are we suggesting that advocates and executive champions who want to bring behavioral insights to an organization need the same level of knowledge as practitioners. Executives and business people are adept at bringing people with different skills and tools together to achieve a common goal. In the same way, one does not need to be a data scientist to recognize the important contribution of data science to organizational strategy. That said, we believe it is important for leaders to increase their knowledge of key concepts in order to enable them to better advocate for such approaches. This is a key reason why the BEworks Academy was created – to educate and empower leaders. Knowledge and skills that are important for leaders to have include the following:

1. An understanding of the theory behind core concepts such as rational choice theory.[10]
2. Awareness of emerging frameworks, such as COM-B,[11] the SHIFT framework,[12] and the BEworks Method.
3. The ability to read a scientific paper and apply critical thinking.
4. Familiarity with other types of interventions (beyond nudges)[13] that drive behavioral change. Examples include "operational transparency"[14] or the "fresh start effect."[15]
5. The ability and willingness to consider the ethical implications of interventions for a given challenge (e.g., knowing when a default may be viewed as a less ethical choice than a boost).[16]
6. An understanding of how incentives and education can be made more effective with behavioral interventions.

Changing the Culture

Although scientists and scientific thinkers need not become business leaders, business leaders ought to become scientific thinkers. We say this because we recognize that many business leaders are grounded, results-oriented people who value materialism, pragmatism, and innovation. We recognize the power and importance of these values and seek to share and cultivate them. We ask our clients and partnering executives to be open-minded and embrace scientific thinking, to put on their scientist's hat, or rather their lab coat. The key components of scientific thinking include:

1. **Curiosity:** Sometimes we have a tendency to accept at face value ideas or practices that should be questioned. Assumptions become tradition; entrenched "wisdom" from leaders can stand as common practice for decades. For instance, when an organization says its fundamental asset is "trust," what does

that really mean? Trust is a presumed level of risk accepted by a customer when engaging with a business; however, the means by which trust is established and exchanged is not typically well understood. Sometimes ideas of this kind are no more than legacy assumptions that have not yet been challenged. Leaders ought to encourage curiosity that might challenge these beliefs.

2. **Empirical observations:** Big data provide transparency on many dimensions of a business, but often data are still lacking where they are most needed. The right measures need to be developed and monitored, and many of the common measures that organizations use need to be vetted for reliability and validity.

3. **Shoulders of giants:** Thousands of papers on topics such as trust, risk, and the science of behavior are published every year. These papers are building upon the culmination of years of scientific research and have been vetted through empirical testing and peer review. Scientific thinkers benefit from conclusions drawn from published research, which offers a treasure trove of unmined intellectual property (IP) to help organizations develop a richer understanding of consumers' thinking and behavior.

Our goals are to engage with our clients, to foster their curiosity, to provide them with an alternative lens through which to view their challenges, to help them become familiar with the language and culture of science, to expand their toolkit, and to enable them to be active players in driving experimentation. We believe that this approach will contribute to more effective business strategies and expand the realm of what is known and understood in the field of behavioral science. Thus, as a collective of individuals who speak the same language and apply the same critical lens to our experiences, we enrich ourselves by sharing and contributing to the pool of communal knowledge.

Embed New Processes

Leaders often encourage employees to be innovative, but making this happen is often very challenging. This is partly because employees are trying to optimize the functioning of their current practice while simultaneously being encouraged to innovatively disrupt that very system. The framework we recommend balances the knowledge and novelty of behavioral insights, the application of different and business-specific project designs, and the rigor of the scientific method to transform both the client experience and the organization that implements it. We call this framework the BEworks Method,[17] and an overview follows.

Discovery: The crucial elements at this stage are the formulation of a strategic hypothesis, the identification of targeted measurable observable behaviors, and the development of reliable and valid measures. This phase takes a vague organizational goal like "increase client trust" and transforms it into "increasing client trust as defined by the degree to which they adhere to our advice." This phase is crucial because there are costly risks to launching a strategy without a reliable way to track its impact. Thus, to avoid politics and/or subjective interpretations of success, agreed-upon goals and how they will be measured need to be established from the start.

This starting phase is difficult for organizations for several reasons. They don't typically think in reductionist terms about the business. Concepts like "trust" are articulated with a vague or inconsistent understanding of what they mean. A useful exercise for leaders is to ask teams to write out the definition of a given term, including how it would be measured. In our experience, a lack of consensus or a shallow understanding of the term is revealed in this stage. The next hurdle is helping organizations realize they either don't have reliable data, or that they have weak or nonexistent processes for gathering data. Some projects spend a significant amount of time in this phase before they move to the next stage.

Behavioral Diagnostics: This is the phase where project teams engage in a root-cause analysis of the challenge. They determine what factors of the challenge are governed by externalities, and what factors are driven by internalities. Internalities can be captured through the Journey Map. The Journey Map studies the behavioral friction points within a journey, including Awareness (i.e., is the client even aware of this product/service?); Perception (i.e., how does the client perceive this product/service; do they see it as novel, expensive?); Evaluation (i.e., do they have the information or other tools to determine if this is desirable?); Decision (i.e., are they prepared to make a decision?); Action (i.e., do they overcome the risk of the intention-action gap?); and finally, Maintenance (i.e., do they sustain the targeted behavior?). The goal of journey mapping is to understand which heuristics clients are using to make decisions. This information can be obtained through a variety of methods, including surveys and data analysis. We also engage in a behavioral audit of the existing experience, assessing where biases might occur. One of the key inputs is to review prior scientific research. For example, those companies interested in increasing trust benefit from reviewing existing research in the area, including tactics that are presumed to increase trust (e.g., operational transparency).

This phase is often exciting for organizations; they start to become familiar with the language of heuristics and biases and develop a rich understanding of how the choice architecture currently designed by the organization can be the biggest barrier to consumer success. However, this phase can also be overwhelming. Conducting a detailed analysis of how a company positions itself and analyzing "what they are doing wrong" can be uncomfortable; nevertheless, sometimes the barriers are obvious and informative when presented in this way. For example, the Journey Map for a large health-benefits insurer identified that at the end of a thirty-minute online enrollment process, the penultimate screen contained a graphic of a large stop sign and an all-caps warning that it was important that the customer's information be valid and truthful. It also contained a "save-for-later" button. At this point in the application process, the likelihood of fraud or erroneous information was relatively low, and the data suggested that the intensity of this page should be toned down to encourage completion. The data showed that a high number of customers saved the application and never returned. The executives had not experienced the enrollment journey themselves and were not aware of this design. While we were presenting and discussing the implications of this on customer behavior, an executive in the room announced that she had just sent an e-mail to her design team to begin work immediately on changing the page.

Ideation: The first two phases of our method provide the research foundation, but the most exciting part is identifying unique solutions and generating the nudges and interventions to overcome the barriers identified in the first two phases. In our experience, companies routinely rely on providing consumers with more information (e.g., they will buy our insurance if we educate them about the benefits of insurance) and focusing on price (e.g., they will buy our insurance only if we are competitively priced). Although we employ a prioritization matrix, which helps identify the ideas that will yield the highest impact for the lowest operational cost and risk, the challenge that organizations face in this phase is the desire to implement simple, tactical solutions without embracing the more radical innovation that behavioral insights might suggest. For instance, we advised insurance clients that embracing a model where a portion of unclaimed insurance funds are directed by policyholders into jointly selected non-profit, prosocial causes would lead to reduced claims as well as greater trust and higher retention. However, these clients were only willing to implement modest design changes to the claims process.

Experimentation: The description of experimentation and its benefits has been provided earlier in this chapter, as have the challenges attached to it. Once experiments take their final shape, they stoke incredible curiosity. New questions emerge, and ideas that were previously regarded as "set in stone" are often added to the list of things to test.

The enthusiasm for the novelty of BE tactics can lead to a reluctance to take the time that experimentation requires. In one of our projects that would have saved a client potentially $20 million a year, they did not want to experiment. BEworks co-founder Dan Ariely asked the CEO, "How long has this problem been a challenge for the organization?" to which she responded, "Years." It was a simple set-up to our response of, "Then does two more months for testing matter to ensure that our hypotheses are right?" We proceeded with the experiment.

Choice Architecture: This is the final stage of a project, where the evidence yielded by experiments is analyzed and interpreted, the recommendations are prepared for stakeholders, and the conditions tested in the experiment are now readied for appropriately scaled deployment.

One of the challenges in this phase is that as the prototypes tested in the experiment are scaled up for broad deployment, the elements tested run the risk of being modified and no longer retain their alignment to the original hypothesis. To give a simple example, we may demonstrate that an advertisement showing a model with her eye gaze directed at a product increases the likelihood that a consumer will also look at the product, thereby increasing their likelihood of purchasing it. But a creative agency may decide to change the direction of the eye gaze elsewhere on the grounds that their "gut" intuition suggests a more desirable image, despite evidence to the contrary.

Conducting Pilot Projects

Beyond providing education, our preferred way to help our clients overcome the barriers to implementing behavioral science and becoming a behaviorally informed organization is to provide guidelines on selecting their first behaviorally informed project. Rather than focus just on insights and information – which can be formulaic, abstract, and inappropriate – we instead seek to collaborate in the development of an appropriate project with clear measures and goals. Depending on the circumstances, we try to conduct pilot projects concurrently with education and culture change, so that clients can learn through a process that is immersive and impactful. This first foray into applied behavioral science helps makes the testing and experimentation process more concrete – directly linked to business outcomes – while it also addresses and reduces the perceived risk of using a new method. This initiative also tends to be the most exciting for our allies and their co-workers, as pilot projects provide the first demonstration of behavioral science in action.

Choosing a Pilot Project

As previously mentioned, there is a temptation to apply seemingly straightforward behavioral insights, such as "The Power of

Free!," "Social proof!," or "Simplification!," in a one-size-fits-all fashion and expect immediate results. The translation from behavioral insights and theory to practice tends to be more difficult. It can be very easy to get BE wrong and launch a project that has no impact or – worse – that backfires. Unless the projects being rolled out are well grounded in theory and based on experiments that are both carefully designed and conducted within similar conditions, the eager organization runs the risk of launching a full-scale application of behavioral insights that will not have the desired impact on business objectives. Having experienced practitioners directly involved with business experts will help to ensure that these risks are minimized. The first project an organization invests in tends to yield more meaningful results if it aims specifically at achieving one of the following goals:

1. Resolve critical business issues and provide direction on decisions that are very high risk, using appropriate experimentation that will provide evidence on the efficacy of said decisions.
2. Resolve problems where other solutions have stagnated, lost efficacy, or failed.
3. Unblock organization jams as well as question or test entrenched assumptions.
4. Serve as a learning project to teach and build the internal resources that are necessary for more widespread adoption of behavioral insights and experimentation.
5. Generate organizational momentum through small-scale experimentation/demonstration projects to address easy targets for behavioral change and, when appropriate, expand the experiment's size and scale.

CONCLUSION

While the barriers to understanding and implementing BE are complex and challenging, let us not lose sight of why overcoming these barriers is critical for organizations. Today's consumers are faced with more choices than ever, whether in the domain of financial decision making, in which they need to make complex investment decisions for retirement, or simply in shopping, for which e-commerce has opened up a seemingly limitless array of choices. The market is changing fast and will likely continue to do so. Furthermore, the pace and intensity of change can send us reeling, constantly on our heels as we struggle to adapt. In some cases, businesses double down on what they have always done in the face of such uncertainty. Given that consumers face more choice than ever, it behooves leaders to add an additional tool to their toolkit, that of understanding the science of decision making. A BE approach provides a tested framework for understanding decision making scientifically, one that provides us with a choice architecture, based on tested findings, that can help keep the consumer–business partnership adaptable, innovative, and in harmony. Our goal is to help leaders understand the role that behavioral insights and experimentation can play in making their products and services better as well as the role that scientific literacy and thinking can play in optimizing their operational strategies.

NOTES

1 Ariely, D. (2009). *Are we in control of our own decisions?* [Video File]. Retrieved from https://www.ted.com/talks/dan_ariely_are_we_in _control_of_our_own_decisions.

2 Thaler, R.H., & Sunstein, C.R. (2008). *Nudge: Improving decisions about health, wealth, and happiness.* New Haven, CT: Yale University Press; Kahneman, D. (2011). *Thinking, fast and slow.* New York: Farrar, Straus and Giroux; and Ariely, D. (2009). *Predictably irrational: The hidden forces that shape our decisions.* New York: Harper.

3 Thaler, R.H., Sunstein, C.R., & Balz, J.P. (2010). Choice architecture. Available at SSRN: https://ssrn.com/abstract=1583509.

4 Kahneman, D., Knetsch, J.L., & Thaler, R.H. (1991, Winter). Anomalies: The endowment effect, loss aversion, and status quo bias. *The Journal of Economic Perspectives, 5*(1), 193–206.

5 Jost, J.T., & Banaji, M.R. (1994). The role of stereotyping in system-justification and the production of false consciousness. *British Journal of Social Psychology, 33*(1), 1–27.

6 Esser, J.K. (1998). Alive and well after 25 years: A review of groupthink research. *Organizational Behavior and Human Decision Processes, 73*(2–3), 116–41.

7 Rabin, M., & Thaler, R.H. (2001). Anomalies: Risk aversion. *Journal of Economic Perspectives, 15*(1), 219–32.

8 Ellsberg, D. (1961). Risk, ambiguity, and the Savage axioms. *The Quarterly Journal of Economics, 75*(4), 643–9.

9 Kaplan, A. (1964). *The conduct of inquiry: Methodology for behavioral science.* New York: Chandler Publishing.

10 Scott, J. (2000). Rational choice theory. In G. Browning, A. Halcli, & F. Webster (Eds.), *Understanding contemporary society: Theories of the present.* London & Thousand Oaks, CA: Sage, 126–38.

11 Michie, S., van Stralen, M.M., & West, R. (2011). The behaviour change wheel: A new method for characterising and designing behaviour change interventions. *Implementation Science, 6*, 1–11.

12 White, K., Habib, R., & Hardisty, D.J. (2019). How to SHIFT consumer behaviors to be more sustainable: A literature review and guiding framework. *Journal of Marketing, 83*(3), 22–49.

13 Johnson, E.J., Shu, S.B., Dellaert, B.G., Fox, C., Goldstein, D.G., Häubl, G., & Wansink, B. (2012). Beyond nudges: Tools of a choice architecture. *Marketing Letters, 23*(2), 487–504.

14 Buell, R.W., & Norton, M.I. (2011). The labor illusion: How operational transparency increases perceived value. *Management Science, 57*(9), 1564–79.

15 Dai, H., Milkman, K.L., & Riis, J. (2015). Put your imperfections behind you: Temporal landmarks spur goal initiation when they signal new beginnings. *Psychological Science, 26*(12), 1927–36.

16 Hertwig, R., & Grüne-Yanoff, T. (2017). Nudging and boosting: Steering or empowering good decisions. *Perspectives on Psychological Science, 12*(6), 973–86.

17 BEworks. (2020). BEworks choice architecture report. Toronto, 2020. Report No.1. Retrieved from www.beworks.com.

PART TWO

Overarching Insights and Tools

CHAPTER FIVE

Seeing Sludge

Daniel Cowen, Niketana Kannan, and Dilip Soman

Whether the task is getting this chapter ready for publication, designing a randomized controlled trial, planning a Behavioral Exchange conference, purchasing groceries, saving for retirement, or returning a product, getting things done is central to the human enterprise.[1] Clearly, people struggle to accomplish tasks like these, as is shown by the demand for self-help books and MBA courses on this topic.

Behavioral scientists have been intrigued by how individuals who plan to get things done fail to accomplish these tasks (see also chapter 3).[2] This intention-action gap is a prominent finding from research in the burgeoning field of behavioral economics.[3] This field portrays human behavior as distinct from that of the "rational agents" often cited in economics textbooks as well as in the central paradigms of business and policy. Economic approaches assume that agents are forward looking, able to execute complex calculations, unemotional, and interested in maximizing their own well-being – essentially, utility maximizers. Meanwhile, humans are characterized as myopic, forgetful, cognitively and physically lazy, and emotional. Pension organizations might assume that consumers are motivated to plan for retirement; financial institutions supply consumers with plentiful information to make informed choices; and retail stores provide many choices because they believe consumers value variety. In contrast, end-users might be unmotivated to plan for retirement and have difficulty in absorbing lots of information and in making choices.

GATES, FENCES, AND FAILURES IN GETTING THINGS DONE

One of the central tenets of human behavior is that getting things done is a function of the person (the actor) but also the situation (the context). The American psychologist Kurt Lewin explains that there are tensions that arise as a function of an individual's motivation and channel factors in the environment that help or hinder progress toward a goal. Lewin calls factors that facilitate behavior *gates*;[4] we call factors that hinder behavior *fences*. Opening more gates facilitates accomplishing tasks, while closing gates (or adding fences) hinders this. Similarly, Thaler and Sunstein write about choice architecture as the changes in context that help individuals in pursuing goals. A nudge is a contextual intervention that opens metaphorical gates and makes things easier; sludge adds fences and makes things harder.[5]

THE EMPATHY GAP AND THE NEED FOR SEEING SLUDGE

The notion of gates (and fences) would be irrelevant to an econ. If the econ knows what is required to accomplish a goal, and the utility is sufficiently high, contextual factors should not influence their eventual success.

Research shows that product and service developers have difficultly empathizing with the end-user because their proximity to product development makes them more like econs.[6] A similar empathy gap arises in thinking about the role of context. For instance, a cognitively sophisticated individual might not see complex information as sludge; and someone with excellent time-planning skills might not see why a delay in an application process causes friction for a myopic and impulsive person.

Given that contextual variables might be sludge for some but not others, it could be *difficult* for many to *see sludge*. Hence, organizations might benefit from a tool that breaks down sludge into its antecedent contextual variables – in other words, a tool that facilitates *seeing sludge*!

NUDGE AND SLUDGE: BEHAVIOR CHANGE AS A PLUMBING PROBLEM

Attempts at behavior change, be it a change in decision or a series of actions needed to accomplish a particular outcome, can be conceptualized as a plumbing problem. In *The Last Mile*, Soman (a co-author of the present article) drew an analogy between moving people from a particular state (say, desiring to open a bank account) to a new state (say, completing everything needed to have a bank account) and the movement of fluid in a pipeline.[7] For fluid to move from one point to another, there needs to be a pressure differential. Similarly, psychology suggests that consumers will not set about trying to accomplish a given task unless there is motivation. Furthermore, the engineer's task is to keep pipe segments clean and leak-free. Knowing that most of the population prefers option B over A leads choice architects to make B the default option. Alternatively, knowing that people struggle with making an annual checkup appointment with their doctor leads choice architects to assign an appointment date and have people opt out if they are unable to attend.

Sludge makes it difficult for fluid to flow through a pipeline. In fluid mechanics, sludge is "a thick, wet mud or similar viscous mixture of liquids and solid components that are typically the product of an industrial or refining process" (*Oxford English Dictionary*). Behaviorally, sludge is any component that makes decisions or accomplishing tasks difficult.

Recently, Soman and Ly wrote about how three segments of people respond differently to a request to change behavior.[8] *Motivated enthusiasts* are motivated to switch behavior. *Diehard opponents* are opposed to the requested behavior change for reasons that include personal beliefs, philosophical positions, or the feeling that they are not a good candidate for that change. *Naive intenders* believe in what is asked of them and plan to do it, but their intentions might never convert to action because of procrastination. For naive intenders particularly, sludge might frustrate them, delay them, and get them to give up. Conversely, sludge might not affect motivated enthusiasts who have high motivation to complete the task immediately.

People routinely fall short in completing seemingly simple tasks. In our interviews, we heard numerous examples of people trying to file taxes, apply for visas and passports, make tuition payments, or transfer money who struggled with technology failures, complex and hence difficult-to-follow instructions, or unanticipated stages in the application process. We also heard of families that could not claim welfare because they needed to receive an authentication code on a mobile phone that they could not afford, and of students from remote parts of the world who could not participate in a case competition because it only accepted online submissions and they did not have access to a reliable Internet connection. As one of us remarked, "Upload your files online" is only a four-word instruction, but one that might trip the end-user up in many ways.

Sludge: A Conceptual Framework

There are two distinct components of sludge. The first is a feature of contextual variables. Does the context remove complexity and *facilitate* decisions or does it add friction and *impede* decisions? Since not all impedances result in bad outcomes, the second dimension is related to the outcome. Does it *increase* or *decrease consumer welfare*? Table 5.1 captures our thinking about nudge and sludge taxonomy (and see table 5.1 in Sunstein's paper).[9]

For the dimension of facilitating versus impeding, there are several interventions that make things easy. Simplified forms,[10] or access to information that allows consumers to make better choices,[11] the presence of sensible defaults that are consistent with consumer preferences,[12] and the reframing of communications to make salient appropriate attributes[13] are interventions that facilitate action and help consumers make the best decision. Much of the work proposed in the book *Nudge* and subsequently done by several "nudge units" around the world in policy, welfare, and business domains is focused on increasing consumer welfare by making it easy to choose and to act upon one's choice. The OECD has summarized these interventions from units across the world in a recent publication.[14]

However, facilitating – making things easy – comes with potential negative consequences. For example, as illustrated in section 1,

Table 5.1 A Framework for Understanding Nudge and Sludge

	Facilitate Decision Making	Impede Decision Making
Helps Consumers	*Nudge*: making things easy for end-users	*Decision Points* or *Cooling-off Periods*: prompting vigilance and thoughtfulness
Harms Consumers	*Nudge-for-Bad* or *Dark Patterns*: making it easy to choose welfare-reducing options (subscription traps, default add-on purchases)	*Sludge*: making it difficult to cancel subscriptions, return products, change privacy settings, etc.

a consumer might be defaulted into taking a magazine subscription that they had no intention of purchasing. Similarly, an inattentive consumer might consent to have their digital footprint shared with businesses interested in customizing products, services, and offers to their customers. In the field of digital interface design, these facilitating interventions might get users to purchase products or services they do not need, or to spend more than they want to.[15] Collectively, these interventions – as well as others that reduce consumer welfare – are referred to as dark patterns.[16] Formally, dark patterns are "user interface design choices that benefit an online service by coercing, steering, or deceiving users into making unintended and potentially harmful decisions."[17] We note that while some may classify dark patterns as a form of sludge, they (a) are conceptually distinct and (b) require different types of solutions. Furthermore, the definition of "dark patterns" implies harmful intent. Sludge, as we conceptualize it, does not necessarily arise from an organization's intention to cause harm.

We next turn to the two cells in table 5.1 where context impedes decision making. Is friction in a process or choice, or the impedance in getting things done, always a bad thing? In previous research, Soman and colleagues argue that sometimes interventions that add friction to the decision-making process might increase consumer welfare.[18] Impedances might help sophisticates, people who have self-control problems who want to do something about it.[19]

Naive intenders routinely say they want to lose weight or save money but simply cannot because of forces they feel are outside their control. In previous work, we contend that these individuals could be encouraged to control their consumption by providing them with *decision points*.[20] Imagine a consumer who purchases a large bucket of popcorn and needs to decide about consuming it. Imagine that in a parallel universe, the same consumer receives the same amount of popcorn but in six equal-sized bags. Would we expect the consumption to be different across these parallel universes?

Based on a series of experiments, researchers Amar Cheema and Dilip Soman found that consumption was significantly greater when the popcorn was in the metaphorical bucket than in the metaphorical six equal-sized bags.[21] When individuals are in the process of consumption, they start off in deliberative mode in which they think about the pros and cons. However, once they start consuming, they shift into automatic mode where continued consumption becomes mindless and habitual.

Ease leads to overconsumption; hence, the provision of a decision point – in this case, whether to open the next bag – can enable the individual to snap back into deliberative mode. For a sophisticate, this entails a call to vigilance and the realization that the consumption was something that they should do in a controlled manner. This impedance, the decision point, allows the planner to take control and transport from an impulsivity zone to a detached view of the choices confronting them.

A decision point is any intervention that adds friction to a process to get an individual to pause and think about their current consumption. There are three methods for creating decision points: (1) inserting a transaction cost that requires individuals to take a positive action, making them think about their consumption decision; (2) providing reminders, or information that draws attention to a neglected activity, providing the impetus to get it done; (3) creating interruptions in the consumption, which allows the individual to refresh their thought process and rethink what is to come next.

The third approach to decision points – creating an interruption – is conceptually identical to introducing "cooling-off periods," interventions that impede quick decision making. In many contractual settings or negotiations, cooling-off periods are windows of time after the transaction or negotiation is completed but before the contract (e.g., a sale) becomes binding. The hot-cold empathy gap is the psychological account that explains the need for cooling off.[22] Loewenstein argues that decisions often get made "in the heat of the moment" and might be suboptimal or based on visceral factors.[23] Allowing these visceral arousals to cool and enabling people to re-examine their decisions over time might get them to be vigilant and make more responsible choices.

To put it differently, there are domains in which friction or impedance can be welfare-enhancing for the end-user. However, it is the bottom right cell of table 5.1 that is most interesting for the present work, and the focus of this chapter – interventions that impede decision making and reduce consumer welfare. The examples quoted earlier and that Sunstein refers to in his research fall into this cell in our two-by-two matrix.[24]

Sources and Moderators of Impedance

In thinking about situations where impedance in the environment reduces consumer welfare, we identified three sources of friction.

1. The first source of impedance could be from the *actual process* required to complete a task. For example, are the channels to accomplish the task easy to use or do they require multiple interfaces, steps, touchpoints, or interactions with service personnel? Do some parts of the process interfere with others? A rich literature in such disciplines as process design[25] and process improvement[26] has identified several principles for maximizing the effectiveness of a process from the end-user's perspective.

One aspect of the process that causes impedance relates to *re-engagement*. Consider a patient who is navigating the healthcare system. Perhaps the biggest source of frustration is the requirement to repeat their medical history or symptoms to different members within a given hospital or clinic, or to healthcare providers across hospitals, clinics, or laboratories.[27] While repetition can be functional, a significant amount could be eliminated by a well-designed electronic health record (EHR).[28] The patient's experience could be a metaphor for many processes in which a user needs to interact with multiple parts of a process, or with the same entity over time. Does a process have memory such that the user navigating the system does not incur the same costs repeatedly? Are parts of the process and system coordinated so that learning in one area can be immediately updated and shared?

2. *A second source of impedance* is the nature of the communication. For example, we know that the human brain is efficient at processing information that is structured, linear, and takes the form of concrete checklists rather than identical information presented in blocks of text. Additionally, simplifying information into blocks or bullet points can increase end-user engagement, simplify communication, and help the user accomplish tasks.[29]

Beyond the complexity of information, there are several other communication features that can create impedances. In thinking about organizational communication, there are three kinds of failures.[30] The first is the *outright failure to disclose information*. Imagine that a consumer clicks through a website and makes a purchase using their credit card. After the credit card has been approved and the order confirmed, they see a message that shipments to the customer's region are subject to an additional surcharge. This information had not been provided during the purchasing process and hence illustrates an outright failure to disclose relevant data. Similarly, financial advisers might fail to disclose fees, and organizations to disclose all their terms and conditions.

A second type of failure is a *delayed or hidden disclosure*. Imagine that a consumer clicks through the same website and is about to make a purchase using their credit card. On the final (purchase) screen, they learn about an additional surcharge for shipping to their region. By the time they see the surcharge, they are psychologically committed, and hence this information does not affect them to the same extent as it would have if it had been presented at the beginning.

A third form of failure is *shrouding* or *obfuscation*.[31] In this case, the firm discloses the surcharge early, but it is not easy to read or interpret. For example, the seller might use difficult-to-read fonts so that it is easy to overlook the information; or they might break down the surcharge into smaller components that require computation; or they might use complicated language about when and where the surcharge becomes relevant so that the consumer is not clear about whether they would incur it.

3. *A third source of impedance* could be direct outcomes of, or emotions generated by, a process that might create differences in inclusivity. Sometimes, someone might be excluded by specific processes built into a system. For instance, an organization that requires forms to be completed in a certain language excludes those not fluent in that language; one that asks for a monetary deposit to process an application excludes people who have liquidity constraints; and one that only accepts electronic applications excludes those who don't have computer or Internet access. Processes could also exclude through a second-order effect. An operations researcher might design an allocation program that assigns temporary workers to shifts on a just-in-time basis to maximize the matching of labor demand and supply. However, single parents unable to organize last-minute childcare could be excluded as a result.

Impedances caused by emotion are prevalent in welfare or poverty programs. The Canada Learning Bond – a welfare program designed to provide low-income Canadians with \$2,000 to support their children's education – had very low take-up rates.[32] One reason was that eligible recipients felt embarrassed about signing up for the education savings account. By doing so, many felt they would be confessing to the banker that they needed aid. It was not the complexity of the procedure but the potential embarrassment associated with it that created the impedance. Many of these frictions cause an impedance because they heighten certain human behavioral tendencies.

Impedance for Humans, Not Econs

Sludge that results from process, communication, inclusivity, and re-engagement issues will not create impedances for econs but will for humans. Five insights from behavioral research magnify the effect of seemingly small contextual frictions. *Procrastination*[33] leads consumers to put off unpleasant tasks and is magnified by processes that introduce delays. *Complex information* creates an excuse to stop working on a task.[34] *Aversion to making choices amongst large assortments*[35] might lead individuals to decline deciding or to make suboptimal choices. *End-users lose trust* when organizations deliberately obfuscate or make *information less transparent*.[36] Finally, *emotions matter*; individuals care about what judgments others make about them and how they are perceived.[37] Our research validates that converting seemingly innocuous aspects of a process into large frictions creates impedance.

TOWARD A DASHBOARD

Methods and Procedure

In developing measurement tools, we used four methods – literature review, surveys, expert interviews, and informal audits of digital interfaces across a seven-step process. In our *literature review* of publications on these behavioral categories we identified the role of contextual variables in facilitating and impeding decisions and actions, developed a conceptual framework for sludge, and classified specific behavioral tendencies that could be exaggerated by contextual variables. Through the fifty responses to our *survey* we were able to collect a compendium of cases where end-users experienced frustration because of sludge. We *interviewed* ten behavioral-science experts for an average of forty-five minutes each to validate the conceptual model and the preliminary list of contextual variables, suggest additional factors, and advise on design choices for the dashboard. Finally, we *informally audited* the digital interfaces of five large financial institutions and five additional consumer-product companies as a preliminary validation of the scorecard and to collect additional insights. The process we used is captured in figure 5.1.

Through this seven-stage process, there were three insights that were particularly relevant.

Figure 5.1 Seven-step process in developing a scorecard and dashboard

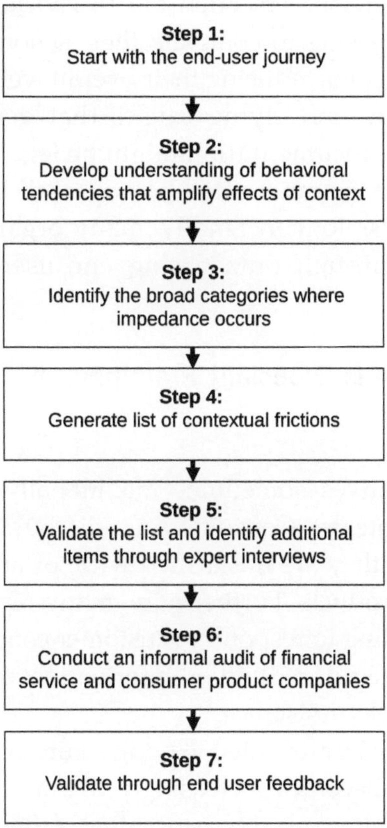

```
┌─────────────────────────────────────────┐
│              Step 1:                      │
│      Start with the end-user journey      │
└─────────────────────────────────────────┘
                    ↓
┌─────────────────────────────────────────┐
│              Step 2:                      │
│   Develop understanding of behavioral     │
│ tendencies that amplify effects of context│
└─────────────────────────────────────────┘
                    ↓
┌─────────────────────────────────────────┐
│              Step 3:                      │
│   Identify the broad categories where     │
│            impedance occurs               │
└─────────────────────────────────────────┘
                    ↓
┌─────────────────────────────────────────┐
│              Step 4:                      │
│   Generate list of contextual frictions   │
└─────────────────────────────────────────┘
                    ↓
┌─────────────────────────────────────────┐
│              Step 5:                      │
│  Validate the list and identify additional │
│     items through expert interviews       │
└─────────────────────────────────────────┘
                    ↓
┌─────────────────────────────────────────┐
│              Step 6:                      │
│   Conduct an informal audit of financial  │
│  service and consumer product companies   │
└─────────────────────────────────────────┘
                    ↓
┌─────────────────────────────────────────┐
│              Step 7:                      │
│    Validate through end user feedback     │
└─────────────────────────────────────────┘
```

Insight #1: Excessive Processes Including Wait Time, Required Documentation, and Difficult-to-Complete Tasks Were the Most Common Impedances.

When we conducted an online scan for negative experiences with financial institutions, we found several in these categories. One customer complained of how it "took 7 months to get [a] bank statement, and [he is] still waiting for the rest of it."[38]

These are also examples of impedances that prevent customers from resolving their initial problem. If a consumer deems that the effort to complete an action is greater than the short-term problems caused by the impedance, the consumer will cease completing that action. However, consumers often fail to consider the long-term consequences of ceasing to complete their action (e.g., additional financial burdens), thus reducing their overall welfare.

There are a few underlying causes that generate excessive processes. Firstly, documentation might be legally required. Secondly, the paperwork must often be reviewed by many people, making the process longer. Finally, many organizations reduce service quality through outsourcing end-user-facing units to save money.

Insight #2: Sludge Is Especially Prominent in Customer Service.

Service representatives sometimes intentionally invoke guilt to serve the bank's interest. Consumers are discouraged from cancelling a service that they are unsatisfied with, or are pushed to purchase irrelevant products. Furthermore, many representatives lack the necessary training to respond to customer concerns. As a result, clients are given false or redundant information, or are put on hold while the agent seeks assistance.

This problem can be attributed to budget cuts or procedural rigidity. As the world becomes increasingly digital, organizations are expected to have online services; hence they reallocate budgets from training service representatives to fund digital processes, decreasing the quality of customer service.

Insight #3: Technology Is a New Breeding Ground for Sludge.

While technology has often been seen as a panacea for inefficiencies, it has also created a new breeding ground for sludge. The most common technological frictions that impede consumer decisions include the following: website/machine/account shutdowns; difficulty navigating and finding information on websites and in apps; outdated websites and information; and slow load times. These technology failures are especially problematic because they have often completely replaced "human touch" solutions.

Scorecards and Dashboard

The scorecard we developed has three components: *Process*, *Com-munication*, and *Inclusivity* (PCI). In the Process and Communica-tion scorecards we assess possible effects on Inclusivity, while the Inclusivity scorecard focuses exclusively on impedance from nega-tive emotional reactions. A list of contextual factors is scored using the sample scorecards in tables 5.2, 5.3, and 5.4. Figures 5.2 and 5.3 provide two ways in which PCI scores are visually represented. The dials mimic an automobile dashboard, providing a snapshot of dimensions in which organizations do well and where they are riddled with sludge. In figure 5.3, scores are represented on a cube in which corner "4" represents a very high-quality end-user experience – a sludge-free environment.

We emphasize three aspects of our approach to creating scorecards:

1. Scorecards will need to be customized for different industries (e.g., banking versus healthcare), and potentially for different processes within the same industry (e.g., opening bank accounts versus credit-card queries). The sample scorecards presented here could be used as a starting point for any industry or process but should not be used as an off-the-shelf solution.
2. Scorecards could be built for various levels of aggregation. For instance, a financial-services firm could build a scorecard for a specific process (e.g., opening a bank account), a product category (e.g., individual bank accounts), a group within the organization (e.g., a branch), or for the whole organization. Our work focused on sludge scorecards for specific processes but could be adapted for more aggregated levels of analysis.
3. Our intention is for each of these three dimensions (P, C, and I) to be scored separately and not aggregated into a single measure. Aggregation will require further analysis to determine what the relative weights of each component should be.

Research in managerial decision making shows that the desire to look good inherently motivates biased responses.[39] Therefore, it is

Table 5.2 Sample Completed Process Scorecard

		Yes	No	N/A
Paperwork	No duplicate questions	x		
	If documents are not provided in preferred language, process to request support or translate is available and easy	x		
	Answering questions does not require additional documentation to be accessed or submitted		X	
	Forms provide options for inclusive demographic categories*		X	
Issue Resolution	The process of how to resolve issue is clear	x		
	Two or fewer interactions required to resolve issue	x		
	Issue resolution takes less than 10 minutes		X	
	Stated process is consistent with actual process		X	
Tasks and Requirements	All forms for all products available and can be shared on all devices		X	
	Three or fewer forms to complete	x		
	No redundancy in supporting documents required	x		
	Forms take appropriate amount of time to complete**		x	
Human Interaction	One or fewer meetings required			X
	Meeting shorter than 15 minutes			X
	Representatives have appropriate availability**	x		
	All contact options available			X
	Contacting takes less than 5 mins (branch location, or remote access)	x		
	Wait for service (in-person, on-phone, or online) less than 2 mins		X	
Total		8	7	3

*Demographic categories refer to all gender and race identifications.
**The determination of appropriateness is at the discretion of the reviewer.
Overall P (Process) Score = 8 / (8+7) = **53.33%**

imperative for external auditors to complete the scorecards. Given that people could see an impedance differently, auditors should be *diverse*, and *representative* of the end-user population.

Furthermore, there are items on the scorecard that require judgment. While diversity among auditors is necessary, we also

Table 5.3 Sample Completed Communication Scorecard

	Yes	No	N/A
Length of process and requirements transparent from beginning		X	
Information about process on landing page for enrolling in service	x		
Information provided online same as provided onsite and on the phone		X	
All available products or services in this category are shown explicitly to end-user	x		
All features of all products or services in category are shown explicitly to end-user	x		
Grade 5 English comprehension level used	x		
Resources available in multiple languages	x		
All information needed to make a choice is presented prior to the end-user making any preliminary commitment	x		
Total	**6**	**2**	**0**

Overall C (Communication) Score = 6 / (6+2) = **75.00%**

Table 5.4 Sample Inclusivity Scorecard

Please rate the following on a scale from 1 to 5.
1: Strongly agree
2: Somewhat agree
3: Neither agree nor disagree
4: Somewhat disagree
5: Strongly disagree

	Anxious	Socially Awkward	Embarrassed	Excluded	Discouraged	Average
When browsing through the web page of the organization, end-users feel ...	1	2	1	3	1	1.6
When completing an online application, end-users feel ...	2	1	2	1	1	1.4
When talking with a representative at the organization end-users feel ...	3	1	1	2	1	1.6
When speaking to a representative on the phone end-users feel ...	1	1	3	1	1	1.4

Table 5.4 *(continued)*

	Socially Anxious	Awkward	Embarrassed	Excluded	Discouraged	Average
When visiting a branch location, end-users feel …	1	2	1	1	2	1.4
End-users limit their interactions with the organization because it makes them feel …	1	1	1	2	1	1.2
Total Average Across Six Rows						8.6

Overall I (Inclusivity) Score: Total Score / 30 = **26.67%**

Figure 5.2 The PCI dashboard for one hypothetical organization

Process	Communications	Inclusivity
Average	Excellent	Poor
P = 53.33%	**C = 75.00%**	**I = 26.67%**

Figure 5.3 The PCI cube

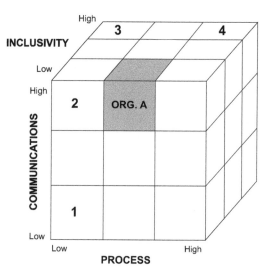

recommend including feedback from a representative panel of end-users. Following best practices, scores across auditors and panelists should be averaged.[40]

DISCUSSION AND CONCLUSIONS

When and How Often Should the Scorecards and Dashboards Be Generated?

Measurements are most useful when they result in dynamic data. A driver looking for data in making decisions about driving gains no insight from the average speed over the past hour, or how much fuel was in the tank last quarter; they need real-time information!

Scorecards should be used on an ongoing basis to measure sludge over time. This helps organizations get a better sense of temporary changes and drive toward a sludge-free environment. For instance, could perceived sludge be higher on certain days of the week? Does the degree of sludge vary as a function of the user demographic?

The ongoing use of scorecards might not be possible in the real world. Hence, we recommend using them – at the very minimum – when one of the following occurs:

1. When the organization launches new products or services, or there is a new set of touchpoints with the end-user.
2. When the user-facing part of the business is reorganized.
3. When a third party is added as an intermediary with end-users. For example, an organization might outsource communications to a call center.
4. When end-user tastes, preferences, or demographics change. For example, as customers get familiar with digital interactions, they likely will experience a greater degree of sludge with nondigital interactions.
5. When there are changes in the overall environment. The level of user experience has gone up over the past few years. Organizations whose processes have not improved could use scorecards to assess the degree of perceived sludge.

How Can the Scorecard Be Used?

While allowing organizations to see sludge, scorecards can be used in two additional ways. First, PCI scores can be tracked over time to assess the impact of the environment and other external factors on perceived sludge and indicate progress over time. If an organization upgrades a sludgy process, a "before-and-after" PCI score measures success. Secondly, PCI scores could be used to benchmark organizations relative to the industry or peers.

How Should the Scorecard Change with Time?

As time passes, the bar for excellent service and experience (therefore, low sludge) rises. However, there is also a need to assess the impact of each contextual variable over time. Consider the notion of waiting time. Two decades ago, asking an end-user to wait was considered especially deleterious because it was a pure cost. Today, however, the exact same wait is less of a cost because individuals have electronic devices through which they stay connected to the rest of their activities. In this case, the same line in a scorecard – *waiting time* – had a higher impact before the advent of mobile technology. Likewise, every variable in the scorecard needs to be monitored for changes in impact over time.

Closing Thoughts

If a scorecard allows an organization to see sludge, who should be tasked with removing it? Often, sludge forms because user touchpoints and processes are created in silos. Process-design teams are trained to maximize throughput and hand over to customer service to implement. This customer-service team might see sludge but be unable to fix it. We suggest that, just as independent auditors are tasked with seeing sludge, a team that is independent from the frontline staff, process designers, and communication representatives be tasked with generating sludge-busting solutions. We note that cleaning sludge is conceptually similar to the conventional "UX" (user experience) exercise, though there are also fundamental differences.

If an organization sees sludge but does not correct it, market-based solutions from other entities will likely emerge. An app that automatically cancels subscriptions after their trial period was recently launched.[41] MasterCard introduced a decision point in automatic billing for subscriptions that were assumed to have been purchased after a free trial.[42] If successful, market solutions improve the welfare of end-users but might reduce the reputation of the offending organization (in this case, the firms that automatically renewed subscriptions). It is therefore in an organization's best interest to see and clean up sludge before such solutions emerge.

Companies spend a lot of time being compliant with the law. Given the increased focus on end-user experience, we believe it is time to start being compliant with human behavior. Behavioral economics does not assume that people's irrationality is negative. We know that organizations tend to design for rational econs rather than humans. However, we need to design for human compliance. Human compliance includes organizations' interactions with end-users and other enterprise functions such as human-resources management, quality control, innovation systems, corporate culture, and strategy formulation. Sludge busting helps organizations understand how they can become human compliant, and scorecards provide insight into internal and external compliance.

Finally, in many organizations, people and teams are rewarded for big thinking, and management emphasizes thinking outside the box.[43] Our work shows that thinking small is also important.[44] To see and clean up sludge one must appreciate the seemingly little and insignificant things. It is only when we can develop the ability to think small and look for the little things that might create impedance that we will be successful in developing more human-compliant organizations.

NOTES

1 Allen, D. (2002). *Getting things done: The art of stress-free productivity*. New York: Penguin Books; and Tu, Y., & Soman, D. (2014). The categorization of time and its impact on task initiation. *Journal of Consumer Research, 41*(3), 810–22. doi:10.1086/677840.

2 Thaler, R.H. (2015). *Misbehaving: The story of behavioral economics*. New York: W.W. Norton & Company.

3 Sheeran, P., & Webb, T. (2016). The intention-behavior gap. *Social and Personality Psychology Compass, 10*, 503–18. doi:10.1111/spc3.12265; and Soman, D., & Ly, Kim. (2018, Winter). The growing market for self-control. *Rotman Magazine*, 36–41.

4 Hobman, E.V., & Walker, I. (2015). Stasis and change: Social psychological insights into social-ecological resilience. *Ecology and Society, 20*(1), 39. doi:10.5751/ES-07260-200139; and Lewin, K. (1939). Field theory and experiment in social psychology. *American Journal of Sociology, 44*(6), 868–96.

5 Sunstein, C.R. (2019, 27 April). Sludge audits. *Harvard Public Law Working Paper No. 19–21*. Published online 6 January 2020 in *Behavioural Public Policy* by Cambridge University Press, 1–20. doi:10.2139/ssrn.3379367.

6 Gourville, J.T. (2006). Eager sellers and stony buyers: Understanding the psychology of new-product adoption. *Harvard Business Review, 84*(6); and Soman, D. (2014, Fall). The innovators challenge: Understanding the psychology of consumer adoption. *Rotman Magazine*, 2–9.

7 Soman, D. (2015). *The last mile: Creating social and economic value from behavioral insights*. Toronto: Rotman-UTP Publishing.

8 Soman, D., & Ly, Kim. (2018, Winter). The growing market for self-control. *Rotman Magazine*, 36–41.

9 Sunstein, C.R. (2019). Sludge audits. *Harvard Public Law Working Paper No. 19–21*. Published online 6 January 2020 in *Behavioural Public Policy* by Cambridge University Press, 1–20. doi:10.2139/ssrn.3379367.

10 Bhargava, S., & Manoli, D. (2015). Psychological frictions and the incomplete take-up of social benefits: Evidence from an IRS field experiment. *American Economic Review, 105*(11), 3489–3529. doi:10.1257/aer.20121493.

11 Richburg-Hayes, L., Anzelone, C., Dechausay, N., & Landers, P. (2017). *Nudging change in human services: Final report of the behavioral interventions to advance self-sufficiency (BIAS) project*. OPRE Report 2017-23. Washington, DC: Office of Planning, Research and Evaluation, Administration for Children and Families, U.S. Department of Health and Human Services.

12 Jachimowicz, J.M., Duncan, S., Weber, E.U., & Johnson, E.J. (2019, November). When and why defaults influence decisions: A meta-analysis of default effects. *Behavioural Public Policy, 3*(2), 159–86. doi:10.1017/bpp.2018.43. Published online 24 January 2019 by Cambridge University Press.

13 Castelo, N., Hardy, E., House, J., Mazar, N., Tsai, C., & Zhao, M. (2015). Moving citizens online: Using salience & message framing to motivate behavior change. *Behavioral Science & Policy, 1*(2), 57–68.

14 OECD. (2017). *Behavioural insights and public policy: Lessons from around the world*. Paris: OECD Publishing. doi:10.1787/9789264270480-en.

15 Mathur, A., Acar, G., Friedman, M., Lucherini, E., Mayer, J., Chetty, M., & Narayanan, A. (2019). *Dark patterns at scale: Findings from a crawl of 11K shopping websites.* arXiv, 1(1). Retrieved from https://arxiv.org/pdf/1907.07032.pdf.

16 Brignull, H. (2018). *Dark patterns.* Retrieved 10 September 2019 from https://darkpatterns.org/.

17 Mathur, A., Acar, G., Friedman, M., Lucherini, E., Mayer, J., Chetty, M., & Narayanan, A. (2019). *Dark patterns at scale: Findings from a crawl of 11K shopping websites.* arXiv, 1(1). Retrieved from https://arxiv.org/pdf/1907.07032.pdf.

18 Soman, D., Xu, J., & Cheema, A. (2010, Winter). A theory of decision points. *Rotman Magazine*, 64–8.

19 O'Donoghue, T., & Rabin, M. (1999). Doing it now or later. *American Economic Review*, 89(1), 103–24.

20 Soman, D., Xu, J., & Cheema, A. (2010, Winter). A theory of decision points. *Rotman Magazine*, 64–8.

21 Cheema, A., & Soman, D. (2008). The effect of partitions on controlling consumption. *Journal of Marketing Research*, 45 (6), 665–73.

22 Loewenstein, G. (1996). Out of control: Visceral influences on behavior. *Organizational Behavior and Human Decision Processes*, 65, 272–92.

23 Loewenstein, G. (2000). Emotions in economic theory and economic behavior. *American Economic Review*, 90(2), 426–32.

24 Sunstein, C.R. (2019). Sludge audits. *Harvard Public Law Working Paper No. 19–21.* Published online 6 January 2020 in *Behavioural Public Policy* by Cambridge University Press, 1–20. doi:10.2139/ssrn.3379367.

25 Evans, J., & Lindsay, W. (2014). *An introduction to six sigma and process improvement* (2nd ed.). Cincinnati: South-Western College Publishing.

26 Boutros, T., & Purdie, T. (2013). *The process improvement handbook: A blueprint for managing change and increasing organizational performance.* New York: McGraw-Hill Education.

27 Ganguli, I. (2012). *Stuck on loop: Why do patients have to repeat their stories?* healthydebate. Retrieved from https://healthydebate.ca/opinions/stuck -on-loop-why-do-patients-have-to-repeat-their-stories.

28 eHealth Ontario. (2019). *What's an EHR?* Retrieved from https://www .ehealthontario.on.ca/en/ehrs-explained.

29 Manoli, D.S., & Turner, N. (2014). *Nudges and learning: Evidence from informational interventions for low-income taxpayers.* NBER Working Paper, No. 20718; and Bhargava, S., & Manoli, D. (2015). Psychological frictions and the incomplete take-up of social benefits: Evidence from an IRS field experiment. *American Economic Review*, 105(11), 3489–3529. doi:10.1257 /aer.20121493.

30 Soman, D. (2015). *The last mile: Creating social and economic value from behavioral insights.* Toronto: Rotman-UTP Publishing.

31 Gabaix, X., & Laibson, D. (2006). Shrouded attributes, consumer myopia, and information suppression in competitive markets. *The Quarterly Journal of Economics, 121*, 505–40; and Brown, J., Hossain, T., & Morgan, J. (2010). Shrouded attributes and information suppression: Evidence from the field. *The Quarterly Journal of Economics, 125*(2), 859–76. doi:10.1162 /qjec.2010.125.2.859.

32 Hardy, E., Khan, H., Audet, M., & Soliman, M. (2018). *Behavioural insights project: Increasing take-up of the Canada Learning Bond.* Government of Canada. Retrieved from https://www.canada.ca/en/innovation-hub /services/reports-resources/behavioural-insights-project.html#inline _content; and Soman, D., Stein, J., & Wong, J. (2013). *Innovating for the global south.* Toronto: University of Toronto Press.

33 O'Donoghue, T., & Rabin, M. (1999). Doing it now or later. *American Economic Review, 89*(1), 103–24.; and Schelling, T. (1992). Self-command: A new discipline. In Loewenstein, G. & Elster, J. (Eds.), *Choice over time,* 167–76. New York: Russell Sage Foundation.

34 Simon, H.A. (1957). *Models of man: Social and rational-mathematical essays on rational human behavior in a social setting.* New York: Wiley.

35 Iyengar, S.S., & Lepper, M.R. (2000). When choice is demotivating: Can one desire too much of a good thing? *Journal of Personality and Social Psychology, 79*(6), 995–1006. doi:10.1037//0022-3514.79.6.995; and Gourville, J., & Soman, D. (2005, Summer). Overchoice and assortment type: When and why variety backfires. *Marketing Science, 24*(3), 382–95. doi: 10.1287 /mksc.1040.0109.

36 Buell, R.W., Kim, T., & Tsay, C.J. (2017). Creating reciprocal value through operational transparency. *Management Science, 63*(6), 1673–95.

37 Rick, S., & Loewenstein, G. (2008). The role of emotion in economic behavior. In L.F. Barrett, M. Lewis, & J.M. Haviland-Jones (Eds.), *Handbook of emotions* (3rd ed.), 138–56. New York: The Guilford Press.

38 Lanford. (2018). Royal bank of Canada [Consumer review]. CONSUMERAFFAIRS. Retrieved 16 September 2019 from https://www.consumeraffairs.com /finance/royal_bank.html?#sort=recent&filter=1.

39 Bazerman, M., & Moore, D.A. (2013). *Judgment in managerial decision-making* (8th ed.). Hoboken, NJ: John Wiley & Sons.

40 Larrick, R.P., & Soll, J.B. (2019). Intuitions about combining opinions: Misappreciation of the averaging principle. *Management Science, 52*(1), 111–27. doi:10.1287/mnsc.1050.0459.

41 Kleinman, Z. (2019). *App that cancels subscriptions launches in UK.* BBC News. Retrieved from https://www.bbc.co.uk/news/amp/technology -49688309.

42 Dellinger, A. (2019). *MasterCard won't let companies bill you after free trials for physical products* (update). Retrieved from https://www.engadget .com/2019/01/16/mastercard-free-trial-protection/.

43 Schwartz, D. (1987). *The magic of thinking big*. New York: Simon & Schuster; and Schmitt, B.H. (2007). *Big think strategy: How to leverage bold ideas and leave small thinking behind*. Boston: Harvard Business Review Press.
44 Service, O., & Gallagher, R. (2017). *Think small: The surprisingly simple ways to reach big goals*. London: Michael O'Mara.

CHAPTER SIX

A Guide to Guidelines

Sophie Duncan, Melanie Kim, and Dilip Soman

The television series *The Good Place* is a satirical account of what it takes for a person to get into "the good place" after death. "The good place" is a heaven-like utopia designed to reward people for living moral and righteous lives that have been marked by good choices and outcomes. Unfortunately, the main characters later realize that no human will ever get into the good place. The reason is that day-to-day decisions have become increasingly complex and mired in layers of other decisions with negative implications – to the point that it is virtually impossible to know what qualifies as good behavior. For instance, a simple decision to buy flowers for a friend might require the consideration of not just their price, quantity, health, and appearance but also a myriad other factors, including the environmental ramifications of growing those flowers, the labor conditions on the farm, and the plastic waste from packaging. As the show illustrates, making the right choice is not as straightforward as optimizing a series of simple utility functions. As a result, even the characters who are consumed by the desire to make all the best decisions to ensure a happy afterlife cannot get into the "good place."

Just as getting into the "good place" is the cumulative result of a lifetime of decisions, so are other important life outcomes, such as health and financial well-being.[1] For instance, good health into one's golden years is the result of a large number of individual choices relating to eating, sleeping, and exercising habits, a string of decisions related to medical adherence or getting regular preventive screenings and checkups, and many other choices. That is, no particular bad health outcome can be attributed to only one or a few instances of bad decisions. Likewise, financial well-being at retirement is a function of a very large number of decisions that people make every day in their lives. Should I spend on an indulgence? Should I refinance my mortgage? Where should I invest? Should I rebalance my portfolio? Should I send my children to private school? Outcomes like good health and financial well-being are the result of what are known as a series of distributed choices.[2] These are choices distributed over time that have significant aggregate impact, even though the impact of each individual choice may be small.

Individuals might have appropriate mental models to make each of these individual decisions. Indeed, there is a wealth of literature and advice on how people should make individual consumption[3] and financial choices.[4] However, each individual choice has implications for other choices in the series of distributed choices. These effects are difficult to anticipate and comprehend,[5] so that the decision maker often gets fixated on trying to optimize the current choice rather than the entire sequence of distributed choices.[6] More generally, human decision making in complex and dynamic environments is inherently difficult despite the best efforts of the individual decision maker. This difficulty is compounded by the presence of sludge (see chapter 5) – that is, frictions in the context that impede decision making and action.

One practical approach to help individuals navigate complex choice environments is to provide them with guidelines – in particular, a roadmap to help them make sequences of either discrete decisions (e.g., should I recommend therapy or surgery?) or allocation decisions (e.g., what percentage of my retirement savings should be in stocks?). In the domain of medicine, clinical-practice guidelines are meant to help physicians make more efficient and effective decisions concerning patient care by providing up-to-date, evidence-based information in easily digestible form.[7] Similarly, there are guidelines for a number of other complex decisions – including guidelines to help Americans choose diets,[8] to help patients reduce cardiovascular risks,[9] to reduce reoffending risks amongst a previously incarcerated population,[10] on using laser technologies in medicine,[11] and more generally on helping people make better choices while shopping, investing, or trying to be physically fit.[12] In all these cases, guidelines play an important role in distilling a large amount of complex and seemingly inconsistent information to guide decision making. They do so by offering a heuristic or rule-of-thumb, prescribing a particular course of action, or just by simplifying information to increase its utility. In this chapter, we delve deeper to understand how and why guidelines affect behavior, and when guidelines are an appropriate tool for behavior change.

The rest of this chapter is organized in three sections. First, we outline the characteristics of good guidelines, and in particular identify design features of guidelines that will likely make them a good behavior-change tool. Second, we develop a taxonomy of guideline types. Third, we present a summary of research prescribing ways to make guidelines more relevant and useful, and conclude with a short guide on how to write guidelines.

FEATURES OF GOOD GUIDELINES

A rich literature in the area of communications provides insights into the roles and design features of good guidelines.[13] In particular, this research suggests that good guidelines do three things. First, they offer a *framework* to help the decision maker dismantle and understand complex choice and allocation environments. For instance, a guideline can help the end-user determine whether they need to make a discrete choice or an allocation decision. Some decisions are about discrete choices (for example, which car to purchase, which fund to invest in, which fitness regimen to enroll in). The magazine *Consumer Reports* provides information and recommendations about multiple options, often highlighting the pros and cons of each. However, a "yes" or "no" response is often inappropriate for more complicated choices, which may instead require allocation decisions.[14] For instance, an individual does not choose between investing in cash or securities, eating carbohydrates or proteins, or spending time working or relaxing. Rather, they choose the level at which they wish to allocate their money, consumption, and time on each of the options.

Guidelines can also provide a mnemonic rule of thumb to allow the end-user to convert a complex choice goal into concrete actions. For instance, instead of needing to think about what it means to consume a healthy and balanced diet, a Canadian can visualize – based on Canada's Food Guide – dividing their plate into roughly one-half fruits and vegetables, one-quarter whole grain foods, and one-quarter protein foods. Food guides like the Healthy Eating Plate, developed at Harvard University, and MyPlate, developed by the US Department of Agriculture (USDA), offer a similar visual rule of thumb. The food guide's image of a plate becomes a mental template to refer back to for faster, easier, informed decision making. In this role, guidelines provide the decision maker with the ability to solve complex problems via bite-sized choices.

Second, good guidelines also provide a *vocabulary* to deal with a particular situation and a set of choices. Prior research suggests that individuals are unable to form preferences if they lack the vocabulary to organize their tastes and, further, that the provision of a consumption vocabulary allows them to better learn, understand, experiment with, and refine their preferences.[15] In the world of consumption, many wineries provide wine-appreciation courses or guides that allow consumers to better express their preferences. Likewise, a guideline for protecting privacy online might introduce users to privacy concepts such as encrypted versus nonencrypted data.[16] Without needing to understand what encryption actually entails, users can identify that encrypted data offer better privacy control than nonencrypted. By offering language with which to distinguish between various options, guidelines help end-users think through their savings, health, or professional-practice goals. They also encourage end-users to weigh the consequences of one sequence of decisions versus another in relation to their ultimate goal.

Third, good guidelines are *expert-driven*, meaning they come from a credible source that uses the latest scientific evidence in developing the guidance. Notably, the selection of experts has important implications for the credibility of the guidelines. For instance, the Healthy Eating Plate is considered particularly trustworthy because it was "not subjected to political or commercial pressures from food industry lobbyists."[17] Past iterations of Canada's Food Guide were received with skepticism by health professionals because of the perceived influence of certain food and agricultural industry players on the development of the guidelines.[18] Moreover, the effectiveness of guidelines is enhanced when they are reinforced by social proof, a form of validation that comes from seeing others engage in the same behavior.[19] For end-users, seeing other people trust and use the guideline will increase the guideline's likelihood of adoption.

Through these features, good guidelines accomplish the goal of translating a vast amount of information into an action-oriented, easily digestible format for individuals to understand and use. In the next section, we look at the different types of guidelines.

A TAXONOMY OF GUIDELINE TYPES

Depending on the kind of information provided and their behavioral goal, guidelines generally fall into three different types. We refer to these as *anchor* guidelines, *procedural* guidelines, and *informational* guidelines. Table 6.1 captures the basic properties of the three types of guidelines.

Each of the three types of guidelines is best suited to particular scenarios that are associated with specific behavioral tendencies. By beginning with an assessment of the decision-making context and behavioral barriers that impede choice and action,[20] practitioners can determine which of these three types of guidelines (or combinations thereof) would best address the problem at hand.

Anchor guidelines serve as a starting point toward distant goals. Many goals relating to health (e.g., improving fitness), personal finance (e.g., saving for retirement), or environmental sustainability (e.g., reducing one's carbon footprint) can feel overwhelming and stressful, leading individuals to delay doing anything about them.[21] In dealing with such inertia, anchor guidelines can be particularly helpful. By suggesting an outcome or a milestone, anchor guidelines allow individuals to assess their current state in comparison with the desired state, and provide a starting place for individuals to embark on the complex

Table 6.1 A Taxonomy of Guidelines

Name	Brief Description	Behavioral Goal	Example
Anchor Guidelines	Provide milestone information, common rules of thumb, or peer comparisons	To motivate users to take action and get started	1) By age 50, most people have $X in retirement accounts 2) Budget by using the 60/20/20 rule
Procedural Guidelines	Provide a sequence of steps to end-users to accomplish a task	To make the process seem less daunting, and reduce sludge	1) Clinical guidelines 2) Guidelines for assembling furniture 3) "How-to" guides
Informational Guidelines	Provide, distil, and simplify complex information as an input into decision making	To reduce informational sludge, and reduce cognitive costs of information processing	1) The Healthy Eating Plate and Canada's Food Guide

series of choices. Using the desired outcome as an anchor, individuals can get started and postpone the burden of making cognitively complex or emotionally laden choices. For instance, for someone overwhelmed by the prospect of saving for retirement, the rule of thumb that 20 percent of monthly income should go into savings offers a point of comparison and something clear to work toward. If at all possible, practitioners should consider implementing anchor guidelines that offer a starting comparison but not an impossible goal.

Procedural guidelines provide a roadmap on how to convert intentions into action. Most people find it difficult to follow through on their intentions. Prior research shows that this intention-action gap can be narrowed by using interventions that give people a clear action path toward completing the task. For instance, research in the area of financial well-being shows that encouraging attendees of a financial literacy program to actively plan specific actions increases the likelihood that they will actually perform those tasks.[22] More generally, implementation intentions that take the form of concrete procedures and actions facilitate goal striving and action.[23]

Procedural guidelines provide a sequence of steps or activities to help accomplish a task – be it performing a clinical procedure, applying to graduate school, or purchasing a house. For instance, clinical-practice guidelines are particularly prominent in healthcare settings, where it is difficult for practitioners to stay abreast of new developments in their field and to implement these changes in the face of habits and a fast-paced decision-making environment. In such situations, these guidelines outlining recommended actions – for instance, in the form of a checklist – could bridge the intention-action gap for clinicians who are trying to shift their practices.[24]

In developing procedural guidelines, the practitioner must be able to determine a clear set of best practices for a specific procedure that are common to a vast majority of users. Practitioners writing such guidelines must be able to explain how to accomplish tasks as a list of activities. This is why procedural guidelines are helpful in some contexts but may have limited use in others where there is greater heterogeneity in what users should do to be successful.

Informational guidelines evaluate, curate, and present complex information in human-compliant language. In contexts with large quantities of seemingly inconsistent information, individuals struggle to make sense of it. For instance, on the Internet, guidance on nutrition, personal finance, and medical conditions takes the form of scientific papers, news reports summarizing those papers, opinions, and other forms of advice. More generally, the complexity of information creates sludge.[25] For instance, in many grocery stores there are elements of choice architecture that may direct shoppers toward highly processed foods instead of fresh vegetables or whole grains.[26] Guidelines can be used to correct for sludge arising from information complexities. However, as chapter 5 suggests, the manner in which information is presented is critical to whether the guideline serves as a nudge, or – conversely – becomes sludge that impedes decision making and action.

Informational guidelines provide additional data to users but package it in a concise and accessible format. Their role is in sense-making and increasing the salience of information. Informational guidelines can also provide users with information they might not otherwise have seen. For instance, most consumers are unlikely to look up nutrition-science journal articles or peer-reviewed research on the benefits of ETFs versus mutual funds, but thanks to food guides or financial guidelines, many still have a general idea about what is included in a healthy diet or a balanced portfolio.[27]

Informational guidelines provide a framework for thinking about the decision. For instance, Healthy Eating Plate and Canada's Food Guide are remarkable for their simplification and sense-making through categorization. Instead of requiring the end-user to learn how much vitamin A versus vitamin D versus saturated fat to consume, Canada's Food Guide groups foods into three categories (fruits and vegetables, protein foods, and whole-grain foods). Users do not need to know exactly what purpose a fruit or vegetable serves; instead they have a practical heuristic for determining what fraction of their plate should be occupied by fruits or vegetables. Categorization increases the likelihood that items across groups (proteins versus grains) are treated differently.[28] As a result, end-users can see that the purpose of a whole grain is different from the purpose of a protein without needing to read the scientific evidence.

The plate-shaped dietary guidelines are not only simple but also intuitively easy to understand; to put it differently, they are written in "human-centric" language. In chapter 1, Soman points out that variables expressed in human-centric terms are more likely to be taken account of in human decision making. Likewise, when a guideline is written in human-centric language, it takes less mental effort to interpret, and there is a higher likelihood that it would actually guide people's behavior.

ENHANCING THE UTILITY OF GUIDELINES: SOME PRACTICAL ADVICE

While guidelines make information simpler and easier to act on for the end-user, information alone is not enough.[29] While a guideline is not all that is needed to change behavior, it can be a good starting point and can be made more effective in combination with other tools. For instance, the food guide is a helpful informational guideline, but it will be most effective in shifting behavior if it is combined with policy interventions that restrict the marketing of particular foods to children, economic interventions that make healthy foods more affordable for all, and industry interventions that shift the choice architecture in grocery stores and the nutritional content of foods. Guidelines themselves can also be constructed in ways that enhance their effectiveness. There are three main considerations in increasing the utility of guidelines: (a) making it easy to convert knowledge into action with a call to action or implementation plan, (b) formatting guidelines for usability, and (c) using co-creation and testing to enhance guidelines' credibility and utility.

Principle 1: Converting Knowledge to Action

Knowing that education and information are not enough, writers of guidelines need to create the motivation to help people act on the guidelines. One way of doing this is to write procedural guidelines that provide concrete steps to help users bridge the intention-action gap.[30] Another approach includes adding a call to action at the end of a guideline[31] or providing an implementation plan. An implementation plan can be as simple as a worksheet that makes the process of applying the guidelines to your life concrete. For example, when offering information about financial well-being, guidelines should include a worksheet with directions on how to open an RRSP and/ or specific questions for the user to ask their financial adviser.

Principle 2: Formatting for Usability

Using appropriate formatting and being concise are immensely important to making guidelines human-centric. In the domain of clinical-practice guidelines, research suggests that three components of formatting can make guidelines more usable. First, guidelines should be "vivid."[32] By carefully choosing which words to highlight or make bold, managers can make the most crucial aspects of a guideline more noticeable. Next, guidelines should be organized and formatted in a way that aligns with the user's process. By "bundling" information around various steps of the user's process, managers can make guidelines feel natural for the end-user.[33]

Many guideline authors also need to write for secondary end-users – middlepersons (such as wealth advisers, dieticians, and fitness trainers) who interpret and advise clients using the guidelines. In order to be useful, guidelines need to align with the "mental models" of users, which are frequently instilled by secondary end-users.[34] This might require "creating multiple tailored versions of the document" to provide information for end-users and for secondary end-users – given their different levels of knowledge and different guideline needs.[35] For example, Canada's Food Guide includes one guideline designed for end-users and one designed for health practitioners. Both guides contain the same framework and recommendations for eating a healthy diet, but they differ in their levels of detail.

Lastly, research shows that using images and figures and being careful to limit the amount of text will improve a guideline's likelihood of being used.[36] For instance, lengthy privacy policy statements written in legal jargon are not very accessible to the average online user, who is likely to ignore information that might otherwise change their decision and to proceed too hastily with a download or purchase. More visual and intuitive labels – such as a "traffic-light" coloring system that captures the key dimensions of privacy – have demonstrated potential for addressing the current deficit in the use of privacy-relevant information in decision making.[37]

Principle 3: Using Co-creation and Testing to Increase the Utility of Guidelines

Finally, it is essential that in addition to being created by credible experts, guidelines are developed through co-creation and repeated testing with both end-users and secondary end-users. After Health Canada determined what body of evidence would be included in the 2019 version of Canada's Food Guide, they ran multiple focus groups with end-users and secondary end-users (such as dieticians and health-advocacy groups) to get feedback on the formatting and language of the guide. This process of co-creation and testing is responsible for many of the formatting changes that made the 2019 Canada's Food Guide far more user-friendly than its predecessor in 2007.[38] Testing with these users may also have added an element of social proof to the guideline, making it appear more credible.[39] In particular, the knowledge that the voices of reputable secondary end-users had been heard by the creators of the guide appears to have made other secondary end-users more likely to trust it. Testing, co-creation, and iteration before a guideline is released are instrumental in determining its credibility, usability, adoption rate, and efficacy. As is the case with any product launch, knowledge of the end-user's needs, behavior, and experience with the guide makes it possible for practitioners to craft guidelines that are readily used.

MAKING GUIDELINES WORK

In this sea of complex choices and information, guidelines bring the most crucial information to the surface, and save individuals from full immersion in the details. Practitioners looking to create or update guidelines should begin by assessing the characteristics of the context – as well as the resulting psychological and behavioral factors at play. After identifying the type of decision-making environment and the behavioral tendencies of potential users, practitioners can match that scenario with an appropriate type of guide.

Life is full of choices whose ultimate "good" or "bad" outcome is dependent on a long sequence of complex and often tiny choices that individuals are often ill-prepared to address. While individuals may be able to analyze the pros and cons of a specific decision, being able to address the full sequence is another story. These situations are where guidelines play a key role, and can help individuals overcome informational, emotional, and behavioral barriers to decision making. By using behavioral insights to craft guidelines, we can create guidelines that are greater than the sum of their parts and are useful tools in a complex environment.

NOTES

1 We deal here with the elements of health and financial well-being that are often within individual control. However, individual health and financial well-being are also the product of factors outside of individual control (i.e., social determinants of health and wealth). For additional details on the social determinants of health see, for example, Office of Disease Prevention

and Health Promotion. (2020). *Social determinants of health / Healthy people 2020*. HealthyPeople.Gov. https://www.healthypeople.gov/2020/topics -objectives/topic/social-determinants-of-health.

2 Herrnstein, R.J., & Prelec, D. (1991). Melioration: A theory of distributed choice. *Journal of Economic Perspectives, 5*(3), 137–56.

3 See, for example Cornil, Y., & Chandon, P. (2016). Pleasure as a substitute for size: How multisensory imagery can make people happier with smaller food portions. *Journal of Marketing Research, 53*(5), 847–64. For a meta-analysis of healthy eating interventions, see Cadario, R., & Chandon, P. (2019). Which healthy eating nudges work best? A meta-analysis of field experiments. *Marketing Science, Articles in Advance*, 1–22.

4 See, for example Benartzi, S., & Thaler, R. (2007). Heuristics and biases in retirement savings behavior. *Journal of Economic Perspectives, 21*(3), 81–104. See also Madrian, B., Herschfield, H., Sussman, A.B., Bhargava, S., Burke, J., Huettel, S.A., et al. (2017). Behaviourally informed policies for household financial decision making. *Behavioral Science & Policy, 3*(1), 27–40.

5 Herrnstein, R.J. (1982). Melioration as behavioral dynamism. In M.L. Commons, R.J. Herrnstein, & H. Rachlin (Eds.), *Quantitative analyses of behavior, vol. II: Matching and maximizing accounts*, 433–58. Cambridge, MA: Ballinger Publishing Co.

6 Herrnstein, R.J., & Prelec, D. (1992). A theory of addiction. In G. Loewenstein & J. Elster (Eds.), *Choice over time*, 331–60. New York: Russell Sage Foundation.

7 Grimshaw, J.M., & Russell, I.T. (1993). Effect of clinical guidelines on medical practice: A systematic review of rigorous evaluations. *The Lancet, 342*(8883), 1317–22.

8 United States Department of Agriculture. (2010). *Dietary guidelines for Americans*. Retrieved from https://health.gov/dietaryguidelines/2010/.

9 Expert Panel on Integrated Guidelines for Cardiovascular Health and Risk Reduction in Children and Adolescents, & National Heart, Lung, and Blood Institute. (2011). Expert panel on integrated guidelines for cardiovascular health and risk reduction in children and adolescents: Summary report. *Pediatrics, 128* (Suppl. 5), S213–S256. doi:10.1542 /peds.2009-2107C.

10 McGuire, J. (Ed.). (1995). *Wiley series in offender rehabilitation. What works: Reducing reoffending: Guidelines from research and practice*. Hoboken, NJ: John Wiley & Sons.

11 Herrmann, T.R.W., Liatsikos, E.N., Nagele, U., Traxer, O., & Merseburger, A.S. (2012). EAU guidelines on laser technologies. *European Urology, 61*(4), 783–95.

12 See, for example, https://www.consumerreports.org/cro/index.htm; https://www.sec.gov/investor/pubs/tenthingstoconsider.htm; and

http://csep.ca/CMFiles/Guidelines/CSEP_PAGuidelines_0-65plus
_en.pdf.

13 See, for example, Farrell-Miller, P., & Gentry, P. (1989). Professional
development: How effective are your patient education materials?
Guidelines for developing and evaluating written educational materials.
The Diabetes Educator, 15(5), 418–22; Grudniewicz, A., Bhattacharyya, O.,
McKibbon, K.A., & Straus, S.E. (2016). User-centered design and printed
educational materials: A focus group study of primary care physician
preferences. *The Journal of Continuing Education in the Health Professions,
36*(4), 249–55; Grudniewicz, A., Bhattacharyya, O., McKibbon, K.A., &
Straus, S.E. (2015). Redesigning printed educational materials for primary
care physicians: Design improvements increase usability. *Implementation
Science, 10*(156), np; and Versloot, J., Grudniewicz, A., Chatterjee, A.,
Hayden, L., Kastner, M., & Bhattacharyya, O. (2015, 31 May). Format
guidelines to make them vivid, intuitive, and visual: Use simple
formatting rules to optimize usability and accessibility of clinical practice
guidelines. *International Journal of Evidence-Based Healthcare, 13*(2), 52–7.

14 For a discussion on allocation versus discrete choices, see Herrnstein,
R.J. (1990). Rational choice theory: Necessary but not sufficient. *American
Psychologist, 45*(3), 356–67.

15 West, P.M., Brown, C.L., & Hoch, S.J. (1996). Consumption vocabulary and
preference formation. *Journal of Consumer Research, 23*(2), 120–35.

16 O'Leary, D.E. (1995). Some privacy issues in knowledge discovery: OECD
personal privacy guidelines. *IEEE Expert, 10*(2), 48–59.

17 Harvard T.H. Chan School of Public Health. (2012, 18 September). Healthy
eating plate vs. USDA's MyPlate. *The Nutrition Source.* Retrieved from
https://www.hsph.harvard.edu/nutritionsource/healthy-eating-plate-vs
-usda-myplate/.

18 Solyom, C. (2019, 23 January). New Canada's Food Guide is a giant
step forward, dietitians say. *Montreal Gazette.* Retrieved from https://
montrealgazette.com/health/new-canadas-food-guide-is-a-giant-step
-forward-dietitians-say; and Schwartz, D. (2012, 30 July). The politics of
food guides. *CBC News.* Retrieved from https://www.cbc.ca/news
/health/the-politics-of-food-guides-1.1268575.

19 For an example of social proof in action at Her Majesty's Revenue and
Customs, as well as greater discussion on the strengths and limitations of
using social norms to encourage behavior, see Cabinet Office Behavioural
Insights Team. (2012). *Applying behavioural insights to reduce fraud, error and debt,*
1–38. Retrieved from http://38r8om2xjhhl25mw24492dir.wpengine.netdna
-cdn.com/wp-content/uploads/2015/07/BIT_FraudErrorDebt_accessible.pdf.

20 Ly, K., Mažar, N., Zhao, M., & Soman, D. (2014, Winter). A practitioner's
guide to nudging. *Rotman Management Magazine*; and Soman, D., & Mažar,
N. (2012). Financial literacy is not enough. *The Hill Times,* 25.

21 Madrian, B., & Shea, D. (2001). The power of suggestion: Inertia in 401(k) participation and savings behavior. *Quarterly Journal of Economics, 116,* 1149–87.

22 Carpena, F., Cole, S., Shapiro, J., & Zia, B. (2017). The ABCs of financial education: Experimental evidence on attitudes, behavior, and cognitive biases. *Management Science, 65*(1), 346–69.

23 Gollwitzer, P.M., & Sheeran, P. (2006). Implementation intentions and goal achievement: A meta-analysis of effects and processes. *Advances in Experimental Social Psychology, 38,* 69–119.

24 Patel, V.L., Arocha, J.F., Diermeier, M., Greenes, R.A., & Shortliffe, E.H. (2001). Methods of cognitive analysis to support the design and evaluation of biomedical systems: The case of clinical practice guidelines. *Journal of Biomedical Informatics, 34,* 52–66.

25 For further exploration of sludge versus nudge, see Soman, D., Cowen, D., Kannan, N., & Feng, B. (2019). Seeing sludge: Towards a dashboard to help organizations recognize impedance to end-user decisions and action. Toronto: Behavioural Economics in Action at Rotman (BEAR) Report series. Available at http://www.rotman.utoronto.ca/bear; and Sunstein, C. (2019). Sludge audits. *Harvard Public Law Working Paper No. 19-21.*

26 Nielsen, K.R., Hansel, P.G., & Skov, L.R. (nd). Do supermarkets really nudge us to eat unhealthily? *iNudgeyou.* Retrieved from https://inudgeyou.com /en/do-supermarkets-really-nudge-us-to-eat-unhealthily/.

27 Duncan, S., Kim, M., Kim, A., Lee, T.Y., Cowen, D., Soman, D., & Dubé, L. (2019). *The role of Canada's Food Guide in the food system: Effects on stakeholder behaviour.* Toronto: Behavioural Economics in Action at Rotman (BEAR) Report series, available at http://www.rotman.utoronto.ca/bear.

28 See https://www.jstor.org/stable/3172864?seq=1#metadata_info_tab _contents. Also see Huh, Y.E., Vosgerau, J., & Morewedge, C.K. (2016). Selective sensitization: Consuming a food activates a goal to consume its complements. *Journal of Marketing Research, 53*(6), 1034–49, showing the substitution effect in food consumption.

29 Soman, D., & Mažar, N. (2012). Financial literacy is not enough. *The Hill Times,* 25.

30 Carpena, F., Cole, S., Shapiro, J., & Zia, B. (2017). The ABCs of financial education: Experimental evidence on attitudes, behavior, and cognitive biases. *Management Science, 65*(1), 346–69.

31 For an example of how a call to action can be used effectively, see Service, O., Hallsworth, M., Halpern, D., Algate, F., Gallagher, R., Nguyen, S., et al. (2015). *EAST: Four simple ways to apply behavioural insights.* Behavioural Insights Team, Cabinet Office, Nesta.

32 Versloot, J., Grudniewicz, A., Chatterjee, A., Hayden, L., Kastner, M., & Bhattacharyya, O. (2015). Format guidelines to make them vivid, intuitive, and visual. *International Journal of Evidence-Based Healthcare,* 52–7.

33 Ibid.

34 Patel, V.L., Arocha, J.F., Diermeier, M., Greenes, R.A., & Shortliffe, E.H. (2001). Methods of cognitive analysis to support the design and evaluation of biomedical systems: The case of clinical practice guidelines. *Journal of Biomedical Informatics, 34,* 52–66.

35 Versloot, J., Grudniewicz, A., Chatterjee, A., Hayden, L., Kastner, M., & Bhattacharyya, O. (2015). Format guidelines to make them vivid, intuitive, and visual. *International Journal of Evidence-Based Healthcare,* 52–7.

36 Ibid.

37 Kelley, P.G., Bresee, J., Cranor, L.F., & Reeder, R.W. (2009). A "nutrition" label for privacy. *Proceedings of the 5th Symposium on Usable Privacy and Security,* SOUPS 2009, Mountain View, CA, 15–17 July 2009. DOI: 10.1145/1572532.1572538.

38 Duncan, S., Kim, M., Kim, A., Lee, T.Y., Cowen, D., Soman, D., & Dubé, L. (2019). *The role of Canada's Food Guide in the food system: Effects on stakeholder behaviour.* Toronto: Behavioural Economics in Action at Rotman (BEAR) Report series, available at http://www.rotman.utoronto.ca/bear.

39 See ibid. for additional discussion of the importance of co-creation in building credibility.

CHAPTER SEVEN

Boundedly Rational Complex Consumer Continuum

Derek Ireland

We all believe that every person including ourselves is unique and distinctive. And yet, economists, regulators, and corporate strategists too often treat the consumer as being of one of two types, with no "shades of gray" in between. The consumer is either sophisticated, rational, well-informed, and demanding or unsophisticated, irrational, vulnerable, and a potential victim (see, for example the distinction between econs and humans in chapter 1). Treating the "representative consumer" as either homogeneous or a binary construct may work for expositional convenience and for mathematical modelling, but the insights from these models often fall far short of reality.

In reality, there is a continuum of bounded rationality, with some consumers being more rational and better informed than others. If policymakers and state and nonstate regulators[1] use vulnerable-and-easily-misled consumers as a benchmark for designing consumer-protection policies, these policies are likely to be overly protective and intrusive for consumers who are reasonably well-informed. Therefore, at the level of a heterogeneous market, these policies will be poorly targeted, ineffective, and costly for taxpayers, companies, and, ultimately, the consumer.

Previous research from the policy and regulatory domain indicates that insights and nuances from the behavioral literatures are best captured through employing continuums rather than binary, either/or dichotomies and distinct categories and types, which are relatively static and provide limited opportunity for learning and change. For these and other reasons, continuums are used extensively in psychology, based on the perspective that distinctions between individuals and their behavior are matters of degree rather than type, and are also employed in the ethics and compliance literatures for similar reasons.[2]

A natural extension is to apply the continuum approach to the various "ideal types" of boundedly rational consumers that are described in the behavioral, psychological, and related literatures (see figure 7.1 below). This chapter contends that the boundedly rational complex consumer continuum (BRCCC hereafter) will enhance our understanding of the complex modern consumer in a manner that will provide guidance to governments, companies, civil society groups, academics, and other behaviorally informed organizations. Two major attributes and advantages of the BRCCC explored in this article are that: (i) it promotes analysis of consumers in the middle between the two extremes; and (ii) consumers can be at different locations along the continuum depending on product, context, mood at the time of purchase, and other variables.

DESCRIBING THE BRCCC "IDEAL TYPES"

Ideal Type 1 – The Highly Sophisticated and "Perfectly Rational" Consumer

The fully rational consumer of the conventional neoclassical-economics model has pre-existing, well-ordered, and stable preferences; is "perfectly" rational, informed, disciplined, self-interested, and predictable; and never allows their emotions, biases, attention span and cognitive limitations, and social norms to influence their preferences and decisions. This "representative" consumer resembles the "homo economicus" posited under the neoclassical rational-choice theory, and therefore matches perfectly with policies that are formulated based on the principles of rational agency and choice models of conventional economics. Under this premise, not

Figure 7.1   The consumer continuum (BRCCC) "Ideal Types"

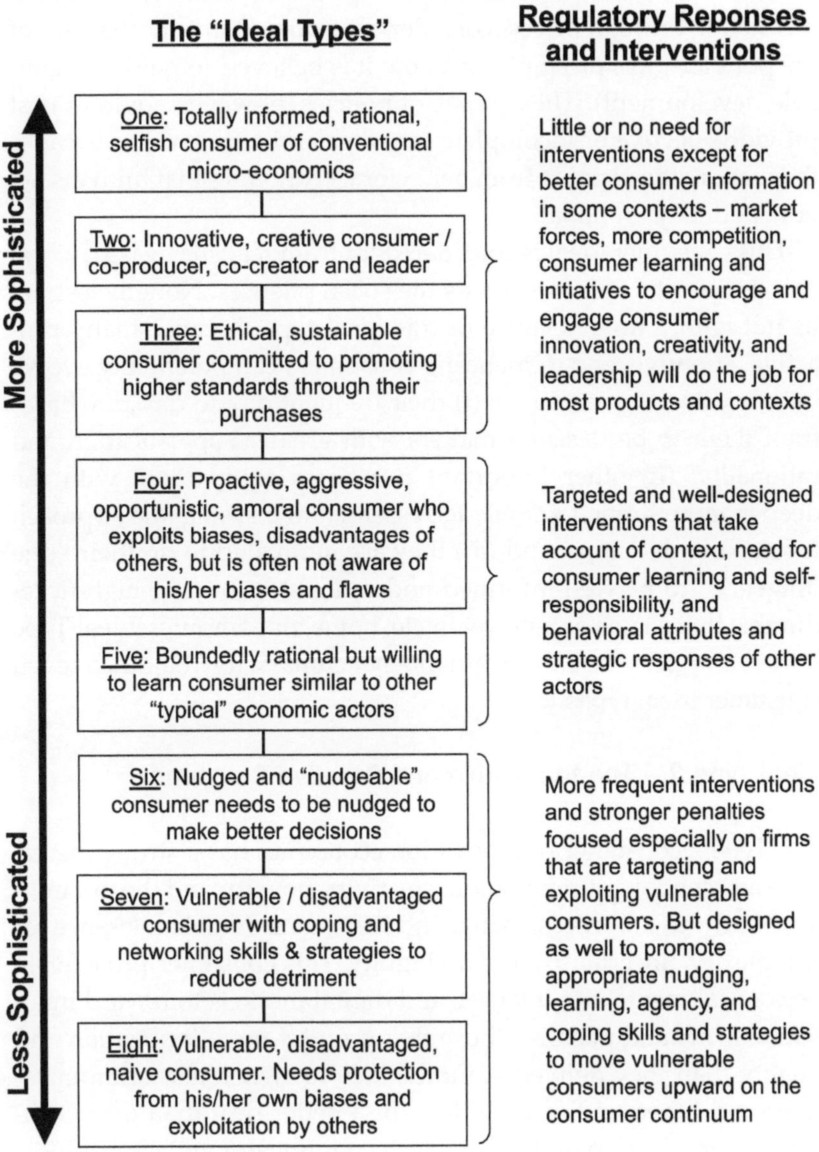

The "Ideal Types"

Regulatory Reponses and Interventions

More Sophisticated ↑

One: Totally informed, rational, selfish consumer of conventional micro-economics

Two: Innovative, creative consumer / co-producer, co-creator and leader

Three: Ethical, sustainable consumer committed to promoting higher standards through their purchases

Little or no need for interventions except for better consumer information in some contexts – market forces, more competition, consumer learning and initiatives to encourage and engage consumer innovation, creativity, and leadership will do the job for most products and contexts

Four: Proactive, aggressive, opportunistic, amoral consumer who exploits biases, disadvantages of others, but is often not aware of his/her biases and flaws

Five: Boundedly rational but willing to learn consumer similar to other "typical" economic actors

Targeted and well-designed interventions that take account of context, need for consumer learning and self-responsibility, and behavioral attributes and strategic responses of other actors

Six: Nudged and "nudgeable" consumer needs to be nudged to make better decisions

Seven: Vulnerable / disadvantaged consumer with coping and networking skills & strategies to reduce detriment

Eight: Vulnerable, disadvantaged, naive consumer. Needs protection from his/her own biases and exploitation by others

Less Sophisticated ↓

More frequent interventions and stronger penalties focused especially on firms that are targeting and exploiting vulnerable consumers. But designed as well to promote appropriate nudging, learning, agency, and coping skills and strategies to move vulnerable consumers upward on the consumer continuum only profit-related issues but even issues with moral or fairness considerations – such as those related to social welfare, environmental conservation, fair competition, and intellectual property rights – could be resolved based solely on the effects of market-based principles acting through prices (consider, for example, the mechanism of the polluter-pays principle and how it is believed to guide sustainable development). These types of policies, however, could at best provide selective or incomplete coverage and effectiveness because they ignore the insights from behavioral economics that humans are not "perfectly" rational.

This consumer ideal is considered far from realistic by behavioral economists and scholars across the social sciences. Nonetheless, let us not ignore the relevance of this ideal type, because many proactive, attentive, and demanding consumers can potentially evolve into the Ideal Type 1 when: (i) their frequent day-to-day purchases train them to be decision makers with greater sophistication and rationality; (ii) other important purchases equip them with the deeper, more refined knowledge essential to a systematic approach for making decisions; and (iii) they are motivated to do their "due diligence" to be well-informed and rational in buying high-ticket durable items such as a new vehicle, home, or computer. Ideal Type 1 therefore provides an invaluable benchmark for the other seven consumer ideal types.

Ideal Type 2 – The Innovative and Creative Consumer

The Type 2 consumer of innovation economics has a strong preference for technology, innovation, creativity, novelty, and the unfamiliar; is curious and risk seeking; and has a considerable tolerance for complexity, uncertainty, and ambiguity. This consumer proactively uses social media, the Internet, and digital markets to reward innovative firms and penalize those that promise more innovation and quality than they deliver; is more likely to switch telecommunications and other service providers for a better deal than other consumers; and is prepared to become a co-innovator and co-producer in product innovation, creation, and development, working with firms and individual innovators and inventors.

The Type 2 consumer not only interacts closely with firms but also plays the role as a consumer leader in the consumer community. Since this consumer is demanding, well informed, highly knowledgeable, "tech savvy," and "risk savvy," they play a leadership role in promoting innovation and ensuring wide acceptance of advanced, transformative, and disruptive technologies; new innovative products and processes; and new platforms and applications in the digital economy. The Type 2 consumer is generally characterized as younger and better educated; but the elderly and people with physical and other challenges are now contributing as co-creators to the development of innovative goods and services that better meet their needs.

Ideal Type 3 – The Ethical and Sustainable Consumer

The ethical and sustainable consumer has a strong interest in and is willing to pay more for products from ethical and environmentally responsible producers and vendors that: (i) protect the environment, ecological systems, biodiversity, and future generations; (ii) reduce greenhouse gas emissions and carbon footprints; (iii) support and invest in recycling and the circular economy; (iv) comply with laws, regulations, and social norms; and (v) conduct their transactions in a fair, equitable, ethical, and socially responsible manner.

Similar to Type 2 consumers, Type 3 consumers are important leaders and role models. They impose substantial "altruistic punishments" on producers, vendors, and service providers that do not comply with laws, regulations, and social norms and violate the public's loyalty and trust. They also influence the preferences and decisions of others in the consumer community through social media, online forums, and social networks.

Committed ethical and sustainable consumers and their associates allocate significant time and effort to the collection and analysis of information on the ethical and sustainable attributes of goods and services, producers, service providers, and vendors and are major sources of complaints and feedback provided to governments, companies, and civil-society groups. Type 3 consumers may also compel a targeted entity to alter its objectionable behavior through boycotts or other forms of consumer activism. One puzzling characteristic of Type 3 consumers is that some of the "less-committed" Type 3s may express stronger preferences for ethical and sustainable consumption in answering surveys than in making actual purchases.

Ideal Type 4 – The Proactive and Overly Aggressive and Opportunistic Consumer

The proactive and overly self-confident, optimistic, aggressive, opportunistic, and amoral consumer believes that he or she is more objective and rational, better informed, and less biased than other market participants, and tries to take advantage of the biases, vulnerabilities, and information disadvantages of other market participants.

Type 4 consumers often possess more information relative to other market participants, either because they have personal interests in the product domain and spend a vast amount of time searching for and analyzing information, or are in a market position with easy access to information. In theory, information can contribute to more efficient markets when used responsibly. However, the opportunistic Type 4 consumer may take advantage of information asymmetry and create unfair market situations for others. Notably, it is not uncommon for Type 4 consumers to be victims of their opportunism and "superior information" – the consequence of their overconfidence, optimism, illusion of competence and control, intention to game the system, cynicism, and tendency to exaggerate their ability to accommodate and cope with privacy and other potential risks and harms.[3] For example, they might buy counterfeit, pirated, and other questionable and "illicit" products, thinking these are "good-deals-that-dealers-won't-tell-you about," when in fact they risk acquiring items of unknown and often inferior quality.

Ideal Type 5 – The Boundedly Rational but Willing to Engage and Learn Consumer

The boundedly rational but willing to participate, engage, and learn consumer is susceptible to judgmental and cognitive biases, and relies quite heavily on heuristics. Nonetheless, Type 5 consumers are consciously aware of these tendencies and are therefore ready to learn from their market experiences in the complex and constantly changing conventional and digital marketplace; their purchasing and related successes and errors; and their social interactions with friends, relatives, neighbours, colleagues, and other market participants. Of note, they are also aware of the bounded rationality of other economic actors. Together, their market experience and consumer literacy nurture them into becoming better consumers over time, thereby mitigating their relative disadvantages compared with suppliers, retailers, service providers, and other vendors.[4]

Ideal Type 6 – The Nudged and "Nudgeable" Consumer

The nudged and "nudgeable" consumer represents the consumer ideal type of Thaler and Sunstein and other asymmetric and soft paternalism behavioral economists. This consumer is often willing to learn and wants to make the right decision but in some contexts requires a nudge from behaviorally informed paternalistic governments, socially responsible employers, producers, vendors and other companies, civil-society groups, and other actors, in order to make better decisions for themselves and for society, the economy, and the environment. As defined by Thaler and Sunstein, a nudge is "any aspect of the choice architecture that alters people's behavior in a predictable way without forbidding any options or significantly changing their economic incentives. To count as a mere nudge, the intervention must be easy and cheap to avoid."[5]

The nudged and "nudgeable" consumer has some uneasiness and awareness about their emotional responses, behavioral biases, flawed heuristics, and cognitive deficiencies; but in some contexts this awareness is not sufficient to modify and improve their conduct and decision making – leading to the concept of the vulnerable but "nudgeable" consumer who requires "nudging" assistance from an outside party.

Governments and other nudgers need to be responsible, ethical, and behaviorally informed. Nudging should not be employed when more direct regulatory interventions are clearly needed, or when using nudging as a "hidden persuader" is both unethical and unnecessary.[6] More specifically, nudgers should make sure that the nudged consumer has general knowledge of the nudging concept, purpose, and intention; is aware that a transaction involves some kind of persuasion attempt; and fully accepts being "nudged" in order to improve decision making and outcomes. Most importantly, nudges should not limit people's freedom of choice and their ability to learn from experience.[7]

Ideal Type 7 – The Vulnerable and Disadvantaged Consumer with Coping Skills

This vulnerable, disadvantaged, and naive consumer is aware of their marketplace deficiencies in terms of product experience, education level, income, and purchasing power. For these consumers, vulnerability and disadvantages may originate from their socioeconomic status and other related attributes such as low income, low consumer literacy, and limited geographic proximity to resources and information. This consumer develops and employs coping skills and strategies to increase their competencies and ability to function in the modern marketplace. They also expand their contacts and social networks through stronger personal connections with more knowledgeable consumers and other market participants – thereby reducing the potential for inferior purchasing decisions and consumer detriment.

Developing and applying coping skills can be extremely challenging for lower-income consumers who live in remote and rural areas, and hence have limited access to higher-quality stores and service providers. Limited access to the Internet and the redress services of governments and consumers' associations would also impede the consumer's coping ability.

One of the more useful insights from the "coping consumer" literature is that many vulnerable consumers may in fact be more aware of their weaknesses than the average consumer. When they do cope, Type 7 consumers can be less vulnerable than "average" consumers, who are less motivated to adopt coping strategies because of their lack of awareness of potential human biases and overconfidence in their capabilities.

Ideal Type 8 – The Vulnerable, Disadvantaged, and Naive Consumer

The vulnerable, disadvantaged, and naive consumer has unstable, inconsistent, and "constructed" preferences that can be readily manipulated and exploited by "unscrupulous" producers, vendors, and service providers, and is unduly influenced by framing, priming, and related marketing techniques. They also lack the emotional and behavioral "self-awareness," consumer literacy and related capabilities, information, attention span, interest, and/or time to develop coping skills and strategies and learn from their purchasing and related errors.

The Type 8 consumer, who is less experienced, informed, sophisticated, self-confident, and "rational," has received most of the attention in the consumer literature and in consumer-protection policies and laws. Policies and laws are typically written with reference to this consumer type. This is because they especially need the "paternalistic protection" provided by government, socially responsible suppliers, vendors, service providers and other companies, and proactive and well-resourced consumers' associations and other civil-society groups. This "paternalistic protection" is provided in order to protect them from their biases; their flawed emotions, heuristics, and cognition; their socioeconomic disadvantages; and the irresponsible, unethical, and disreputable behavior of vendors, marketers, producers, and other companies and market participants – including Type 4 disreputable consumers in electronic and more conventional peer-to-peer transactions.

While all consumers are vulnerable at one time or another, there are more profound states of vulnerability and disadvantage where some consumers are susceptible to particular forms of detriment and harm. This may occur when consumers live in poverty and have low financial- or functional-literacy skills, have limited computer skills and experience and Internet access to the digital economy, and/or live in geographically isolated communities – including more isolated Aboriginal and Indigenous communities in Canada and elsewhere – where opportunities to gain market capabilities and experience and seek consumer redress are limited.[8]

APPLYING THE BRCCC TO PRIORITY CONSUMER POLICY ISSUES IMPORTANT TO BEHAVIORALLY INFORMED ORGANIZATIONS

The BRCCC was first developed to provide assistance and guidance to state and nonstate regulators, regulated entities, other companies, civil-society groups, and other regulatory actors, including the final consumer. This section will summarize some of the more important BRCCC insights from the perspective of different regulatory actors that are behaviorally informed and/or that wish to become more behaviorally informed in the future.

Prioritizing Consumer Policy Issues

For the more sophisticated consumers at the first three locations on the continuum, improved product and market information, expanded competition and inter-firm rivalry, and the operation of market forces should be sufficient to remedy most of the market problems they encounter in their purchases, other transactions, and contract negotiations. Consumer protection, competition policy, privacy and other consumer-related initiatives by regulators will more often be required for the less sophisticated and more vulnerable consumers on the lower half of the continuum (Types 5 to 8). Special attention would be given to regulated entities that are targeting and exploiting these more vulnerable consumers. However, regulatory interventions should be designed in a manner that promotes appropriate nudging, learning, agency, and coping skills and strategies in these consumers, in order to help them move upward on the continuum.

The "nudged and nudgeable consumer" under Type 6 within the BRCCC raises a number of issues. Nudging consumers is an important contribution from behavioral economics, but more research and practical experience are needed on the types of consumers who possess the attributes that make them "nudgeable" and therefore most likely to respond to and benefit from responsible nudging. Likewise, more research is needed on the products and market contexts where nudging will be more and less effective. There is a caution that self-interested governments and their policymakers, regulators, and officials will apply nudges to the wrong consumers for the wrong products, market contexts, and reasons. There are also concerns that these agencies will employ inappropriate, poorly designed, and highly intrusive nudging based on Big Data, data fusion, the "Internet of Things," algorithmic intelligence, and other forms of artificial intelligence. Companies are reportedly employing their own "dark nudges," through learning scientifically tested nudge techniques from the behavioral sciences in order to exploit consumers rather than promote consumer welfare.

The Type 4 consumer – the more aggressive, opportunistic, self-confident, and amoral consumer – poses special challenges for state and nonstate regulators, firms, other regulated entities, and other final consumers. In many respects, the harms experienced by these consumers are self-imposed and therefore could arguably be ignored by regulators. The major exception is when their purchases of counterfeit, pirated, and other questionable products have substantial negative spillover effects on other consumers and market participants, and on market efficiency and competition. In these cases, interventions under trademark, copyright, other intellectual-property, and product-safety laws may provide the required remedies.

The anxiety, stress, pressures, and unrealized expectations generated by the anticipated slower-growth and more turbulent economies in the coming years could result in substantial increases in the number and market influence of Type 4 consumers. These consumers will be even more motivated to search for "the best bargains possible" in order to compensate for stagnant incomes and lower purchasing power.

Addressing Market Challenges

The high individual and social costs of free goods on the Internet and other markets are an important theme in recent behavioral consumer research. Applying the BRCCC will bring greater clarity to the actual costs of free goods to consumers in terms of privacy, personal security, consumer choice and variety, and potential long-term reductions in competition. The BRCCC will illustrate how the high

costs and potential harms of free goods are important to all consumer types, and also how these harms vary significantly for the
different consumer types. These different potential harms should be
addressed through different nudges, laws, and regulations.

The expanding digital economy poses other challenges that would
benefit from the BRCCC. The unease, uncertainty, reduction in psychological well-being, and loss of self-confidence, self-reliance, and control
associated with breaches of privacy, private information and personal
identities, and cyber threats and bullying could have substantial negative externality effects that make some consumers more vulnerable,
disadvantaged, and susceptible to exploitation than others.

The BRCCC also enhances our understanding of the role of competition in market operations. Economists have provided theoretical insights and empirical evidence on why enhanced competition
and more suppliers in many markets do not necessarily enhance
consumer welfare and consumers' satisfaction with their purchases.
This is especially true for experience and credence goods, financial
products and advice, and other more complex products and product
bundles sold in conventional and digital markets, and for markets
driven more by product quality than price competition.[9]

Applying the BRCCC could strengthen the positive association
between competition and consumer welfare and make it more operational as consumers move upward on the continuum and become
more sophisticated, informed, attentive, and demanding. Studies
on the interactions between the complex behavioral consumer and
competition also suggest that, for many consumers and contexts, the
negative effects of consumer biases on competition and consumer
detriment may not be substantial, and may simply represent irritants
and annoyances that do not warrant investigation by regulators.[10]

Long-Term Advantages of Applying the BRCCC

Recent advances in the behavioral literatures underline the need
for behaviorally informed organizations to employ a nuanced
approach to consumer sophistication, rationality, and diversity that
takes account of all eight ideal types. All eight should be addressed
when   behaviorally   informed   organizations   are   conducting

regulatory-impact and benefit-cost analyses, including the separate analyses conducted on consumer, competition, business, and government impacts. Applying the BRCCC would be especially helpful when assessing unintended and unanticipated consequences and the distribution of predicted impacts, benefits, and costs among different consumer groups and market segments, and among consumers, producers, governments, and other actors.

In addition, employing the continuum even in a conceptual way would reduce the risks and errors that emerge when organizations presume that all of their consumers and target groups are located at either the top or the bottom of the BRCCC. In particular, the continuum would help behaviorally informed organizations to avoid what could be called "lowest-common-denominator" product and social-marketing strategies that can be seen as patronizing, demeaning, and insulting by many consumers/individuals.

Another advantage of employing the BRCCC is that, over time, policymakers, state and nonstate regulators, and other regulatory actors would come to focus more on the objective characteristics of individual consumers "as they really are" – rather than apply generalizations, categorizations, stereotypes, biases, and related inaccurate judgments that result from grouping consumers together based on age, gender, ethnicity, socioeconomic status, immigrant status, and other personal characteristics. Using the continuum would reduce the risk that policymakers, analysts, and others will simply presume, with limited evidence, that

- most women or most men, depending on context and the analyst applying the stereotype;
- all or most consumers over age sixty-five;
- most consumers in rural locations and smaller communities and most consumers with lower incomes and less education; and,
- consumers who are Indigenous, or members of other ethnic minorities, or recent immigrants from a developing economy

are less sophisticated and "rational" and more vulnerable and disadvantaged than other groups, and therefore need to be protected from deception, frauds, and scams.

Furthermore, the vulnerable and disadvantaged consumer and "the consumer as victim" are too often the unstated and unexplained "default option" in the consumer and related analysis and policy development of regulators, academics, and other groups. Using the BRCCC will, it is hoped, make these presumptions more transparent, tractable, credible, and meaningful. One other major advantage is that the continuum approach allows consumers to move upward on the continuum in response to experience, learning, higher-quality information, new attitudes and skills, positive changes in market context and product attributes, and assistance from relatives, friends, and other social networks.

Identifying the Different Ideal Types of Consumers

A major challenge is how to identify consumers at the different locations along the continuum without employing questionable categorizations, stereotypes, and generalizations. One source of evidence and information would be the kinds of marketing and advertising directed by corporations at their target market. One would expect that successful corporations with effective marketing programs would know whether their target market comprises relatively more sophisticated or less sophisticated consumers.[11]

A second source would be surveys and focus groups of consumers who represent the relevant market when, for example, competition, consumer-protection, privacy, sectoral, and other agencies are investigating and considering an enforcement action against a specific company, industry, or market. A third source would be consumer and civil society complaints to governments, consumers' associations, seniors' associations and other civil society groups, and better business bureaus; as well as media reports and consumer advisories on the Internet. Consumer and other complaints and advisories separate the more informed, demanding, and proactive consumers and consumer leaders from other consumers along the continuum. Complaint information also helps to identify regulated entities that are underestimating or purposely ignoring the sophistication of their consumers and customers, or are intentionally exploiting their weaknesses.

Finally, as noted at the outset, individual consumers and consumer groups can belong to different ideal types along the continuum depending on: (i) consumer characteristics such as mood, attention span, interest, self-awareness, and self-confidence at the time of purchase; (ii) characteristics of the situation including the complexity, ambiguity, and related "wicked" characteristics of the consumer transaction, contract, problem, or other matter; and (iii) characteristics of the decision process, including whether the purchase involves a relatively simple search good, or a more complex experience and credence good and product bundle.[12]

CONCLUDING COMMENTS

The BRCCC is little more than a conceptual construct that requires significant multidisciplinary research across a large number of behavioral, economics, industrial-organization, institutional, consumer-policy-and-law, regulatory, governance, organizational, and other literatures.

Making precise estimates of the number of consumers at each location along the continuum would be virtually impossible, but more behavioral analysis is needed on how final consumers might be distributed across the BRCCC's eight locations. Hypotheses hinted at in this article and the literature generally are as follows: Type 1 consumers are a "rare bird" relevant mainly to purchases of search goods. Innovative and creative consumers, ethical and sustainable consumers, and consumer leaders under Types 2 and 3 are expanding in number and influence, but their numbers are still relatively small.

The opportunistic and amoral consumer under Type 4 could expand significantly in size and influence during periods of market turbulence, economic crisis, and slower economic growth. The Type 5 boundedly rational but learning consumer and the Type 7 vulnerable but coping consumer have received limited attention but can be very important to consumer policy, corporate strategy, and behaviorally informed organizations. In particular, the learning consumer should receive much greater attention in future consumer and behavioral research.

Simplistic interpretations of the abundant literature on nudging may have led some practitioners to overestimate the number and representativeness of nudged and nudgeable consumers under Type 6. More insights are also needed on the positive and negative interactions between: nudging and related "soft interventions" of persuasion and motivation; nudging and consumer learning, agency, and autonomy; nudging and the coping skills and strategies of more vulnerable and other consumers; and the positive and negative interactions between nudging and the more conventional competition, consumer-protection, privacy, and other policy and regulatory interventions.

The vulnerable and disadvantaged consumers under Type 8 are clearly important but are often context- and product-dependent, and their numbers, challenges, mistakes, and detriment can be miscalibrated. Many who are considered to be vulnerable under the representative consumer, binary, and "consumer as victim" concepts would be better categorized as aggressive, nudging, learning, and coping consumers under the BRCCC.

The major theme of this chapter and research is that governments and their policymakers and regulatory authorities should clearly identify and articulate the attributes of the consumer ideal type or types to be targeted by their proposed policies, laws, regulations, rules, and regulatory functions and messages. Behaviorally informed companies and industry associations, consumer associations, other civil-society groups, and other stakeholders should display similar discipline when addressing consumer attributes and interests and advocating policy, legal, and regulatory remedies. The era of the "representative, homogeneous, and binary consumer" in policy analysis should come to an end.

NOTES

1 Nonstate regulators include: compliance officials and divisions of firms; consumer associations and other civil-society groups; standards organizations; advisory websites on the Internet; and well-informed and demanding consumers who are prepared to complain and punish wrongdoers.

2 Maesschalck, J. (2005). Approaches to ethics management in the public sector: A proposed extension of the compliance-integrity continuum. *Public Integrity, 7*(1) (Winter 2004–5), 21–41.

3 Hoffmann, C.P., Lutz, C., & Ranzini, G. (2016). Privacy cynicism: A new approach to the privacy paradox. *Cyberpsychology: Journal of Psychosocial Research on Cyberspace, 10*(4), article 7. http://dx.doi.org/10.5817/CP2016-4-7.

4 Delsys Research. (2009). Consumer literacy and its effect on consumer detriment: Report on project findings and analysis. Prepared for the Office of Consumer Affairs, Government of Canada; and OECD. (2010). Consumer policy toolkit. Paris: OECD Publishing. doi: 10.1787 /9789264079663-en.

5 Thaler, R.H., & Sunstein, C.R. (2008). *Nudge: Improving decisions about health, wealth, and happiness.* New Haven, CT: Yale University Press.

6 Oliver, A. (2013). From nudging to budging: Using behavioural economics to inform public sector policy. *Journal of Social Policy, 42*(4), 685–700. doi:10.1017/S0047279413000299; Loewenstein, G., & Chater, N. (2017). Putting nudges in perspective. *Behavioural Public Policy, 1*(1), 26–53. doi:10.1017/bpp.2016.7; and Reisch, L.A., & Zhao, M. (2017). Behavioural economics, consumer behaviour and consumer policy: State of the art. *Behavioural Public Policy, 1*(2), 190–206. doi: https://doi.org/10.1017 /bpp.2017.1.

7 Puaschunder, J.M. (2019). Towards a utility theory of privacy and information sharing and the introduction of hyper-hyperbolic discounting in the digital big data age. In *Research Association for Interdisciplinary Science Collective Volume on Economic Science,* 4–46.

8 Delsys Research. (2009). Geographic isolation and its effect on consumer detriment. Prepared for the Office of Consumer Affairs, Government of Canada.

9 Huck, S., & Zhou, J. (2011). Consumer behavioural biases in competition: A survey. Report for UK Office of Fair Trading. Retrieved from http:// ssrn.com/paper=1944446.

10 Heidhues, P., & Kőszegi, B. (2018). Behavioral industrial organization. In D. Bernheim, S. DellaVigna, & D. Laibson (Eds.), *Handbook of Behavioral Economics,* 1: 517–612. Amsterdam: Elsevier.; and Ireland, D., & Kofler, G. (2012). Behavioral economics and competition policy and law in emerging market economies. Paper presented to the Canada Law and Economics Association Conference in Toronto, Canada, 28–29 September 2012.

11 Deng, Y., Staelin, R., Wang, W., & Boulding, W. (2018). Consumer sophistication, word-of-mouth and "false" promotions. *Journal of Economic Behavior and Organization, 152,* 98–123.

12 Dulleck, U., Kershbamer, R., & Sutter, M. (2011). The economics of credence goods. *American Economic Review, 101*(2), 526–55; Tor, A. (2016). Justifying antitrust: Prediction, efficiency, and welfare. Retrieved from

SSRN: https://ssrn.com/abstract=2730670; and Chirita, A.D. (2016). The rise of big data and the loss of privacy. Consumer protection and IP law – towards a holistic approach? In M. Bakhoum, B. Conde Gallego, M.-O. Mackenordt, & G. Surblytė-Namavičienė (Eds.), *Personal data in competition, consumer protection and intellectual property law*. MPI Studies on Intellectual Property and Competition Law, 28: 153–89. Berlin, Heidelberg: Springer. doi: 10.1007/978-3-662-57646-5_7.

CHAPTER EIGHT

A Scarcity of Attention

Matthew Hilchey and J. Eric T. Taylor

Mandated disclosure is a common policy tool that requires firms to provide information about their goods and services to help prospective consumers make better choices. If implemented in a human-centric way, disclosures should make it harder for firms to conceal relevant product information from their consumers and therefore should empower the consumer. However, the reality is that traditional mandated-disclosure policies have not proven satisfactory at improving or influencing consumer choice.[1] For example, studies in the domain of financial decisions show that making annual percentage rates (APRs) more salient by increasing their font size, as mandated by an amendment to the Truth in Lending Act (TILA), has little effect on credit-card-choice share.[2] Field studies show that savings-account holders are unlikely to switch accounts even when provided with salient, direct comparisons between their interest rates and better alternatives in their annual statements.[3] Other field studies show that highlighting versus concealing the trade-offs of credit cards offered by a bank's website has a weak effect on consumer credit-card choice.[4] Many studies show either weak or no effects of information provision on various financial choices.[5]

One reason information disclosures fail is that people do not pay much attention to them. For example, the Australian Securities and Investments Commission (ASIC) and the Dutch Authority for the Financial Markets (AFM) report that only about 20 percent of individuals read the long text-based disclosure documents about financial products. To increase the probability of attracting attention, some researchers have attempted to transmit information using visually salient infographics instead. This approach is particularly prominent in dietary and tobacco-consumption studies on mandated-information disclosures. The research there shows that salient, graphic health warnings can be especially effective at stimulating healthier choices.[6] While such warnings can indeed increase the probability of drawing attention[7] – which can affect choice in many different ways – we also know that mere increases in visual salience do not guarantee corresponding increases in visual attention.[8]

With this in mind, this chapter's goal is to provide a fuller understanding of visual attention by harnessing the behavioral insights from basic laboratory research. We begin by introducing the concept of visual selective attention. We then identify broad forces that drive it. We will explain why neither mere information provision nor the salience of an object is sufficient for attracting or sustaining attention by discussing other factors that can be as important, if not more so. By doing so, we hope to inspire practitioners and policymakers to innovate with other, more successful ways of drawing attention to the information that matters most.

VISUAL SELECTIVE ATTENTION

Broadly construed, selective attention refers to any instance of asymmetric information processing. Asymmetries can occur at the earliest stages of information acquisition (when we take in information from the world around us) all the way through to the response-selection and planning stages (when a specific response and action plan are chosen).[9] When selectivity occurs at relatively early visual stages of processing, we refer to it as "visual selective attention." For example, we know how difficult it can be to find a familiar face in a crowd, a phone on a cluttered desk, a car in a parking lot, or – worst-case scenario – the proverbial needle in a haystack. Many of us have spent too long looking for Waldo (or Wally) in the popular Martin Handford picture-book series. If all visual information could be processed fully in parallel, then we would not experience such difficulties. Instead,

Figure 8.1 Image from a video used in the now-famous gorilla experiment. Most participants failed to notice the person wearing the black gorilla suit.[13]

Source: Image provided by Dan Simons. Learn more about inattentional blindness and see the video at www.dansimons.com.

our visual systems are faced with capacity limits that lead to highly selective forms of visual information processing.[10]

Attention to one place or thing implies inattention to other places and things. There are caveats to this claim that we will discuss later on in this chapter, but it is often true that unattended-to information is lost somewhere in the stream of visual information processing. Now-famous examples of inattention are provided by the "gorilla experiments," in which a visually salient person in a gorilla suit gesticulates amid a group of undergraduates tossing around a basketball. In the canonical demonstrations, spectators are told to focus on something in particular, like the number of times that the basketball is passed between people wearing white shirts. Some studies show that the gorilla is overlooked by 73 percent of the spectators.[11] This textbook example is called inattentional blindness (see figure 8.1).[12]

It is just one among many demonstrations showing that neither unexpected, visually salient, nor downright bizarre events obligatorily attract or hold attention.

BASIC TERMINOLOGY IN VISUAL SELECTIVE ATTENTION

To most, "attention" means taking notice of something or someone. To researchers studying visual selective attention, "attention" refers more broadly to the many systems in the human brain that determine information throughput. These systems are referred to as "networks of attention."[14] One key idea is that attention is an umbrella term for many different cognitive and neural processes. Another is that the allocation of visual selective attention need not necessitate or result in awareness. Many of the networks that drive visual selective attention can do so subconsciously.[15]

Broad distinctions are also commonly drawn between different modes of visual selective attention. One famous distinction is between externally triggered (exogenous) and internally triggered (endogenous) modes.[16] Attention that is shifted reflexively by an event in the environment may be referred to as exogenously driven. Researchers have historically characterized exogenous attention as automatic, fast, transient, powerful, and capacity unlimited. For example, a sudden flash of light in the visual periphery may rapidly orient attention even if it is irrelevant to the individual.[17] In such cases, the relative visual salience of the signal rapidly dominates the competition for attention. A good example is an emergency vehicle's siren. All else being equal, relatively bright, flashy, colorful lights exogenously orient attention.

In contrast, attention that is guided by the individual's goals and motivations is referred to as endogenous. Endogenous attention can be engaged explicitly to select one thing over another. For example, an individual who has a newborn baby may be motivated to search for debt-management suggestions that they would otherwise not pay attention to when childless. An individual who is operating within a shoestring budget may have a goal to reduce spending, and may show a greater tendency to fixate on price information than an individual who is not working within the same financial constraints.[18] Researchers have historically characterized endogenous attention as effortful, slow, sustained, and capacity limited.

In practice, the distinction between endogenous and exogenous modes is relative rather than absolute. Paraphrasing attention luminary Michael Posner, a signal may only capture attention exogenously if it is "important" to the subject.[19] Yet, importance is determined by goals, motivations, contexts, learning, and experience. In other words, exogenous attention can be strengthened or weakened by endogenous forces. Nowadays, there is a growing consensus that many behavioral effects ultimately reflect some amalgam of endogenous and exogenous attention rather than just one or the other.[20]

FORCES THAT DRIVE VISUAL SELECTIVE ATTENTION

The most important question for policymaking is how these different modes of attention interact to determine our "final" attention. Perhaps policymakers who propose mandated disclosure hope that displaying important credit-card information prominently in large fonts will attract a bit of attention from unmotivated individuals. However, attention is determined not by any singular force but by many forces that modify the neural-activation levels of brain regions that are known as "attentional priority maps."[21] Notably, the visual salience of an object represents just one such force that contributes to these neural-activation levels; other inputs that can significantly modify the neural-activation levels are the individual's current search goals and motivations and the individual's selection history with a scene and the objects within it. These forces conspire to reduce or enhance the attention-grabbing potential of a visually salient object. We next discuss these three key inputs to the attentional-priority maps and implications for attention.

Relative Visual Salience

While many experiments show that a visually salient object may exogenously draw attention,[22] many others show that a visually salient object may not draw any attention at all. Take, for example, the following question: if credit-card companies displayed overdue interest rates in relatively large or visually salient fonts, would individuals inevitably pay more attention to them? The answer is "no," as evidenced by many laboratory experiments and real-world simulations. The gorilla experiment is one compelling demonstration. In the laboratory, search efficiency may be unaffected by the presence or absence of a visually salient distractor falling within the visual field, depending on previously established search strategies and incentives to search for a particular object feature or dimension.[23] Outside of the laboratory, a staged physical assault that is visible to joggers for at least thirty seconds is more likely to be overlooked if the joggers' attention is instead focused narrowly on monitoring the gesticulations of the lead runner.[24]

Momentary Goals and Motivations

Visually salient signals are insufficient to drive attention because they can be overpowered by our momentary goals and motivations. This basic premise receives strong empirical support from many basic laboratory studies on attention. We have mentioned earlier that our goals and motivations represent endogenous forces that can exert control over exogenous shifts of attention toward salient objects. Here, we will discuss two basic, generalizable examples: spatial focus and feature focus, the understanding of which will help us design and implement more scientifically sound interventions.

Spatial focus. Not all space within the visual field (the entire area that can be seen) is assigned the same information-processing priority, and the position of the eye is not a reliable indicator of where attention is allocated.[25] Information can be covertly attended – without eye movements – at locations far away from where the eye is oriented. Colloquially, information can be attended out of the corner of one's eyes. Often, attention is not fully concentrated on a particular region. Attentional gradients emanate out from prioritized regions, such that information near them is preferentially processed.[26] These gradients can also conform to the contours of objects within the environment.[27]

Ultimately, attention can be concentrated on particular regions, at the expense of the processing of other regions.[28]

We can think about spatial focus informally by drawing on any number of sports analogies. For example, from a young age, hockey players are trained to handle the puck with their heads up. Players are trained in this way because we know that if attention is focused in on the puck or the act of handling it, then there are high risks that the player will (1) be blindsided by a hit from an opposing player, and (2) miss opportunities to make a play. You can also think back to the famous gorilla example that we provided at the outset of this chapter. If attention is focused exclusively on the space that is occupied by the ball because the spectator is counting the number of passes that are made, then the information around it is unlikely to attract attention, no matter how bizarre or visually salient. The same common sense holds true in policymaking contexts: if the financial player is focused in on some region at the expense of another – for example, the "sign here" line in a cardholder agreement – then they will miss opportunities to make sounder financial plays and/or will get hit hard later on with various fees and penalties that were disclosed elsewhere.

We can think about spatial focus more formally by considering some basic laboratory research. In the lab, one way to alter the spatial distribution of attention is by making one region disproportionately relevant. Consider an experiment in which we manipulate whether it is or is not necessary to monitor a stream of rapidly presented letters in central vision before searching through an array of visual stimuli in peripheral vision.[29] When it is necessary to monitor the letter stream – and thus the information at this location is highly relevant – your average search speed is unaffected by the presence of a salient distractor in peripheral vision. In short, because your attention is focused on processing the central letter stream, the salient distractor in peripheral vision does not capture your attention. When it is not necessary to monitor the central letter stream, your average search speed is longer when the visually salient distractor is present. In short, because your attention is not focused on processing the letter stream (i.e., it was "diffusely distributed"), the salient distractor captures your attention. Collectively, the results suggest that a visually salient item will not reliably capture attention if attention is already focused on a different region. It may also be helpful to think about this as an example of "tunnel vision."

Feature focus. Information processing can be attuned to particular features (e.g., red) and dimensions (e.g., color) in the visual environment. Providing advance knowledge about a search object's defining attributes can boost its perceived relative salience. If you know what it is that you are looking for, then the signal strength of the search-defining attribute(s) may be upweighted, altering the signal-to-noise ratio in the visual cortex and biasing the competition for attention.[30]

We can develop a better sense of this by building on our hockey analogy. Any kid who grew up playing hockey (or any team sport for that matter) may recall how difficult it is to attend to a teammate when jersey features cannot be used to reliably distinguish between teams. However, as soon as the team-defining jersey features are known, it becomes trivially easy to preferentially attend to teammates. In the famous gorilla example, if you comply with the instruction to pay close attention to something in particular (e.g., the color of the ball or the white shirts), then other information in the environment that does not resemble it becomes much less likely to attract attention. Again, the same point rings true in policymaking contexts. For example, if the financial player is focused on obtaining a credit card that offers the best travel rewards, then other information that does not signal travel reward (e.g., annual percentage rate or annual fee) is much less likely to attract or sustain attention. To put it most simply, unexpected, surprising, or visually salient objects will attract and sustain attention reliably if, and only if, the goals and motivations of the individual are relatively weak or if the object is perceived as congruent with the individual's search goals and motivations.

In the laboratory, the most well-known demonstration of feature-based attention is provided by the contingent-capture cueing procedure.[31] In this procedure, you are instructed to find some object that is defined by its unique color (say red or green) in an array of colored visual distractors. A split second before the appearance of the search array, a visually salient stimulus (i.e., a cue) appears somewhere in your visual periphery. When this visually salient cue resembles what it is that you are looking for (e.g., the same color), we find that your average search speed is faster when the thing that you are looking for appears near it; in short, your attention is captured by the salient cue. However, when this visually salient cue does not resemble the thing that you are looking for, we find that your search speed is no faster when the thing that you are looking for appears near the cue relative to elsewhere; in short, your attention is not captured by the salient cue.[32] Painting in even broader strokes, a great deal of laboratory research demonstrates that information that is currently being held in memory to accomplish some goal has powerful effects on where and toward what attention is allocated.[33]

Selection-History Effects

Up to this point, we have acted as though attention is shaped only by the information that is available in the present. However, attention does not exist in a temporal vacuum. The brain subconsciously keeps a meticulous record of the things and places that you have attended to and the relative value associated with them. In broad theoretical strokes, relatively high-value things and places that have been noticed are more likely to grab attention later on. Relatively low-value things and places that have been noticed are less likely to grab attention later on. Such findings are often referred to broadly as selection-history effects. These refer to how your experience of selecting in favor of or against various things or places influences their likelihood of attracting your attention later on. Although attentional biases generated by selection history are fundamentally determined by endogenous forces – in that they are determined by earlier goal states, motivations, contexts, and feedback structures – they can occur so quickly and independently of your current goals and motivations that they can appear to be driven in a purely exogenous fashion.[34]

Selection-history effects across uncorrelated sequences of events. Let's start off with a rudimentary laboratory example. Suppose that you are the unfortunate research participant who has to repeatedly find red and green objects embedded in arrays of blue and yellow distractor objects. The colors of the search object and distractor objects just happen to vary randomly from one visual search environment to the next. One basic finding is that you are faster to find a search object when its defining features stay the same than when they change (i.e., attention tends more easily toward information that was recently useful for signalling the target). Another is that you are faster to find a search object when distractor features stay the same than when they change (i.e., information that was recently useless for finding something is more easily discounted later on).[35] These kinds of effects can strongly influence eye movements and search scan paths.[36] Broadly construed, features that were recently useful for finding the search object may be upweighted (perhaps because they were associated with the intrinsic reward of discovery), whereas features that were useless for finding the search object may be down-weighted (perhaps because they were perceived as valueless for discovery).[37]

To contextualize, we will return to our hockey analogies, this time taking the perspective of a referee. Suppose that two players are involved in an altercation and that the referee assigns a penalty to just one of them. If the penalized player later becomes involved in an altercation with a different player (who has not been penalized), then in theory the referee should be more likely to pay attention to the previously penalized player than to the previously unpenalized player. In this case, an asymmetry in the allocation of attention can lead to a bias in the decision to call a penalty. Returning to the gorilla example, suppose that you first attend to the gorilla (perhaps you are forewarned of it), and then count the number of times that the ball is passed. Assuming that there was some value in having attended to the gorilla in the first place (e.g., discovery), then attention will occasionally revisit or keep track of this gorilla even though your principal, explicit goal is to keep track of the ball. In fact, the gorilla will be quite hard to ignore if your attention was drawn to it in the first place.

For mandated-disclosure policies, attentional biases due to selection history may pose interesting challenges. The purpose of mandated disclosure is to ensure that the individual has ready access to potentially relevant information that might have been previously ignored or filtered out at some stage of information throughput. However, because of the individual's selection history, information that was previously downplayed will likely remain so, and thus its attention-grabbing potential will remain suboptimal. We would suggest that the optimal strategy for the policymaker interested in attracting attention is to play into these selection-history biases. Render the information that you want processed in such a fashion that it is congruent with the things that the individual historically looks for. In practice, this means that information that you want seen should maximally take on features that the individual historically prizes while minimally taking on features that the individual historically discounts.

Selection-history effects across correlated sequences of events. Other laboratory studies include manipulations of the probabilities at which a given search object (i.e., the thing that you are looking for) or distractor (i.e., the thing that you are not looking for) consistently appears at the same place. One interesting aspect of these studies is that the researchers do not inform individuals of the fact that some locations are more likely to contain the thing that is being looked for than others or that some locations are more likely to contain the thing that is not being looked for than others. More interesting still, formal tests reveal that individuals usually do not become aware of these relationships. Despite this, these studies tend to show that a highly salient distractor will capture attention progressively less if it appears more or less consistently at the same location. In the same vein, a highly salient distractor will capture attention progressively more when it appears in the same place that the search object usually does. An additional finding is that a search object is found progressively faster when its location is more or less consistent.[38]

Something partly related is called contextual cueing.[39] In contextual-cueing procedures, some search environments appear more than once, with their reappearance usually being separated by many different search environments. When the search environment repeats, so too does the search object's location, but, importantly, across all search environments the search object is no more likely to appear at any one location than any other is. The key finding is that search performance progressively improves with repeated exposure to the same or similar search environments.[40] That is, attention is rapidly oriented to the likely location of the search object, given the environment, even though people are generally unaware of the relationship between search object and environment.[41] Findings like these dovetail with research showing that regions in natural environments that are historically associated with a search object are preferentially attended.[42]

The main practical point of this research is that there is a multitude of processes that implicitly keep track of where, in the context of certain search environments, search objects and distractors have historically been likely to occur. Attention is biased accordingly. From a policymaking perspective, the lessons are straightforward. It pays to know where in the environment the individual usually finds what it is they are looking for. To increase the likelihood of attracting attention, disclose the information that you want seen at that location or somewhere very close to it. Location, location, location – it matters a lot.

Value-driven selection-history effects. We will briefly address one final class of selection-history effect. Things and places that are imbued with social, appetitive, or financial value, by virtue of their associations with certain kinds of feedback, can bias attention in ways that appear to be independent of awareness, current goals, and motivations.[43]

We will start off by illustrating the principle with a simple laboratory example. Consider a value-driven attentional-capture procedure.[44] In this procedure, there is an initial training phase that involves searching through environments over and over again for one of two objects that are defined by some basic visual property (e.g., red or green; i.e., each environment contains either a red or green search object). Importantly, one of the search objects, once found and identified, results in a larger financial payout than the other. This incentivizes performance and creates an association between the search-defining feature of the search object and reward. In a subsequent transfer phase, (1) search is no longer extrinsically rewarded, (2) the search object is defined by its unique shape (as opposed to color), (3) people are explicitly told that color cannot be used to find the search object, but (4) on occasion, a distractor takes on the color that was associated with the high or low payout during the training phase. The key finding is that search performance is worst when a value-laden distractor appears in the environment during the transfer phase. Put simply, even though this distractor object no longer yields any financial gains (or losses)[45] and is irrelevant to the present goals, it still attracts attention. These effects can become quite context-specific, in that a valued object is less likely to attract attention if it occurs outside the environment that it acquired value in.[46] Through the use of different procedures, value-associated objects have been shown to modify eye-movement trajectories and landing sites.[47] There is even some evidence to suggest that stimuli imbued with value can break through strategically focused spatial attention to reorient attention![48]

Think back to the basketball gorilla example of inattentional blindness. This time, let us imagine that some of the people who are asked to count the number of passes just happen to be part of a gorilla-conservation group. Assuming that such people have associated gorillas with relatively high value, on some level, the gorilla should attract their attention even if they are focusing their attention on the ball or jerseys. At the very least, their gorilla miss rates will be lower than average. From a policymaking perspective, an understanding of the things that people value is indispensable, in large part because perceived value drives attention. It is theoretically possible to break through someone's focus entirely and to reorient it on the things that you want by ensuring that the information you provide takes on something of idiosyncratic value.

BRINGING IT TOGETHER

An understanding of the fundamental behavioral principles of attention that have arisen from basic laboratory work is essential when it comes to designing and implementing interventions for behavior change. We hope that the practitioner will take away at least two important and broad ideas from the attention laboratory to more natural environments. First, appreciate that attention is a gatekeeper to perception, judgment, decision making, and other cognitive processes. Information left unattended cannot influence behavior, and this is the fate of many mandated information disclosures. Second,

Figure 8.2 Simplified illustration of three forces determining visual selective attention

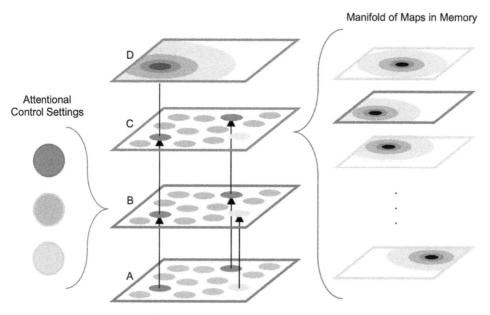

Source: (*A*) Sensory input. Relative visual salience between elements increases the activation of the more uncommon items, dark and light gray. (*B*) Attentional-control settings. The individual is looking for something dark gray, so dark gray objects receive greater activation in the maps than non-dark gray objects. (*C*) Selection history. The individual remembers circumstances prioritizing the bottom-left, perhaps because a search object there was rewarding, resulting in greater activation of this location. (*D*) The resultant attentional-priority map is the aggregate of these three forces.

passing through the gateway of attention is not a trivial matter. Visual selective attention is driven fundamentally by attentional priority maps whose activation levels are determined by three broad forces that we refer to as relative visual salience, momentary goals and motivations, and selection history (see figure 8.2). Any attempt to change behavior by focusing on only subsets of these forces, or ignoring them altogether, is not likely to produce the desired behavioral result.

With these lessons in mind, how can we improve information disclosure to attract individuals' attention? First, let us consider an inadequate policy, which fails to exploit these drivers. In online credit-card-search environments, the annual interest rates, grace periods, annual fees, and so forth associated with a credit card must be disclosed in a summary table at the beginning of the cardholder agreement, pursuant to the Cost of Borrowing (Banks) Regulations in Canada. The legislated presentation standards are such that all titles and numbers be highlighted in relatively large, bolded font. Problematically, visual salience is diluted when multiple objects possess the same basic feature properties, so that nothing is especially salient. The information box is mandated to appear at the beginning of the cardholder agreement. At this time, the individual has already completed their search and is, in all likelihood, more motivated to complete the process (i.e., to search the environment for information that signals the "Continue" button) than to orient to or examine additional credit-card attributes. None of the information in the disclosure is likely on the individual's mind when it appears. Finally, the average individual does not have much experience in navigating a federally mandated information box, has little familiarity with its content, and does not directly associate the information in it with any value or recent selection-history experience. The policy exploits either very few or no attention drivers.

The likelihood that an information source will attract and sustain attention increases if it is visually salient and made more important than other information, and if it is rendered in such a way as to be congruent with the individual's feature search goals and selection history. As far as goals and motivations go, this means that if we want an information source to be attended to, we ought to piggyback the information on the regions or features that the individual is likely to prioritize given their goals and motivations at the time the information is provided. If the individual is preferentially processing information that is near the beginning of a communication (e.g., when the section is too long to read), then the information we most want to be seen should appear there. If the individual is preferentially processing feature information that signals some outcome, then the information we most want to be seen should appear in those features. For example, if readers are racing through the disclosure and are searching for a clickthrough button that is consistent with the website's blue template, we might also consider attracting their attention toward the critical disclosure information with a blue outline. In short, effective disclosure depends critically on under-standing the goals and motivations of the people who should be consuming the information at the time it is disclosed.

Beyond this, it is important to take into account the historical search patterns of the individual. Put simply, this is because it is possible to disrupt the goals and motivations that guide search by piggybacking information that you want seen onto features that the individual has historically perceived as useful or valu-able. In online environments, we believe that many social-media platforms, search engines, and retailers may try to take advan-tage of selection-history effects by applying machine-learning algorithms to user-input data in order to customize information provision. In offline environments, there may be few empirical precedents for the most substantial drivers of attention in any given context in which an information disclosure is mandated. In practice, a sensible solution is to behaviorally test the effective-ness of information disclosures precisely in those circumstances in which they are expected to make a behavioral difference, and to revise the manner in which the information is provided accord-ing to the results.

Taking a wider lens, we can look at research and practice using attention interventions in behavioral economics outside of mandated disclosure. We find that virtually all interventions and experimental manipulations equate attention with visual salience, omitting the influence of goals and motivations and selection history altogether. This is a stunning departure from the literature on visual selective attention from basic research that we have reviewed here. It is especially surprising because, as we have seen, one cannot expect saliency manipulations to have an effect if they are counteracted by control settings (focus) or selection history. Arguably, many interventions aimed at alter-ing attentional priority never had a chance at significant success, and the ones that have worked are unlikely to be explained by differences in visual salience alone. We address this challenge by pointing out that practitioners are faced with an opportunity to optimize disclosures by considering all three forces described here prior to implementation.

NOTES

1 See Day, G.S. (1976). Assessing the effects of information disclosure requirements: Experience with past information disclosures is a useful guide for those trying to understand and respond to new requirements. *Journal of Marketing, 40*(2), 42–52; Cude, B.J. (2005). Insurance disclosures: An effective mechanism to increase consumers' insurance market power? *Journal of Insurance Regulation, 24*(2), 57–80; Ben-Shahar, O., & Schneider, C.E. (2011). The failure of mandated discourse. *University of Pennsylvania Law Review, 159*(3), 647–750; Loewenstein, G., Sunstein, C.R., & Golman, R. (2014). Disclosure: Psychology changes everything. *Annual Review of Economics, 6*(1), 391–419; Ontario Securities Commission. (2019). Improving fee disclosure through behavioral insights (Staff Notice 11-787). Retrieved from https://www.osc.gov.on.ca/documents/en/Securities-Category1/sn_20190819_11-787_improving-fee-disclosure-through-behavioural-insights.pdf; and Australian Securities and Investments Commission and the Dutch Authority for the Financial Markets. (2019). Disclosure: Why it shouldn't be the default (Rep 632). Retrieved from https://asic.gov.au/regulatory-resources/find-a-document/reports/rep-632-disclosure-why-it-shouldn-t-be-the-default/.

2 Braunsberger, K., Lucas, L.A., & Roach, D. (2004). The effectiveness of credit-card regulation for vulnerable consumers. *Journal of Services Marketing, 18*(5), 358–70; and Braunsberger, K., Lucas, L.A., & Roach, D. (2005). Evaluating the efficacy of credit card regulation. *International Journal of Bank Marketing, 23*(3), 237–54.

3 Adams, P.D., Hunt, S., Palmer, C., & Zaliauskas, R. (2019). *Testing the effectiveness of consumer financial disclosure: Experimental evidence from savings accounts* (No. w25718). National Bureau of Economic Research.

4 Buell, R.W., & Choi, M. (2019). Improving customer compatibility with operational transparency. *Harvard Business School Technology & Operations Management Unit working paper* (20-013).

5 Seira, E., Elizondo, A., & Laguna-Müggenburg, E. (2017). Are information disclosures effective? Evidence from the credit card market. *American Economic Journal: Economic Policy, 9*(1), 277–307.

6 For examples, see: Enax, L., Krajbich, I., & Weber, B. (2016). Salient nutrition labels increase the integration of health attributes in food decision-making. *Judgment and Decision Making, 11*(5), 460–71; Borland, R., Wilson, N., Fong, G.T., Hammond, D., Cummings, K.M., Yong, H.H., et al. (2009). Impact of graphic and text warnings on cigarette packs: Findings from four countries over five years. *Tobacco Control, 18*(5), 358–64; Donnelly, G.E., Zatz, L.Y., Svirsky, D., & John, L.K. (2018). The effect of graphic warnings on sugary-drink purchasing. *Psychological Science, 29*(8), 1321–33. We also acknowledge that even if a disclosure is attended, it can have perverse or unintended

downstream effects on consumer choice and preference: see Lunn, P.,
McGowan, F.P., & Howard, N. (2018). *Do some financial product features
negatively affect consumer decisions? A review of evidence.* Research Series No.
78; and Sussenbach, P., Niemier, S., & Glock, S. (2013). Effects of attention to
graphic warning labels on cigarette packages. *Psychology & Health,* 1192–
1206.

7 Shankleman, M., Sykes, C., Mandeville, K.L., DiCosta, S., & Yarrow, K.
(2015). Standardised (plain) cigarette packaging increases attention to
both text-based and graphical health warnings: Experimental evidence.
Public Health, 129, 37–42; Graham, D.J., Orquin, J.L., & Visschers, V.H.M.
(2012). Eye tracking and nutrition label use: A review of the literature
and recommendations for label enhancement. *Food Policy, 36,* 378–82;
Meernik, C., Jarman, K., Towner Wright, S., Klein, E.G., Goldstein, A.O., &
Ranney, L. (2016). Eye tracking outcomes in tobacco control regulation and
communication: A systematic review. *Tobacco Regulatory Science, 2,* 377–403;
and Byrne, S., Kalaji, M., & Niederdeppe, J. (2018). Does visual attention
to graphic warning labels on cigarette packs predict key outcomes among
youth and low-income smokers? *Tobacco Regulatory Science, 4,* 18–37.

8 Munafo, M.R., Roberts, N., Bauld, L., & Leonards, U. (2011). Plain
packaging increases visual attention to health warnings on cigarette packs
in non-smokers and weekly smokers but not daily smokers. *Addiction,
106,* 1505–10; Maynard, O.M., Munafo, M.R., & Leonards, U. (2012). Visual
attention to health warnings on plain tobacco packaging in adolescent
smokers and non-smokers. *Addiction, 108,* 413–19; and Peschel, A.O.,
Orquin, J.L., & Mueller Loose, S. (2019). Increasing consumers' attention
capture and food choice through bottom-up effects. *Appetite, 132,* 1–7.

9 For some general overviews of attention, see Chun, M.M., Golomb, J.D., &
Turk-Browne, N.B. (2011). A taxonomy of external and internal attention.
Annual Review of Psychology, 62, 73–101; Klein, R.M., & Lawrence, M.A.
(2012). On the modes and domains of attention. In M. Posner (Ed.),
Cognitive neuroscience of attention (2nd ed.). New York: Guilford Press,
11–28; and Oberauer, K. (2019). Working memory and attention – A
conceptual analysis and review. *Journal of Cognition, 2(1),* 36.

10 Desimone, R., & Duncan, J. (1995). Neural mechanisms of selective visual
attention. *Annual Review of Neuroscience, 18(1),* 193–222.

11 Most, S.B., Simons, D.J., Scholl, B.J., Jimenez, R., Clifford, E., & Chabris,
C.F. (2001). How not to be seen: The contribution of similarity and selective
ignoring to sustained inattentional blindness. *Psychological Science, 12,*
9–17.

12 Simons, D.J. (2000). Attentional capture and inattentional blindness. *Trends
in Cognitive Sciences, 4(4),* 147–55.

13 Simons, D.J., & Chabris, C.F. (1999). Gorillas in our midst: Sustained
inattentional blindness for dynamic events. *Perception, 28,* 1059–74.

14 See Corbetta, M., & Shulman, G.L. (2002). Control of goal-directed and stimulus-driven attention in the brain. *Nature Reviews Neuroscience, 3*(3), 201–15; Petersen, S.E., & Posner, M.I. (2012). The attention system of the human brain: 20 years after. *Annual Review of Neuroscience, 35,* 73–89; and Vossel, S., Geng, J.J., & Fink, G.R. (2014). Dorsal and ventral attention systems: Distinct neural circuits but collaborative roles. *The Neuroscientist, 20*(2), 150–9.

15 Mulckhuyse, M., & Theeuwes, J. (2010). Unconscious attentional orienting to exogenous cues: A review of the literature. *Acta Psychologica, 134,* 299–309.

16 See, for example, Posner, M.I. (1980). Orienting of attention. *Quarterly Journal of Experimental Psychology, 32*(1), 3–25; Jonides, J. (1981). Voluntary versus automatic control over the mind's eye's movement. *Attention and Performance,* 187–203; Müller, H.J., & Rabbitt, P.M. (1989). Reflexive and voluntary orienting of visual attention: Time course of activation and resistance to interruption. *Journal of Experimental Psychology: Human Perception and Performance, 15*(2), 315–30; Klein, R. (2009). On the control of attention. *Canadian Journal of Experimental Psychology / Revue canadienne de psychologie expérimentale, 63*(3), 240–52; Carrasco, M. (2011). Visual attention: The past 25 years. *Vision Research, 51*(13), 1484–1525; Klein, R.M., & Lawrence, M.A. (2012). On the modes and domains of attention. In M. Posner (Ed.), *Cognitive neuroscience of attention* (2nd ed.). New York: Guilford Press, 11–28; and Carrasco, M., & Barbot, A. (2019). Spatial attention alters visual appearance. *Current Opinion in Psychology, 29*(56–64), 1.

17 Jonides, J., & Yantis, S. (1988). Uniqueness of abrupt visual onset in capturing attention. *Perception & Psychophysics, 43*(4), 346–54; Theeuwes, J., Kramer, A.F., Hahn, S., & Irwin, D.E. (1998). Our eyes do not always go where we want them to go: Capture of the eyes by new objects. *Psychological Science, 9*(5), 379–85; and Hilchey, M.D., & Pratt, J. (2019). Hidden from view: Statistical learning exposes latent attentional capture. *Psychonomic Bulletin & Review, 26*(5), 1633–40.

18 Tomm, B.M., & Zhao, J. (2016). Scarcity captures attention and induces neglect: Eyetracking and behavioral evidence. In A. Papafragou, D. Grodner, D. Mirman, & J.C. Trueswell (Eds.), *Proceedings of the 38th annual conference of the Cognitive Science Society,* 1199–1204. Austin, TX: Cognitive Science Society.

19 See page 19 in Posner, M.I. (1980). Orienting of attention. *Quarterly Journal of Experimental Psychology, 32*(1), 3–25

20 Anderson, B.A. (2018). Controlled information processing, automaticity, and the burden of proof. *Psychonomic Bulletin & Review, 25*(5), 1814–23.

21 See, for example: Fecteau, J.H., & Munoz, D.P. (2006). Salience, relevance, and firing: A priority map for target selection. *Trends in Cognitive Sciences, 10*(8), 382–90; Gottlieb, J. (2007). From thought to action: The parietal cortex

as a bridge between perception, action, and cognition. *Neuron, 53*(1), 9–16; Bisley, J.W., & Goldberg, M.E. (2010). Attention, intention, and priority in the parietal lobe. *Annual Review of Neuroscience, 33*, 1–21; and Bisley, J.W., & Mirpour, K. (2019). The neural instantiation of a priority map. *Current Opinion in Psychology, 29*, 108–12.

22 Here are a few relatively recent examples: Barras, C., & Kerzel, D. (2017). Target-nontarget similarity decreases search efficiency and increases stimulus-driven control in visual search. *Attention, Perception, & Psychophysics, 79*(7), 2037–43; Gaspelin, N., Ruthruff, E., & Lien, M.C. (2016). The problem of latent attentional capture: Easy visual search conceals capture by task-irrelevant abrupt onsets. *Journal of Experimental Psychology: Human Perception and Performance, 42*(8), 1104–20; and Hilchey, M.D., Taylor, J.E.T., & Pratt, J. (2016). Much ado about nothing: Capturing attention toward locations without new perceptual events. *Journal of Experimental Psychology: Human Perception and Performance, 42*(12), 1923–7.

23 A few good examples include: Leber, A.B., & Egeth, H.E. (2006). It's under control: Top-down search strategies can override attentional capture. *Psychonomic Bulletin & Review, 13*(1), 132–8; Müller, H.J., Geyer, T., Zehetleitner, M., & Krummenacher, J. (2009). Attentional capture by salient color singleton distractors is modulated by top-down dimensional set. *Journal of Experimental Psychology: Human Perception and Performance, 35*(1), 1–16; and Gaspelin, N., Leonard, C.J., & Luck, S.J. (2017). Suppression of overt attentional capture by salient-but-irrelevant color singletons. *Attention, Perception, & Psychophysics, 79*(1), 45–62. For some theories, see Geng, J.J., Won, B.Y., & Carlisle, N.B. (2019). Distractor ignoring: Strategies, learning, and passive filtering. *Current Directions in Psychological Science.* DOI:10.117/0963721419867099; Gaspelin, N., & Luck, S.J. (2018). The role of inhibition in avoiding distraction by salient stimuli. *Trends in Cognitive Sciences, 22*(1), 79–92; and Theeuwes, J. (2013). Feature-based attention: It is all bottom-up priming. *Philosophical Transactions of the Royal Society B: Biological Sciences, 368*(1628), 20130055.

24 Chabris, C.F., Weinberger, A., Fontaine, M., & Simons, D.J. (2011). You do not talk about Fight Club if you do not notice Fight Club: Inattentional blindness for a simulated real-world assault. *i-Perception, 2*(2), 150–3.

25 Hunt, A.R., Reuther, J., Hilchey, M.D., & Klein, R.M. (2019). The relationship between spatial attention and eye movements. In T. Hodgson (Ed.), *Current topics in behavioral neurosciences*, vol. 41, 255–78. Berlin, Heidelberg: Springer.

26 Egly, R., Driver, J., & Rafal, R.D. (1994). Shifting visual attention between objects and locations: Evidence from normal and parietal lesion subjects. *Journal of Experimental Psychology: General, 123*(2), 161; and Goldsmith, M., & Yeari, M. (2003). Modulation of object-based attention by spatial

focus under endogenous and exogenous orienting. *Journal of Experimental Psychology: Human Perception and Performance, 29*(5), 897–918.

27 Taylor, J.E.T., Chan, D., Bennett, P.J., & Pratt, J. (2015). Attentional cartography: Mapping the distribution of attention across time and space. *Attention, Perception, & Psychophysics, 77*(7), 2240–6; and Taylor, J.E.T., Rajsic, J., & Pratt, J. (2016). Object-based selection is contingent on attentional control settings. *Attention, Perception, & Psychophysics, 78*(4), 988–95.

28 Yeshurun, Y. (2018). The spatial distribution of attention. *Current Opinion in Psychology, 29,* 76–81.

29 Belopolsky, A.V., & Theeuwes, J. (2010). No capture outside the attentional window. *Vision research, 50*(23), 2543–50.

30 Bichot, N.P., Rossi, A.F., & Desimone, R. (2005). Parallel and serial neural mechanisms for visual search in macaque area V4. *Science, 308*(5721), 529–34; and McAdams, C.J., & Maunsell, J.H. (2000). Attention to both space and feature modulates neuronal responses in macaque area V4. *Journal of Neurophysiology, 83*(3), 1751–5.

31 Folk, C.L., Remington, R.W., & Johnston, J.C. (1992). Involuntary covert orienting is contingent on attentional control settings. *Journal of Experimental Psychology: Human Perception and Performance, 18*(4), 1030–44; Irons, J.L., Folk, C.L., & Remington, R.W. (2012). All set! Evidence of simultaneous attentional control settings for multiple target colors. *Journal of Experimental Psychology: Human Perception and Performance, 38*(3), 758–75; and Belopolsky, A.V., Schreij, D., & Theeuwes, J. (2010). What is top-down about contingent capture? *Attention, Perception, & Psychophysics, 72*(2), 326–41.

32 Büsel, C., Voracek, M., & Ansorge, U. (2018). A meta-analysis of contingent-capture effects. *Psychological Research,* 1–26.

33 For some perspectives and demonstrations, see Oberauer, K. (2019). Working memory and attention – A conceptual analysis and review. *Journal of Cognition, 2*(1), 36; Olivers, C.N., Peters, J., Houtkamp, R., & Roelfsema, P.R. (2011). Different states in visual working memory: When it guides attention and when it does not. *Trends in Cognitive Sciences, 15*(7), 327–34; and Soto, D., Hodsoll, J., Rotshtein, P., & Humphreys, G.W. (2008). Automatic guidance of attention from working memory. *Trends in Cognitive Sciences, 12*(9), 342–8.

34 Theeuwes, J. (2018). Visual selection: Usually fast and automatic; seldom slow and volitional. *Journal of Cognition, 1*(1), Article 29, 1–15.

35 Here are some examples: Lamy, D., Antebi, C., Aviani, N., & Carmel, T. (2008). Priming of pop-out provides reliable measures of target activation and distractor inhibition in selective attention. *Vision Research, 48*(1), 30–41; Rangelov, D., Müller, H.J., & Zehetleitner, M. (2013). Visual search for feature singletons: Multiple mechanisms produce sequence effects in visual search. *Journal of Vision, 13*(3), 1–16; Hilchey, M.D., Antinucci, V.,

Lamy, D., & Pratt, J. (2019). Is attention really biased toward the last target location in visual search? Attention, response rules, distractors, and eye movements. *Psychonomic Bulletin & Review, 26*(2), 506–14; Kristjánsson, Á., Saevarsson, S., & Driver, J. (2013). The boundary conditions of priming of visual search: From passive viewing through task-relevant working memory load. *Psychonomic Bulletin & Review, 20*(3), 514–21; and Goolsby, B.A., & Suzuki, S. (2001). Understanding priming of color-singleton search: Roles of attention at encoding and "retrieval." *Perception & Psychophysics, 63*(6), 929–44.

36 McPeek, R.M., Maljkovic, V., & Nakayama, K. (1999). Saccades require focal attention and are facilitated by a short-term memory system. *Vision Research, 39*(8), 1555–66; Van der Stigchel, S., & Meeter, M. (2017). Negative versus positive priming: When are distractors inhibited? *Journal of Eye Movement Research, 10*(2), 6–13; and Hilchey, M.D., Antinucci, V., Lamy, D., & Pratt, J. (2019). Is attention really biased toward the last target location in visual search? Attention, response rules, distractors, and eye movements. *Psychonomic Bulletin & Review, 26*(2), 506–14.

37 Kruijne, W., & Meeter, M. (2017). You prime what you code: The fAIM model of priming of pop-out. *PloS One, 12*(11), e0187556.

38 For some examples and reviews, see: Shaw, M.L., & Shaw, P. (1977). Optimal allocation of cognitive resources to spatial locations. *Journal of Experimental Psychology: Human Perception and Performance, 3*(2), 201–11; Geng, J.J., & Behrmann, M. (2002). Probability cuing of target location facilitates visual search impicitly in normal participants and patients with hemispatial neglect. *Psychological Science, 13*(6), 520–5; Jiang, Y.V., Koutstaal, W., & Twedell, E.L. (2016). Habitual attention in older and young adults. *Psychology and Aging, 31*(8), 970–80; Leber, A.B., Gwinn, R.E., Hong, Y., & O'Toole, R.J. (2016). Implicitly learned suppression of irrelevant spatial locations. *Psychonomic Bulletin & Review, 23*(6), 1873–81; Wang, B., & Theeuwes, J. (2018). Statistical regularities modulate attentional capture. *Journal of Experimental Psychology: Human Perception and Performance, 44*(1), 13–17; and Ferrante, O., Patacca, A., Di Caro, V., Della Libera, C., Santandrea, E., & Chelazzi, L. (2018). Altering spatial priority maps via statistical learning of target selection and distractor filtering. *Cortex, 102*, 67–95.

39 Chun, M.M., & Jiang, Y. (1998). Contextual cueing: Implicit learning and memory of visual context guides spatial attention. *Cognitive Psychology, 36*(1), 28–71; and Jiang, Y., & Leung, A.W. (2005). Implicit learning of ignored visual context. *Psychonomic Bulletin & Review, 12*(1), 100–6.

40 Jiang, Y., & Song, J.H. (2005). Hyperspecificity in visual implicit learning: Learning of spatial layout is contingent on item identity. *Journal of Experimental Psychology: Human Perception and Performance, 31*(6), 1439–48.

41 Chun, M.M., & Jiang, Y. (2003). Implicit, long-term spatial contextual memory. *Journal of Experimental Psychology: Learning, Memory, and Cognition, 29*(2), 224–34; and Jiang, Y.V. (2018). Habitual versus goal-driven attention. *Cortex, 102,* 107–20.

42 Võ, M.H., & Wolfe, J.M. (2015). The role of memory for visual search in scenes. *Annals of the New York Academy of Sciences, 1339*(1), 72–81.

43 For some helpful reviews, see Failing, M., & Theeuwes, J. (2018). Selection history: How reward modulates selectivity of visual attention. *Psychonomic Bulletin & Review, 25*(2), 514–38; Anderson, B.A. (2017). Reward processing in the value-driven attention network: Reward signals tracking cue identity and location. *Social Cognitive and Affective Neuroscience, 12*(3), 461–7; and Bourgeois, A., Chelazzi, L., & Vuilleumier, P. (2016). How motivation and reward learning modulate selective attention. *Progress in Brain Research, 229,* 325–42.

44 Anderson, B.A., Laurent, P.A., & Yantis, S. (2011). Value-driven attentional capture. *Proceedings of the National Academy of Sciences of the United States of America, 105*(25), 10367–71.

45 Wang, L., Yu, H., & Zhou, X. (2013). Interaction between value and perceptual salience in value-driven attentional capture. *Journal of Vision, 13,* 1–13; Wentura, D., Muller, P., & Rothermund, K. (2014). Attentional capture by evaluative stimuli: Gain- and loss-connoting colors boost the additional singleton effect. *Psychonomic Bulletin & Review, 21,* 701–7; and Muller, S., Rothermund, K., & Wentura, D. (2016). Relevance drives attention: Attentional bias for gain- and loss-related stimuli is driven by delayed disengagement. *The Quarterly Journal of Experimental Psychology, 69,* 752–63.

46 Anderson, B.A. (2015). Value-driven attentional priority is context specific. *Psychonomic Bulletin & Review, 22*(3), 750–6.

47 Hickey, C., & van Zoest, W. (2012). Reward creates oculomotor salience. *Current Biology, 22*(7), R219–20; and Hickey, C., & van Zoest, W. (2013). Reward-associated stimuli capture the eyes in spite of strategic attentional set. *Vision Research, 92,* 67–74.

48 Munneke, J., Belopolsky, A.V., & Theeuwes, J. (2016). Distractors associated with reward break through the focus of attention. *Attention, Perception & Psychophysics, 78*(7), 2213–25.

PART THREE

Examples of Behavioral Initiatives from Business and Policy

CHAPTER NINE

Workplace Habits and How to Change Them

Kyle Murray and Shirley Chen

For years, there has been an ongoing, seemingly unsolvable problem in many organizations. Journalists dubbed it a crisis. It even became the focus of a book on leadership for rising-star managers.[1] We are referring, of course, to the theft of workplace cutlery.

Although a pernicious problem – one study estimated that to keep just 70 teaspoons in communal eating areas required the purchase of 250 spoons each year[2] – the London Borough of Hounslow found a solution. It did take a few tries, however, and required the application of behavioral science. At issue was the fact that the borough's onsite cafe served 2,000 staff who regularly brought their lunches back to their desks and then failed to return the spoons, forks, and knives.[3]

The first attempt to address the problem was a simple educational campaign. Under the clever caption of "We Don't Want to Fork Out More!," signs were posted letting borough staff know that the "Parkside Cafe has reported that much of its metal cutlery has disappeared. If you have any cutlery in your desk, please return them as their supplies are running low." Nobody returned any cutlery, and some suspected that the problem got worse. The cafe then instituted a "Cutlery Amnesty" and offered customers the opportunity to make anonymous returns. They even promised to donate to charity for every dozen pieces they got back. This resulted in a grand total of twelve returns!

Feeling frustrated, the cafe decided to do some research. They found that the employees had simply developed a habit of putting cutlery in their desks after finishing their lunches. Walking the cutlery back to the cafe would take two to three minutes, a price that was apparently too high to pay. It was a small friction (or sludge, in the language of chapter 5) that was at fault, not any criminal intent.

The borough devised a solution. They simply made it more convenient to return the cutlery by placing a bin – that was easy to put cutlery into, but hard to remove it from – closer to borough staff. In the first month, they received 100 pieces of cutlery back, and that grew in the second month to a return of 180 pieces. The bins were 1400 percent more effective than the amnesty campaign and infinitely better than the educational campaign. The crisis was averted.

This is just one, somewhat tongue-in-cheek, example of how seemingly simple individual habits can be difficult to change. In practice, productive workers have many routines that improve efficiency and allow mundane tasks to be completed without much thought. Saving two to three minutes, as in the cutlery example, can be more than enough to lock people into a pattern of behavior. In fact, research has shown that saving even a few seconds can be a powerful driver of human decision making.[4] From coffee breaks to complex tasks, experienced workers rely on habits to increase efficiency and productivity. Most of the time this is a good thing, but too often these habits become ruts that make organizational change challenging and inhibit innovation.

This chapter is about better understanding habitual behavior and how to change it. In the next section, we will briefly review the behavioral science of associative learning and the process that creates (often unproductive) routines. We will discuss why change is often challenging and how habits can inhibit innovation. Then, our focus will turn to how change happens. We propose three paths to positive habitual-behavior changes. We will wrap up with our thoughts on the potential of emerging technologies to help us break bad habits and build healthy ones.

THE BEHAVIORAL SCIENCE OF HABITS AND CHANGE

A habit is *an association between a cue and a response that is created through repetition* and, in many cases, in the presence of a reward.[5] For example, an employee of the Super Productivity Corporation might learn that when their computer is not working as expected, they should call the IT department for help. The cue is a malfunctioning machine, the response is a phone call, and the reward is a computer fix that allows the employee to get back to being super productive.

The first time an employee's computer broke down, it probably wasn't that simple. Not having dealt with the situation before, the employee would have gone through a number of steps that required conscious attention to solve the problem. They had to recognize that the computer was not working as expected, decide it was not something they could manage alone, figure out who could assist them and how to ask for help, then pick up the phone and make the call. After this had happened a few times, much of the process would have become routinized. Eventually, a computer problem would automatically trigger dialling a memorized number. This habit would improve the efficiency of the process and minimize the employee's downtime.

Such habits can also become significant barriers to organizational change. For example, imagine that the IT department at Super Productivity Corporation learns of an automated process for IT help based on an electronic helpdesk. This technology works through an app on the employee's computer or mobile device. It is demonstrably faster than the inevitable hold queue of the old phone-in process. It also allows the IT department to better manage requests for assistance, and it provides a great deal of data that can contribute to ongoing improvements. IT is very excited about this new technology, and they deploy it throughout the organization. Given the clear superiority of the new process, IT does not anticipate any problems with adoption, but just to be safe, they inform everyone at Super Productivity Corporation through a series of e-mails in the weeks leading up to the change. They even go out of their way to host luncheons and workshops to demonstrate how the new process will benefit everyone. Feeling confident that the Super Productivity Corporation is prepared for this simple shift in a relatively minor corporate process, they launch the new app and disconnect the old helpdesk phone number.

We have all seen similar approaches to change in the organizations where we work. On one level it makes sense. The new approach is better. The fact that it is better has been clearly communicated throughout the organization. So why would anyone use the old process?

The underlying, but erroneous, assumption here is that people spend their workday making a series of conscious and reasonable (even if not perfectly rational) choices. As discussed in chapters 1 and 7, a great deal of evidence suggests that classical notions of rationality do not adequately characterize real-world human behavior. Most likely, when the employee runs into a computer problem, they are going to habitually pick up the phone and call the same number they have repeatedly dialled in the past to get IT help. When that habit does not produce the desired result, the employee is likely to feel stressed and frustrated. At an aggregate level across the organization, when many employees experience the same broken habit, there is a negative reaction to the change, a general loss in productivity, and damage to employee morale – none of which seems like a rational reaction to the introduction of a superior workflow process. Organizations facing such a situation tend to find themselves spending substantial resources to re-create the old process temporarily while they attempt to reintroduce a very simple, but now widely unpopular, change.

In this way, routines inhibit organizational innovation. This IT scenario is a relatively simple example that illustrates what can be a much larger problem. Research indicates that 55 percent of our workday behaviors are habitual.[6] In other words, the majority of what we do at work every day is respond automatically to cues in ways that have previously resulted in some kind of reward or positive feedback. This feedback cycle of cue→ response→ reward is at the core of habitual behavior. Ultimately, the habit can become so ingrained that positive feedback is unnecessary and the cue produces the response, even if that behavior is unrewarded.

In the past, employees called IT and their computers worked again. Then they called IT and no one answered. Chances are they hung up and tried again later. This might have happened multiple times before the employee broke the habitual response and tried to figure out why it wasn't working. This is responding to a cue, even without the desired reward. When the employee does finally learn about the app and is told that it is a superior process for IT help, it doesn't feel superior because they have to spend time and energy learning to do something that used to be effortless. As a result, otherwise rational and reasonable people can become outraged at a relatively simple process change. A similar pattern plays out with changes big and small – ranging from when an old coffee maker is replaced with a novel machine to when a retail store is redesigned with an unusual layout, to when a business revises its order-fulfilment process. In many cases, the new machine, store layout, or process is objectively superior to what came before it. But these changes may not be subjectively superior for those employees who have developed habitual behaviors that made the old machine, layout, or process feel easy.

Another example of this phenomenon comes from the early days of online shopping. Initially, pundits believed that e-commerce would be a race to rock-bottom prices and the death of brand value because consumers could shop the competition with a single click of the mouse. How could any business create loyalty online when search costs were close to zero? Yet, as it turns out, most people do very little price comparison online and instead return to familiar retailers to make their purchases repeatedly. Amazon is not the low-price leader for many of the products it sells, yet it has a nearly 40 percent market share of e-commerce sales in the United States.[7] Research has demonstrated that a great deal of this loyalty can be explained by the development of habitual shopping behavior.[8] If you want to buy a book, you go to Amazon, search for that book, and buy it. The desire to make that purchase cues a specific set of behaviors that feel easy and lead to the desired outcome. For the habitual shopper, going to a new website, finding the right book, and going through an unfamiliar check-out process is not worth the extra effort. In fact, this effect is so powerful that there is even a formal name for it – *cognitive lock-in*.[9]

HOW HABIT CHANGE HAPPENS

Information and Education

Habits are automatic behaviors that do not require conscious control, and that therefore make life easier and our actions more efficient. After lunch, employees take cutlery back to their desks without really thinking about it. If a computer isn't working properly, we call IT. When a new employee joins the organization, we follow our onboarding process.

What if we didn't have these habitual organizational behaviors? What if every workday behavior required making decisions from scratch? This would involve searching for information on possible responses, deciding which response to engage in, and going through the effort of executing that unpracticed behavior. Our habitual routines save us from this drudgery by focusing on well-learned cues, minimizing the search for new information, ignoring possible alternative behaviors, and biasing us toward what we have done in the past.[10] In other words, what makes habitual responses easy and efficient also makes such behavior resistant to new information. As a result, and as we saw in the case of the stolen cutlery, information and education tend to be inadequate as behavioral-change interventions. Simply telling someone to stop stealing cutlery or use a new IT app is unlikely to work. Even if you can get people to pay attention to the message (which won't be easy), having to learn to do something new (and probably more difficult, at least initially) isn't very appealing to a habitual responder.

Behavioral Insights for Organizational Change

Although this chapter focuses on habit change, it is worth pointing out that many of our habits are positive. As we have discussed, 55 percent of our work tasks are completed habitually because doing so makes life easier and work more efficient. When we get a cue, we know what to do. We tend to follow the same route to work every day. When an order comes in, we follow a familiar script to fulfil it. When we have data to analyse, we turn to familiar software and

Table 9.1 Three Paths to Habit Change

Make it easy

Habits make deciding and acting easier. When alternative behaviors are easy to adopt, the value of a habitual response is reduced, and a door opens to behavior change.

Make it personal

Connecting behavior to an individual in a relevant and meaningful way – for example, through normative feedback – creates a personalized incentive to break existing habits and replace them with behaviors that lead to improved performance.

Make it (about) money

Ultimately, habits save us time and make our behavior more efficient, an outcome that is valuable in a time-starved world. When we want someone to change their habits, compensating them for the value lost with incentives to engage in alternative behaviors can be a powerful path to change. Disincentives, such as taxes or financial penalties applied to bad habits, can also be effective.

---

statistical models. Without these habits, work would be difficult and we would get a lot less done every day. Consequently, people resist habit change.

Fortunately, for organizations hoping to avoid habits that inhibit innovation, insights from behavioral science provide a roadmap for facilitating change. Work on habit change goes back to the early days of psychological research and has produced a large academic literature about how humans (and other animals) learn to associate a cue with a response that generates a reward. In this chapter, we focus on three well-established paths to positive habit change: making it easy, making it personal, and making it about money (table 9.1).

Make It Easy

To overcome this resistance, organizations should make the adoption of alternative behaviors as easy as possible. We already saw how this can work in the cutlery example. People didn't really want to steal cutlery, but they also didn't want to walk back to the cafe to return it. Convenient bins made returns easy, and employees began to put back the spoons, knives, and forks.

In another example, Google found that small changes in presentation can make a big difference in the company's efforts to encourage healthy eating. Specifically, Google made it less convenient for employees to habitually grab a sugary soda or snack of M&Ms. This was done by placing these unhealthy options out of sight and behind opaque glass. At the same time, Google made it easier for employees to find water, fruit, and nuts by putting these at eye level and behind clear glass. Over a seven-week test period, employees in Google's New York office consumed 3.1 million fewer calories from M&Ms![11] The company also saw a 47 percent increase in the amount of water consumed and a 7 percent decrease in calories consumed from sugary beverages.[12] Google didn't take choice away from people – they could still eat M&Ms and drink Coca-Cola if they wanted to – but the company made it easier for employees to find healthier choices, and that had a substantial effect on eating habits.

A similar approach was used by Walt Disney World in an attempt to improve food choices among children who visited the park. Instead of offering traditional combos with soda and fries as the side dishes, they made juice, fruits, and vegetables the default option. Research in behavioral economics has consistently found that default options nudge people, in a powerful way, toward one choice while still allowing them to opt in to an alternative behavior if they so desire. At Disney World, the result was a substantial reduction in calories (21.4 percent), fat (43.9 percent), and sodium (43.4 percent) consumed by kids at the park.[13] For many families, Disney's defaults made it easy to change eating habits and make healthier choices.

Beyond the domain of food, "making it easy" has been successful in helping people improve their personal finances. For example, Thaler and Benartzi (2004)[14] devised a creative way to make saving easier with what they called the "Save More Tomorrow" program (SMarT). The basic idea behind SMarT was to get people to commit to save more by allocating a portion of future salary increases toward retirement savings. They found that 78 percent of eligible employees joined the plan, and 80 percent of those remained in the plan through four pay raises. Over three and a half years, the average savings rates increased from 3.5 percent to 13.6 percent. The basic premise of the SMarT plan was that it might be difficult to save more today, but it is relatively easy to save more in the future. Rather than just breaking the old habit (saving little), this approach helped create new habits by setting up a cue (pay raise) that triggered a response (save more) and rewarded people with enhanced savings.

Make It Personal

It is not always possible to just "make it easy" to change habits within an organization. Work habits can be complex. In many cases, we would like to change behavior in a direction that is as difficult, or possibly even more difficult, to enact than current processes. For example, as an organization grows, it often becomes necessary to introduce more formal processes for a variety of common work tasks. This can range from expense reimbursement to hiring practices to dealing with customer or employee complaints. If a salesperson has a habit of simply handing in receipts for whatever they deemed a reasonable expense while the new process requires the use of an online portal (along with a new set of allowable spending rules), then "making it easy" might be difficult. Sometimes innovation at the organizational level requires employees to adopt new behaviors that, at least initially, are more challenging.

In such cases, making it personal helps. By this, we mean connecting the new behavior to the individual in relevant and meaningful ways. One way to accomplish this is to provide feedback that links the task to the individual. Research has shown that normative feedback, which compares an individual's task performance to the performance of others, is especially effective in this regard. For example, research looking at video gameplay has found that providing normative feedback about scores and performance relative to other players can break the cognitive lock-in that comes from habitual patterns of play and encourages willingness to switch styles and approaches.[15] This works because it gets people to focus on themselves and their self-efficacy rather than on the ease with which they can habitually play the game. In this way, normative feedback can motivate people to be more innovative in an attempt to improve their performance relative to their peers.

Another example comes from studies of new-employee onboarding. For most organizations, the goal of onboarding is to introduce a company's culture and outline the requirements of the job.

Employers would like to see new hires fit into the company as easily as possible. Old habits from prior work experience can interfere with this process. As discussed above, an educational approach – telling people what they need to do and how to do it – is unlikely to displace habits developed over years of doing similar work. In one study,[16] looking at Wipro BPO, an India-based company built on outsourced business processes, researchers found that onboarding was more successful when the focus was put on the new employee rather than the company. For example, in a controlled experiment, one set of new employees were asked to talk about themselves and their decision making rather than hear about the company and its culture. They were given a badge and a shirt with their names on them. In the other condition, employees were taught about the company and given a badge and shirt adorned with the company's name. The onboarding that "made it personal" enhanced adaptation to new work routines and resulted in 33 percent greater employee retention over the first six months – when old habits are being broken and new habits and processes are being learned. In general, this line of research has demonstrated that a more personal approach to onboarding improves job satisfaction, employee engagement, and task performance, as well as employee retention. Making it personal focuses people on thinking about how they can do better and nudges them away from simply responding habitually.

Make It about Money

When it isn't feasible to make alternative behaviors easy or to make task performance more personal, behavior can be modified with financial incentives – that is, people can be paid to change their habits, or a disincentive can be introduced to penalize those who continue the unwanted behavior. Speeding tickets and "swear jars" are examples of disincentives meant to discourage behaviors that are habitual for many people.

This straightforward approach to behavior change has been effective even when the habit is driven by a strong physiological desire, as in the case of smoking cigarettes. Today, it is well known that cigarette smoking is a leading cause of premature death, with hundreds of thousands of people in the United States dying each year from smoking-related diseases.[17] While this is a habit that 70 percent of smokers would like to break, only about 3 percent of smokers quit successfully because nicotine is highly addictive.[18] Yet, a tax on cigarettes has been an effective disincentive. Research looking at US cigarette sales in the fifty states from 1955 to 1988 found that when taxes were increased, cigarette consumption declined significantly, leading the authors to conclude that this disincentive was an effective public-health intervention.[19]

Although smoking is an extreme example, incentives can be used to address more mundane workplace behaviors. This is true in part because it is relatively easy to provide bonuses or cash incentives for habit changes that allow employees to hit key performance indicators. If you want salespeople who have habitually sold product X to move more of product Y, then pay more for selling product Y. If the goal is a safer workplace, then provide bonuses to units that work accident-free. Financial incentives compensate the individual for the extra effort they have to put into learning a different response to a familiar cue. The downside of this approach is that it directly increases the cost of doing business. In many cases, it might be preferable to focus on the ease of alternative behaviors or on making it personally relevant to employees. Nevertheless, financial incentives can be an effective habit-modification tool as they offset the employee's "cost" in time and effort of learning a new way of doing things, and they can, like normative feedback, draw attention to performance over efficiency.

THE FUTURE OF HABIT CHANGE

In concluding this chapter, we turn our attention to how technology can be helpful when a little nudge is needed to encourage good habits and combat rotten ones in organizations. In particular, recent increases in computational power combined with the availability of intelligent analytic tools can help identify habits that inhibit innovation, thereby improving corporate efficiency and employee well-being.

Consider, for example, that the average employee spends about 37 percent of their time at work in meetings.[20] This has become a well-established routine. The cue in the case of meetings can range from new information (e.g., government regulations affecting business) to the time of day (e.g., team meets every Monday morning) to the problem of stolen cutlery. The response to these cues is to habitually schedule a meeting. Microsoft partnered up with an analytics firm to study the value of this behavior. Their research analysed data from a variety of digital sources, including calendars and e-mails, and found that meetings – especially large group meetings – were driving down employee satisfaction. Specifically, employees who were unhappy at work and those who left the organization tended to have more meetings with larger groups. These employees were less efficient and had less time for innovation. They were also more likely to work overtime and on weekends. By taking an analytical approach to this large dataset of workday behaviors, Microsoft was able to modify the ingrained organizational meeting habit, improving both employee satisfaction and retention.

Driving is another classic example of habitual behavior. Initially, driving is an overwhelming and frightening experience, but in time we learn how to respond automatically to particular cues to stay safe and get where we want to go. However, those driving habits can also lead to complacency and errors when the ingrained response to an environmental cue is not the correct response. Research conducted by the US Department of Transportation[21] attributed 87 percent of 78,000 fatal crashes to human error. In an attempt to improve driving habits in the trucking industry, the United States and Canada have introduced an electronic logging device (ELD) mandate. ELDs capture driving data that can help predict when ingrained behaviors put drivers at risk.[22] These data can be used to identify potentially dangerous situations and intervene to prevent accidents before they happen. For example, Schneider National, Inc., uses data on speed, acceleration and deceleration, and driving times to form a predictive model of safety.[23] Supervisors are then alerted when the algorithm perceives that the behavior of certain drivers is putting them at risk. This allows the organization to intervene and correct poor habits before an accident occurs.

We are just at the very beginning of being able to leverage data and analytics to identify problematic habits and opportunities to introduce behavioral change. Simple examples at a personal level include wearable devices that encourage users to take a certain number of steps every day or remind employees to get up and move around once in a while. These small interventions provide personalized feedback that directly addresses the habitually sedentary nature of many modern work environments. The rise of new technologies that are immersive and shape our environments have the potential to further affect habit change.

SUMMARY AND CONCLUSION

Ultimately, habits are at the core of efficient and productive human behavior. Without well-established routines, we would struggle to get through our daily lives. Yet, as work evolves, many of the habits that made us efficient are at risk of becoming ruts that slow change and inhibit innovation. In this chapter, we have highlighted three paths to habit change: make it easy, make it personal, and make it (about) money. Whether we want to avert the crisis of stolen cutlery, improve new product sales, make meetings more efficient, or reduce traffic fatalities, we can all benefit from a better understanding of the behavioral science behind habits and how to change them.

NOTES

1 Hoyle, C. (2017, 15 April). Who stole all the forks? The science of missing office cutlery. Retrieved from https://www.stuff.co.nz/business /91303980/who-stole-all-the-forks-the-science-of-missing-office-cutlery.

2 Admittedly, this example is a bit tongue-in-cheek. Although stolen cutlery has a cost, it isn't a life-or-death problem for most organizations. It is, however, an interesting case study in how dysfunctional habitual behavior develops within an organization and how those habits can be changed.

3 Norfield, C. (2014, 7 August). A simple nudge to stop staff stealing cutlery. Retrieved from https://chrisnorfield.wordpress.com/2014/08/07/a -simple-nudge-to-stop-staff-stealing-cutlery/.This cutlery case study is

described in detail on Chris Norfield's blog: https://chrisnorfield
.wordpress.com/2014/08/07/a-simple-nudge-to-stop-staff-stealing
-cutlery/. (Chris is a public health manager at the London Borough of
Hounslow, specializing in behavior change).

4 Murray, K.B., & Häubl, G. (2007). Explaining cognitive lock-in: The role of
skill-based habits of use in consumer choice. *Journal of Consumer Research*,
34(1), 77–88.

5 Wood, W. (2019). *Good habits, bad habits: The science of making positive changes
that stick*. New York: Farrar, Straus and Giroux.

6 Ibid.

7 Lipsman, A. (2019, 27 June). US commerce 2019. Mobile and social
commerce fuel ongoing commerce channel shift. Retrieved from https://
content-na1.emarketer.com/us-ecommerce-2019.

8 Murray, K.B., & Häubl, G. (2007). Explaining cognitive lock-in: The role of
skill-based habits of use in consumer choice. *Journal of Consumer Research*,
34(1), 77–88.

9 Johnson, E.J., Bellman, S., & Lohse, G.L. (2003). Cognitive lock-in and the
power law of practice. *Journal of Marketing*, *67*(2), 62–75.

10 Verplanken, B., & Wood, W. (2006). Interventions to break and create
consumer habits. *Journal of Public Policy & Marketing*, *25*(1), 90–103.

11 Kang, C. (2013, 1 September). Google crunches data on munching in office.
Retrieved from https://www.washingtonpost.com/business/technology
/google-crunches-data-on-munching-in-office/2013/09/01/3902b444
-0e83-11e3-85b6-d27422650fd5_story.html.

12 Ibid.

13 Peters, J., Beck, J., Lande, J., Pan, Z., Cardel, M., Ayoob, K., & Hill, J.O.
(2016). Using healthy defaults in Walt Disney World restaurants to
improve nutritional choices. *Journal of the Association for Consumer Research*,
1(1), 92–103.

14 Thaler, R.H., & Benartzi, S. (2004). Save more tomorrow™: Using
behavioral economics to increase employee saving. *Journal of Political
Economy*, *112*(S1), S164–S187.

15 Bellman, S., & Murray, K.B. (2018). Feedback, task performance, and
interface preferences. *European Journal of Information Systems*, *27*(6), 654–69.

16 Cable, D., Gino, F., & Staats, B. (2015). The powerful way onboarding can
encourage authenticity. *Harvard Business Review Digital Articles*, 2–5.

17 Benowitz, N.L. (2010). Nicotine addiction. *New England Journal of Medicine*,
362(24), 2295–2303.

18 Ibid.

19 Peterson, D.E., Zeger, S.L., Remington, P.L., & Anderson, H.A. (1992).
The effect of state cigarette tax increases on cigarette sales, 1955 to 1988.
American Journal of Public Health, *82*(1), 94–6.

20 INFOCOM. (nd). Meetings in America. A study of trends, costs, and attitudes toward business travel and teleconferencing, and their impact on productivity. Retrieved from https://e-meetings.verizonbusiness.com /global/en/meetingsinamerica/uswhitepaper.php#INTRODUCTION.

21 Federal Motor Carrier Safety Administration Office of Research and Analysis. (2007, July). The large truck crash causation study – analysis brief. Retrieved from https://www.fmcsa.dot.gov/safety/research-and -analysis/large-truck-crash-causation-study-analysis-brief.

22 Federal Motor Carrier Safety Administration Office of Research and Analysis. (2018, 20 December). Electronic logging devices. Retrieved from https://www.fmcsa.dot.gov/hours-service/elds/electronic-logging -devices.

23 Mitchell, R.L. (2008, 22 May). IT hits the highway: Big rigs go high tech. *Network World*. Retrieved from https://www.networkworld.com /article/2279855/it-hits-the-highway–big-rigs-go-high-tech.html.

CHAPTER TEN

Humanizing Financial Services with Behavioral Science

Jane Howe, Alex Henderson, Jennifer Nachshen, and Sarah Reid

The past two decades have seen a resurgence of interest in applied behavioral science. With the introduction and subsequent popularization of concepts like nudging and choice architecture in the 2000s,[1] policymakers across the globe have begun applying techniques from the social sciences to design programs and policies that go with the grain of human psychology. Perhaps as a result of Thaler and Sunstein's focus on public policy, the conversation around nudging has tended to focus on public-sector applications of behavioral science. With the exception of the technology sector, where the same concepts have become foundational elements of user-experience design and human-computer interaction,[2] business has been slow to harness the potential of these techniques. As consultants and practitioners in this field, we are excited by the untapped potential of using behavioral science to improve the services, products, and experiences private-sector organizations offer their customers. In this chapter, we will share real-world examples of how these techniques have been applied in financial services, and provide some thoughts on how to think about commercial applications of behavioral science more broadly.

We would like to start by addressing the ethics of applying nudge techniques in a for-profit context. Recent scandals related to the use of behavioral techniques to influence public opinion (e.g., Cambridge Analytica) have prompted long-overdue conversations about the responsibility that comes with applying the insights of behavioral science to influence citizens, customers, and other groups. As practitioners in the field of behavioral insights and design, we take these cases seriously and believe they illustrate the importance of grounding applied behavioral science in an ethical framework that puts the interests of the user/customer/citizen at the center of the work (see also chapter 11 for a discussion of ethics in policy). While the misuse of behavioral science should serve as a cautionary tale, it should not overshadow the conversation or discourage practitioners from applying these techniques in a business context. As we will show, behavioral science is one of the most powerful tools organizations have to make their products and services more customer-centric and to positively impact the lives of the people they serve.

In this chapter we divide our discussion into two sections, each highlighting a different facet of applying behavioral techniques in the private sector. The first section focuses on understanding customers better by applying a behaviorally informed lens to the design of products and services. Our approach integrates behavioral science with human-centered design, a practitioner-rooted discipline that uses deep empathy derived through qualitative inquiry to create solutions that respond to the unmet needs of the user. This combined approach allows for a more expansive and contextualized understanding of customers and the choice environments in which they operate.[3] This integrated approach brings behavioral science into the conversation earlier in the design process (see, in particular, the discussion on the behavioral scientist as a designer in chapter 2). For example, one of the cases we feature shows how a behavioral approach to customer segmentation disrupted orthodoxies at a major Canadian bank about the type of customer who used their direct-investing platform. Our research uncovered fundamental differences in how certain types of customers thought about investing that led them to engage with the platform in very different ways. This lens revealed patterns of behavior that classic demographic approaches were unable to uncover and enabled our client to meaningfully pivot the design and marketing of their product in ways that were more useful to their users. While these insights would not have been unearthed in the absence of behavioral science, it is equally true that they would not have been unearthed if we had applied behavioral insights only to problems that were solvable with randomized controlled trials. The heart of this first section is about how to apply behavioral science to cases where understanding your customer's decision-making process is vital, but where the exact outcome may be unclear or even unknown.

Our second section shifts from understanding to action, highlighting two case studies where we worked with clients to develop customer-centric nudges to actively influence the way customers experienced products and services. The first case takes a design-led, behaviorally informed approach to imagining and bringing a new insurance-quoting tool to market. The second illustrates how a behavioral approach to customer-centricity equipped one Canadian bank with the tools it needed to improve one of the most difficult client interactions they face – denying someone a loan. Collectively, these cases illustrate how behavioral science can be a driver of both better (and less risky) products and better customer experiences. The theme that runs through each of them is a focus on developing a deep appreciation of the context in which customers make their decisions and using behavioral science as a tool for making products, services, and interactions more responsive to the real needs of the people whom organizations serve.

PART 1: UNDERSTANDING YOUR CUSTOMER

Organizations often seek to evolve their products or services to meet changing customer needs. Traditionally, organizations have used surveys or experimental research to measure customer responses to product concepts. While this may work well for products that already exist in the market, it is not especially helpful when a business has a customer-focused challenge that is ambiguous, future-focused, or requires generative thinking, such as adapting customer behavior in response to the COVID-19 crisis. Incorporating the rigorous experimental methods of behavioral science into the empathy-based, qualitative, human-centred design process enables us to engage in evidence-based innovation by layering deep insights with scientific evidence. It is this process of leading with the user – and the science – that has enabled us to support major shifts in the ways organizations think about their customers' decision making, de-risk innovation by building solutions on what is already known about human behavior, and tailor those solutions to the current customer context. Our discovery process begins with a thorough literature review to unearth what is already known about decision making and behavior in both the immediate context and related ones. This review feeds into the development of the primary research protocol and enables us to incorporate focused areas of inquiry into the interview or observation process. It also provides a framework within which to interpret our research findings. Below, we present two examples of how this combined approach enabled organizations to differentiate their offering by understanding their customers in a different way.

Taking a Behavioral Lens to Customer Segmentation

Traditional segmentation approaches tend to over-rely on demographic variables, including gender, age, and socioeconomic status. Although these demographics can offer some predictive value when little else is known about a customer, they do not provide insight into the nuances that differentiate individuals within groups. We know that millennials do not all share a unifying love for craft beer and a hate for home ownership, so why do our segmentation models treat them as if they do?

A behavioral approach to customer segmentation uses deep insight into customer experiences to base prediction of future behavior on past behavior. We recently used this approach when we helped a large Canadian bank to understand how their active-trader segment was making decisions about using online trading platforms. We began with a review of the literature that suggested that certain cognitive phenomena (e.g., overconfidence, sunk-cost effect, confirmation bias, and regret aversion) explained how active traders made decisions about buying and selling stocks. In-depth interviews and platform walkthroughs with active traders revealed that they actively battled their biases. For example, they specifically selected trading tools to reduce their feelings of stress and make what they

Figure 10.1 Four segments of traders

felt were smarter, less emotionally influenced, decisions. There were two major variables that influenced the way active traders thought about and used online trading platforms:

1. traders' sense of personal control over their trading outcomes (whether they felt that outcomes were more heavily influenced by their own decisions versus the market); and
2. their need for information when making decisions (whether they are a maximizer, requiring lots of information from diverse sources, or a satisficer, preferring more curated information to reduce noise).

By placing these two variables on a two-by-two grid (figure 10.1), we were able to identify four customer segments of traders based on how they chose their online trading platform.

We humanized the data by creating personas that described each of the four segments in terms of individual risks and needs:

1. **The Curator:** In order to manage their emotions, Curators have chosen to limit the wave of information they receive by carefully selecting their trusted sources. They believe they can beat the market if they trust their own intuition and their inner circle.

    a. **Risks**: Curators may fall prey to confirmation bias, seeking opinions and information that match their currently held beliefs.

    b. **Need**: Curators need a way to trust and integrate new information that doesn't match what they already know.

2. **The Security Seeker:** Security Seekers manage their feelings of powerlessness over the market by relying on a few trusted resources to guide their actions, because they certainly don't trust themselves.

    a. **Risks:** Security Seekers fall prey to the familiarity bias, showing preference for investments that fit in with what they already know.

    b. **Need:** Security Seekers need a way to feel empowered to seek out and evaluate different sources of information (and diversify their portfolio).

3. **The Power Player:** Power Players believe that with enough knowledge and the best tools, they have the power to beat the market. They've had some big wins – and probably some big losses.

    a. **Risks:** Power Players may fall prey to the attribution bias, attributing success to themselves and failures to external factors, like bad information, leading to over-confidence and over-trading.

    b. **Need:** Power Players need a way to manage and organize a wide range of information to enable more balanced decision making.

4. **The Trend Trader:** Trend Traders look to lots of different sources of information, but don't have faith in an internal compass. As a result, they look for trends – in the market, in advice, in opinions – and tend to go with the crowd.

    a. **Risks:** Trend Traders deal with regret aversion, playing overly safe to avoid anticipated regret over losses, and may make decisions based on proven performers using out-of-date information.

    b. **Need:** Trend Traders need a way to trust themselves to make decisions with unknown variables and use information to anticipate future trends.

This kind of segmentation is useful for a number of reasons:

1. It enables us to predict future behavior based on customers' past behavior, instead of potentially misleading demographic variables.
2. It bases segmentation on psychological and behavioral dimensions that can be measured through either observed behavior or survey methods.
3. It allows for people to switch segments when their relevant behaviors change.

This type of work reinforces the need for the researcher to go beyond typical behavioral approaches and incorporate primary methodologies common to human-centred design, such as ethnographic research, to uncover the psychological and behavioral dimensions at work. Doing so allows organizations to develop accurate, dynamic portraits of the customers they serve and to respond to those needs as people's behavior shifts. It's a paradigm shift from segmentation orthodoxy that, inaccurately, assumes people's preferences and behaviors are static and demographically driven.

Understanding the Context of Decision Making

As chapters 1, 2, and 5 in this book highlight, human behavior is embedded in the context in which choices and actions are made. In any given context, there are likely to be a large number of contextual variables and resulting cognitive phenomena that will be at work to influence behavior. Applying behavioral design rules of thumb (e.g., "make it easy") in the absence of a deep understanding of the customer's context can cause behavioral approaches to misfire. For that reason, behavioral designers should make a special effort to understand the context in which customers are making their decisions (see also the discussion on the behavioral scientist as an auditor in chapter 2).

When a large Canadian bank sought to create a mortgage-renewal process based on the classic behavioral strategy to reduce hassle costs and "make it easy," they faced some unexpected results. Faced with a simple, transparent, and fast renewal process – customers were distrustful. Our research helped uncover why they felt this way.

In-depth interviews with recent mortgage renewers revealed a common journey. Many of our interviewees reported a feeling that they had been taken advantage of in obtaining their first mortgage. With a limited credit history, many felt they had had little choice and were forced to accept terms that were not balanced. Over the years their lives had changed significantly. They were financially better off and more confident in their financial literacy and their ability to negotiate. Our research also revealed that customers use the mortgage renewal as an opportunity to take stock of their broader financial standing – fast-tracking the process deprived them of this opportunity and reduced their trust in the legitimacy of the process itself.

By reducing "hassles" in order to nudge behavior, the bank had unwittingly removed the key elements needed to build trust. As chapter 5 in this book argues, the optimal level of friction/impedance in the environment is not always zero. Our research allowed us to target the key behavioral biases that influenced customer confidence and use empathic interviewing to understand how they affected customers in the context of this surprisingly emotion-driven process. By incorporating this research into the design of their mortgage-renewal process, the bank was able to streamline the process while preserving the key moments that allowed the customer to take stock of their situation and build trust with the institution.

PART 2: CUSTOMER-CENTRIC NUDGING

Today's consumers are more aware than ever of tactics aimed at getting them to buy and buy more. This is a good thing for those of us who want to design consumer experiences that provide value to both customers and companies beyond profits alone. This objective requires us to bend and extend the ways in which behavioral insights have typically been used in organizations. This means that behavioral science should be generative and participatory, speculative and design-led, as well as evaluative, sticky, and scalable. It also means that we need to bring two parties into the design process more fully: end-consumers as well as service providers or employees, who play a critical role in shaping the overall experience and relationship.

Designing Compelling Experiences

Designing compelling customer experiences means we need to be designing seamless interactions between service providers and end-customers. Although this might seem obvious, the service providers are often overlooked in the design process in ways that can have negative unintended consequences and can limit impact (e.g., produce limited and uneven uptake) or backfire (e.g., result in outright rejection or sabotage). With the service provider in mind, we helped a large national insurance provider imagine and bring a new digital insurance-quoting tool to market.

Using a design-led and behaviorally informed[4] methodology, we assembled a panel of insurance brokers who served as our co-designers in the end-to-end process. We engaged in ethnographic research with this cohort to understand the insurance-quoting context:

- What are the preconceptions of different insurers out there?
- Whom do you trust/not trust and why?
- What motivates you?
- What is your current go-to process and what workarounds have you devised over time to make the workflow work for you?

We also accompanied brokers into the real world to hear and observe how they engage with potential and current customers. These "ride-alongs" helped us understand the interactions we needed to get right above and beyond the choice architecture in a digital experience.

The insights gleaned from this generative use of behavioral design fed into a series of wireframes that outlined the core elements of a compelling quoting experience – from getting the right language to attract brokers to the tool; to a simple, fast, quoting and binding process; through to defining a clear path forward to renewal. We then tested these as wireframes and clickable prototypes with a larger set of brokers to determine if our design resonated more broadly – and we iterated based on the feedback. Finally, we designed a beta version to pilot, as well as a rollout strategy that involved a national roadshow of the quoting tool. The roadshow brought the insurer closer to brokers, giving them a chance to learn about the tool and even experiment with it together. This simultaneously built deeper connections as well as demystified a new tool on the market. This generative and participatory approach to behavioral design manifested in a real-world product that has high adoption, conversion, and renewal rates.

Supporting Thoughtful, Long-Term Decision Making at the Moments Where It Can Be Most Difficult

A positive experience can make the difference between having a customer return to do more business and having a customer tell their friends how awful the organization was. Using principles from behavioral science, organizations can create more positive interactions and experiences for their customers. This can be beneficial in acquiring and retaining customers. It can also set an organization apart from its competitors.

This is exactly what one Canadian bank focused on in order to do better for their customers over the long term. Not all interactions with a bank are positive. Being denied a loan or a line of credit can make customers feel that *they* are being rejected. However, it is important for banks and other financial institutions to understand how to support thoughtful, long-term financial decision making in order to foster better financial health, especially in these types of difficult moments.

We helped one Canadian bank rethink an applicant's experience of being denied a loan to discover how it might use this challenging interaction to play a role in supporting the customer's financial health over the long-term. Our research revealed that customers were not always clear on why they were being denied a loan or what they could do to be in a better position to be approved for a loan next time. Telling a customer that they need to build their credit – the typical explanation banks provide – is not always useful to customers. Credit is an abstract concept for most people, and many people do not understand what they can do to improve it.

The point in the process where customers receive the loan decision (approval or rejection) is critical in their experience and has a lasting impact on how they view their bank. Unfortunately, it's also the last interaction many customers have with their bank. But it doesn't have to be. What if the bank helped the customer understand how they might start to create good financial habits, and what specific actions they can take to build their credit? Moreover, what if the bank showed them other people who were in similar situations and the actions they took in order to build their credit? We worked with our client to develop prototype tools that could help their front-line employees facilitate these types of long-term conversations with customers when they are denied a loan. This has the potential to create a more positive experience for the customer, build trust between the bank and the customer, and ultimately help to put the customer in a better position financially over the longer term.

CONCLUSION

Private-sector organizations have an opportunity to do better for their customers. Behavioral science is a tool that should be considered to support the achievement of both the organization's goals and the customer's goals. Of course, it is only one tool in an organization's toolkit but an important one if an organization wants to understand its customers deeply. In this chapter, we looked at examples of ways to better understand customers and gave examples of customer-centric nudges designed to influence the way customers experience products and services. While the cases we share are predominately in financial services, they run the gamut from designing digital products to innovating new ways to improve in-person, branch-level interactions.

First, we looked at examples of ways to better understand your customer. Understanding your customers always starts with listening to them and observing what they do. This type of customer research can help organizations to go beyond demographic profiles of their customers and move to a deeper understanding of what motivates customers to do what they do. Through it, organizations can better understand the real drivers of past customer behavior and make informed predictions about what services, products, and interactions customers are likely to respond to in the future.

"Context matters" is the number one golden rule in behavioral science. Without careful consideration of the context in which the customer experiences the interaction, behavioral interventions can backfire. In our example, we looked at the mortgage application and renewal process. Buying a house is the biggest investment that many customers will make. Making this process too easy made customers feel that something was not right and reduced their trust in the process. In this context, it was important for customers to be more involved in the process, because the act of applying for mortgage renewal was itself a beneficial opportunity to take stock of their financial situation. Streamlining the process might have made it easier, but it also made it feel less legitimate and deprived customers of the opportunity to take stock of their overall financial health.

Second, we looked at examples of customer-centric nudges designed to influence the way customers experience products and services. We believe that organizations must put the customer at the center of everything they do. Doing so can help organizations better achieve their goals while helping customers satisfy their needs and achieve their own respective goals. Our first example focused on using techniques and principles from behavioral science to design compelling experiences for customers. In the case of one insurance company, they were able to design seamless interactions for their customer in the quoting process. Taking a design-led and behaviorally informed approach ensured a more compelling experience for customers and ultimately greater adoption and conversion rates for the service provider, because it incorporated the service provider into the design of the tool from the outset

We must also remember that experiences may not always be positive and that we cannot always design for the optimal outcome. In this case, we can still take a design-led and behaviorally informed approach in order to do right by our customers. This was the case for one Canadian bank that wanted to help improve the financial health of customers who had been denied a loan. The interventions were focused on supporting improved financial decision making in order to help customers improve their credit score and, ultimately, their financial well-being. These moments are critical in the experience of the customer and can shift an experience from a negative transaction to a positive opportunity.

The foregoing examples provide some insight into the potential ethical considerations that arise when applying behavioral science in the private sector. As we have tried to illustrate, most industries are replete with missed opportunities for improving *both* the organization's bottom line and the customer's satisfaction and well-being. Behavioral science is a positive force for ethical business practice because it allows organizations to understand what their customers actually need and to deliver it to them in ways that are intuitive and maximally helpful. Like any tool, the techniques of behavioral science can be and have been abused by people with bad intent. But these cases are rare and are eclipsed by the far more common problem of products and services that fail to account for human behavior and leave customers underserved, frustrated, or confused. We believe that behavioral-science practitioners have something unique to offer organizations as they try to serve customers better; and we have seen at first hand the tangible benefits that come to both consumers and businesses when behavioral design is done right. We encourage organizations interested in this opportunity to focus on developing a deep appreciation of the context in which customers make their decisions and to use behavioral science as a tool for making products, services, and interactions more responsive to the real needs of the people they serve.

NOTES

1 Thaler, R.H., & Sunstein, C.R. (2003). Libertarian paternalism. *American Economic Review, 93*(2): 175–9; and Thaler, R.H., & Sunstein, C.R. (2008). *Nudge: Improving decisions about health, wealth, and happiness.* New Haven, CT: Yale University Press.

2 Fogg, B.J. (2003). *Persuasive technology: Using computers to change what we think and do*. San Francisco: Morgan Kaufmann Publishers Inc.
3 Reid, S., & Schmidt, R. (2018, 17 September). A new model for integrating behavioral science and design. *The Behavioral Scientist*. Retrieved from https://behavioralscientist.org/a-new-model-for-integrating-behavioral -science-and-design/.
4 See ibid.

CHAPTER ELEVEN

Choice Architecture in Programs and Policy

Elizabeth Hardy, Lauryn Conway, and Haris Khan

The opportunity to deliver better outcomes for citizens through behaviorally informed, evidence-based public policy continues to gain traction globally. Governments at the local, provincial, and federal levels are increasingly designing and redesigning public services to better reflect the needs and perspectives of the citizens who use them by placing the end-users – humans who behave, think, and feel – at the center of service delivery. Importantly, rigorous testing of design options at a low stake and scale using behaviorally informed methodologies allows us to generate "gold-standard" evidence of what works and what does not.

The current chapter explores the application of choice architecture to program and policy design in the Government of Canada. We start by defining choice architecture and contextualizing the Canadian federal system. Next, we examine design and implementation considerations for public servants, with a focus on guiding principles and ethics. Lastly, we conclude with three case studies that demonstrate the use of choice architecture to create better outcomes for Canadians.

DEFINING CHOICE ARCHITECTURE

The term "choice architecture" encapsulates the idea that even small and seemingly insignificant details in the environment can have substantial impacts on people's behavior.[1] For example, default options have been shown to have powerful effects on the decisions we make. Individuals are more likely to save for retirement when automatically opted-in to 401(k) plans;[2] children consume fewer calories when pre-set meal choices swap soda for juice and fries for fruit;[3] and doctors are more likely to prescribe generic medications when electronic health record systems automatically replace brand-name medications with their generic alternatives.[4]

The examples above illustrate that decisions are not made in a vacuum. The way in which choice options are presented can have a substantial impact on how we behave, even when the reasoning behind choice presentation is arbitrary. It follows that, by redesigning the choice environment, we can prompt individuals to make better decisions while also respecting freedom of choice. Thaler and Sunstein refer to an individual who is responsible for organizing the context in which people make decisions as a "choice architect." In line with a growing consensus that there is no such thing as a "neutral" choice environment, public-sector institutions around the world are increasingly adopting choice-architecture methodologies as an additional tool in the government's toolkit.

GOVERNMENT OF CANADA CONTEXT

Canada operates in a federated system whereby each province and territory has specific powers that are sometimes different from those at the federal level. The Government of Canada primarily administers policies and programs that are of national interest – including taxation, national defense, and foreign affairs, to list a few. The government consists of "line" departments and agencies, which are tasked with delivering and implementing policies and programs in their specific policy area. For example, the Public Health Agency of Canada (PHAC) is a federal institution working to protect the health and safety of Canadians. Its activities focus on preventing chronic diseases, preventing injuries, and responding to public-health emergencies and infectious-disease outbreaks.

In Canada, there has been a growing interest in the use of behavioral insights (BI) and experimentation at all levels of government in an effort to improve outcomes. In 2015, the Privy Council Office,

Government of Canada, launched the Innovation Hub (renamed the Impact and Innovation Unit in 2017), which was mandated, in part, to build a BI practice for the organization. Since that time, the team has grown from a two-person start-up operation to a full-service practice, offering BI and experimentation expertise to the government at large.

Despite this growth and interest from senior leadership in the practice of BI, challenges exist in the application of BI in the federal system, in part as a result of the low number of accessible touchpoints. For instance, while PHAC plays an important role in the overall health of Canadians, the oversight and responsibility for immunization is diffused to the provinces and territories. This diffusion adds a layer of complexity in, for example, running trials to increase vaccination rates, because of the need to first create a partnership with another jurisdiction. From a user's or citizen's perspective, however, as long as the service they are receiving is satisfactory, the level of government responsible for the particular initiative, policy, or service is of little concern.

This diffusion of oversight increases the complexity for the design and testing of BI experiments at the federal level. The limited access to touchpoints requires the creative development of partnerships with other levels of government and nongovernmental organizations in order to achieve desired outcomes. An example of a multijurisdictional partnership can be found in "Case Study 3: Social Benefit Bundling," later in this chapter.

WHAT DOES BEHAVIORALLY INFORMED CHOICE ARCHITECTURE LOOK LIKE?

A behaviorally informed approach to the architecture of choice has three fundamental core tenets. First, it places users at the center of service design and delivery, asking how every decision serves the user, not the service provider. Second, it minimizes any excessive or unjustified friction that is not aligned with the best interests of the user, or that hinders the user in making progress toward a goal[5] (otherwise known as "sludge," see chapter 5). Third, a behaviorally informed approach prioritizes an iterative cycle of testing, learning, and adapting, in order to, first, determine what works and what doesn't, and then to feed these insights back into the policy and program design process.[6]

Thaler and Sunstein outline six principles of good choice architecture (see also Professor Sunstein's Foreword to this volume). We find these principles helpful as starting points for policymakers and program designers who are interested in driving the creation of behaviorally informed choice environments in public-service delivery.

- **Consider the default**. The "path of least resistance" refers to our human tendency to choose whatever option requires the least effort, even if this option is not in our best interest. As described earlier, default options are inevitable in a choice environment and, as such, tend to have powerful effects on the decisions we make. In program and policy design, it is important to consider what happens when the end user "does nothing," and whether the choice of the default option serves to make the user's life easier or whether it adds more friction. Further, when defaults are intentionally designed using insights from behavioral science to nudge citizens' behavior in a particular direction, transparency is paramount. See the section "The Ethics Discussion," later in this chapter, for steps to mitigate ethical issues from the outset.
- **Expect error.** Given that humans are not perfectly rational beings, we tend to make errors. An ideal choice environment expects users to make mistakes, is designed to be as forgiving as possible, and makes it easy for people to carry through on their intentions. For example, to account for unexpected differences in traffic flow, the city of London designs for visitor safety by including "Look right!" signs on the pavement at street crossings in neighborhoods that are frequented by tourists.
- **Give feedback.** Feedback is a powerful tool for encouraging individuals to improve their performance. Well-designed choice environments inform users when they are doing well and when they make mistakes (e.g., including feedback on utility bills that advises consumers of their energy consumption relative to previous months or to that of others in their neighborhood).

Feedback may not always influence the current decision; however, it can aid in improving the next one.

- **Improve the ability to "map."** Complex choices – like choosing among options for medical treatment – are often tied to a complex set of possible outcomes, such as quality of life, length of life, different shades of possible side effects, and so on. Choices can be hard because often no option seems clearly better than the others, and the consequences of choice options are rather abstract (think of "reduced quality of life" – what does it mean?). A well-designed choice environment helps users to map the relation between an option and the result of choosing that option (i.e., the possible benefits or consequences). One way to improve the user's ability to map involves ensuring that the available information about each choice option is comprehensible. For example, healthcare providers are encouraged to use plain language instead of medical terms when they talk to patients – for example, by using the phrase "helps swelling and irritation go away," instead of the term "anti-inflammatory"; or by saying "soft, brittle bones," instead of "osteoporosis." Similarly, we can transform numerical information into easy-to-understand and easy-to-use units, such as translating cell-phone storage space from gigabytes to the number of pictures or songs that the device can hold.

- **Structure complex choices.** As the number and complexity of available choice options increases, people tend to move away from comparing the attributes of each alternative and instead turn to simpler decision-making strategies. Structuring available options is an effective way to make the decision-making process easier for the end-user. This could include, for example, providing decision aids, organizing options by category or theme, or creating an opportunity to filter options by relevant factors (such as price, calories, safety rating, etc.) to enhance comparability.

- **Use incentives.** Many decisions are driven by incentives. A well-designed choice environment matches the right incentives with the right people. This can be accomplished by considering four key questions: *Who uses? Who chooses? Who pays?* and *Who profits?*

THE ETHICS DISCUSSION

No matter how a program or policy is designed, it requires policy-makers to make decisions on the design of the choice architecture to be presented to a citizen. Even the most basic government service presents citizens with a choice as to how they would like to use it. For example, a driver chooses either to obtain a driver's license or to drive without a license and face whatever consequences may arise. The licensing system, as mandatory as it may seem, still presents users with a choice. A BI approach takes the additional step of con-sciously designing a service in a way that prompts individuals to make better decisions while also respecting their freedom of choice. BI practitioners do so by working with behavioral biases, rather than assuming that they do not exist.

When designing, testing, and iterating on choice environments in a public-sector context, it is important to take stock of any ethical considerations that may arise. This lens is not exclusive to BI proj-ects; whenever a new approach is being used in government, there is a higher level of scrutiny placed upon it. The Organization for Economic Co-operation and Development (OECD) provides a com-prehensive guide to the ethical application of BI to policymaking[7] and recommends identifying and addressing ethical considerations at certain stages of a BI project (table 11.1). These steps, which are explained fully in the OECD's BASIC Manual, can be applied to any project or initiative.

For BI practitioners in government in particular, the following additional steps can help support project success:

- **Ensure executive buy-in:** It is important for executives to understand that BI and experimentation are being applied to programs and policies and to be comfortable with the approach.
- **Consult with corporate functions:** Corporate functions such as legal, finance, and communications bring invaluable perspectives to a BI project and should be engaged at an early stage to help support implementation.
- **Collaborate with academic researchers**: The academic community can be helpful partners. Engaging academics as

Table 11.1 Summary of OECD Recommendations for Identifying and Addressing Ethical Risks at Each Stage of a BI Project

Stage of Project	Recommendations
Before starting the project	• Appoint one member of the team to supervise data collection, use, and storage. • Observe existing ethical guides and codes of conduct, and exercise sound judgment where they do not necessarily apply.
Identifying and defining the problem	• Discuss and establish procedures for how the team handles ethics issues in a way that protects honesty, anonymity, and whistleblowing. • Refrain from targeting behaviors that cannot be defended in public and the wider BI community. Evaluate the existing evidence for targeting a behavior as an ethical guide (i.e., what else has the organization tried?).
Analyzing why people act as they do	• Anonymize participation. • In situations where research involves a vulnerable population, consider additional safeguards. • Ensure secure handling of data.
Designing strategies for behavior change	• Ensure that interventions are designed to preserve choice.
Testing BI strategies	• Demonstrate the benefit and necessity of experimentation. • Protect data privacy and confidentiality. • Double-check analysis to ensure ethical data analysis.
Implementing behaviorally informed policies	• Ensure proper stakeholder engagement. • Share results of experiments publicly. • Report on what works, and what does not. • Monitor long-term outcomes and side effects.

subject-matter experts in the design, implementation, and analysis of a BI project, as well as in the experimental and intervention design, can further improve results and help contribute to the evidence base.

- **Apply "The Newspaper Test":** A good mental exercise for evaluating any issues around a project is to ask how it would be reported on by the media. Government's work should be in the public interest, and if it is difficult to convey the public benefit of a given project, there may be important issues to address.

- **Involve a "red team"**: A "red team" is an independent group whose role is to challenge assumptions and identify issues in a project plan. Using a separate team can help bring diverse perspectives to the exercise.

We have provided a roadmap that guides policymakers through the use of BI to inform choice architecture and policymaking. However, it is of the utmost importance for policymakers to ensure that their programs and policies are designed to maximize positive outcomes for the public. Policymakers are tasked with implementing government programs in ways that ensure these programs are as effective as possible. By designing services that are difficult to use, policymakers would be falling short of that goal.

Government of Canada employees are bound by the Values and Ethics Code for the Public Sector – the Public Sector Code.[8] The code establishes five core values: respect for democracy, respect for people, integrity, stewardship, and excellence. This code outlines the values and expected behavior that should guide staff in all work-related activities. As such, public servants strengthen the ethical culture of the organization and support public confidence by adhering to the expected behaviors, and to do so is a term and condition of employment. Further, because government services are provided using taxpayer money, every opportunity should be taken to maximize the value-for-money of these funds. By designing policies and programs with users in mind, policymakers are fulfilling their obligation to ensure policy and program effectiveness and efficiency.

CASE STUDIES

This section outlines three case studies that demonstrate choice architecture in action to create better outcomes for Canadians, with a focus on organ-donor registration,[9] government-survey response rates,[10] and the uptake of social benefits.[11] Versions of these case studies have been published elsewhere and are referenced as appropriate.

CASE STUDY 1: ORGAN-DONOR REGISTRATION

Overview

In the Province of Ontario, more than 1,500 people are currently waiting to receive life-saving organ transplants. Every three days, one of these individuals dies while waiting. Increasing organ-donor registration rates is critical. While studies show that the majority of people across the province are willing to register as an organ and tissue donor, only 25 percent of Ontarians do so.

Opportunity

The Province of Ontario has a prompted-choice system to register organ and tissue donors – this means that Ontarians are asked whether they consent to be a donor during health-card, driver's-license, and photo-card transactions at government service centers across the province.

Individuals can also proactively register online at BeADonor.ca. The registration rate remains significantly lower than in other jurisdictions that use a prompted-choice system, despite the fact that research shows a broad public support of the program and willingness among Ontarians to register.

In an effort to increase registration rates in the province, the Ontario Behavioural Insights Unit partnered with the University of Toronto's Behavioural Economics in Action at Rotman (BEAR), the Trillium Gift of Life Network, ServiceOntario, and the Ministry of Health and Long-Term Care to pilot the use of behavioral insights in organ-donor registration.

Solution

To begin with, a number of barriers were identified that could prevent individuals from registering. These barriers included a complex registration form that was difficult and time consuming to complete, and customer-service representatives who at times, because of the lengthy process and the high volume of customer traffic, did not always prompt individuals to register.

After careful analysis of the donor-registration process, the team designed a pilot project based on the established principles of behavioral insights. The goal of the project was to improve the in-person organ-donor registration process and increase registration rates. Four types of interventions were tested:

- *Simplification*: providing a simplified version of the current donor-registration form
- *Timing*: handing the form out sooner, at the reception desk, rather than at the service counter
- *Nudge*: adding one of three nudge statements to the top of the simplified form
- *Information*: handing out the current Trillium Gift of Life Network brochure, rather than not handing out anything

Results

The pilot project was a success. Registration rates increased by up to 143 percent compared to current registration rates. Three of the conditions outperformed all others, each significantly increasing an individual's likelihood of registering compared to the control condition. The best three conditions applied behavioral-insights interventions that included simplification of the form, timing, nudge statements, and adding an information brochure to the simplified form. As a result of this trial, the simplified form with the best performing nudge statement, handed out as soon as the individual arrives at the center, is being implemented.

Once implemented, these successful changes could garner over 450,000 new registrations in Ontario annually, approximately 200,000 more than the status quo.

CASE STUDY 2: STATISTICS CANADA SURVEY RESPONSE

Overview

During the past several years, there has been a steady decline in Canadians' rate of response to the Government of Canada's mandatory and voluntary surveys. This issue makes it harder for government to design policies and programs in an evidence-based way, and to evaluate those actions once they are implemented. For example, in the last five years, there has been a 4 percentage point decrease in the overall response rate to Statistic Canada's household surveys.

Opportunity

To address this problem, in Spring 2016, Statistics Canada approached the Privy Council Office's Impact and Innovation Unit (IIU) for consultation on how to increase response rates to these surveys. After a careful review of a number of Statistics Canada surveys, the investigators decided to focus on the Farm Financial Survey for a research project. The Farm Financial Survey, an initiative by Agriculture and Agri-Food Canada and Statistics Canada, provides data on farm assets, liabilities, revenues, expenses, capital investments, and capital sales. This information is critical to understanding the effects of federal and provincial agriculture programs and policies on different farm operations. The survey uses the Census of Agriculture to create a list stratified by province, farm type, and farm size. The target population for the survey consists of all active Canadian agriculture operations.

Participation in the survey by selected farms is mandatory. Currently, selected participants are informed by mail via a notification letter that includes a copy of the paper questionnaire for reference and preparation. Several weeks after the notification letter is sent, Statistics Canada employees call participants to collect data via a twenty-five-minute telephone interview. If a participant declines to answer questions during the first phone contact, Statistics Canada continues to attempt to collect responses until the end of the data-collection period.

Solution

The IIU worked with BEAR to develop an experiment to test the effect of two simple, low-cost, behavioral interventions on Farm

Financial Survey response rates: a reminder letter; and a reminder letter that includes a process change.

The reminder letters incorporated principles of behavioral science, including framing and imposing a deadline, to encourage participants to respond to the survey. An initial notification letter, letting participants know about the survey and asking them to complete it, was sent out in June 2016.

Intervention 1 – Soft Reminder Letter

This version of the reminder letter involved a relatively simple "soft" reminder, incorporating BI principles such as framing, grouping, and simplification. Extensive research in the field of behavioral science has shown that simplifying processes, incorporating plain language, and grouping concepts together can increase cognitive ease and result in improved outcomes.

Intervention 2 – Reminder Letter with Process Change

This version of the reminder letter not only incorporated framing, grouping, and simplification principles but also included the addition of a process change. In Statistics Canada's usual practice, staff phone participants at various times of the day in the hope that they will have time available to complete the twenty-five-minute survey. With this intervention, participants were given a five-day deadline to call Statistics Canada to schedule an appointment to complete the survey. The idea of encouraging participants to call to schedule an appointment builds on the research findings that individuals are more likely to follow through with an action, such as a medical appointment, once the date and time are scheduled. Additionally, existing research in the behavioral sciences shows that imposing a short deadline (here, five days) can create a sense of urgency and motivate people to take action. The reminder letter also included a tear-away feature to help prevent missed appointments by encouraging participants to write down the date and time of their appointment.

The Randomized Controlled Trial

An RCT was designed to test and compare the effectiveness of the two reminder letters against the control group (no reminder letter). On 14 July 2016, a total of 4,542 participants who had not yet completed the Farm Financial Survey were randomly assigned to one of three categories:

- Control Group: No Reminder Letter
- Intervention 1: Soft Reminder Letter
- Intervention 2: Reminder Letter with Process Change

Results

The randomized controlled trial results show that the reminder letter with process change (intervention 2), in which participants were given a five-day deadline to call Statistics Canada to schedule an appointment, significantly increased response rates to the Farm Financial Survey. This intervention increased the overall response rate from 59.1 percent (the control group) to 63.1 percent, a statistically significant ($p < .05$) increase of 6.8 percent relative to control (% change). The soft reminder letter (intervention 1) also had a greater response rate than the control group (61.4% versus 59.1%), but this difference was not statistically significant.

CASE STUDY 3: SOCIAL BENEFIT BUNDLING

Overview

The Canada Learning Bond (CLB) is an education savings incentive administered by Employment and Social Development Canada (ESDC). It is designed to encourage and reinforce the importance of saving for a child's postsecondary education through a Registered Education Savings Plan (RESP). Eligible children from low-income families can have up to $2,000 deposited to their RESP at a participating organization, such as a bank, credit union, or group scholarship plan dealer. Despite the benefits of opening an RESP and accessing the CLB, only 36.5 percent of eligible children received the CLB as of 2017.

Approximately 1.9 million eligible children have yet to receive the CLB, and increasing uptake of the CLB and other government benefits for low-income families is a key priority for the Government of Canada. Importantly, research has found that having a Registered Educational Savings Plan at the age of fifteen is associated with higher postsecondary enrolment rates by age nineteen, independent of family income.

Opportunity

To help increase the uptake of educational savings programs, the IIU worked with Employment and Social Development Canada and other levels of government to integrate registration for Registered Educational Savings Plans into existing government processes that eligible individuals undertake. Bundling multiple processes reduces the "friction cost" of accessing the program from the point of view of the client, resulting in increased access to financial support.

Solutions

In the Province of Ontario, parents of newborns use an online birth-registration platform to access key services such as birth certificates and social insurance numbers. In the first of these projects, the Government of Canada worked with the Government of Ontario to integrate a Registered Educational Savings Plan referral mechanism into the Ontario online birth-registration service. In the new service, the option to pursue an RESP is included as part of the bundle of existing services already available to parents.

In addition, the Government of Canada partnered with the City of Toronto to encourage the uptake of educational savings incentives among recipients of social assistance in the city. Recipients of social assistance are required to meet with a case worker regularly to discuss their financial situation, and this offers an opportunity to promote and discuss educational savings. City staff encouraged case workers to discuss the CLB in these meetings and added behavioral-insights interventions to the appointment-notice letters to further improve CLB sign-up rates. These interventions included the up-front provision of key information regarding the CLB, the inclusion of an online self-serve sign-up link, and a short form for clients to fill out before attending the meeting, to ensure that they had all the required documents to open an RESP in the meeting.

Results

The results from the integration of RESP sign-up into Ontario's birth bundle have been very positive, with 70 to 75 percent of new parents scheduling appointments to open registered educational savings accounts in Ontario. To help more Canadian families start saving early for postsecondary education, the Government of Canada will continue to work with its provincial and territorial partners to scale this service.

In the City of Toronto project, a randomized controlled trial found that bundling Registered Educational Savings Plan sign-up with these meetings more than tripled the baseline uptake rate among this population, once again providing an evidence-based model that could be scaled nationally.

CONCLUSION

As part of their core activity, governments create decision environments for citizens through the design and implementation of policies. Both at home and abroad, public servants are increasingly leveraging BI as an additional tool in government toolkits and are placing the needs and experiences of end-users at the center of service design and delivery. To support the growing appetite for BI and experimentation in the public service, this chapter outlines and describes guiding principles and ethical considerations that can be used as a starting point for policymakers and program designers who are interested in maximizing outcomes through intentional and behaviorally informed choice architecture. The case studies provide tangible examples of choice architecture in action as a way to create better results for Canadians, with solutions that range from tweaking existing touchpoints, to creating new processes, to bundling multiple services – all with the goal of generating impact by making the decision-making process easier for users.

NOTES

1 Thaler, R.H., & Sunstein, C.R. (2008). *Nudge: Improving decisions about health, wealth, and happiness*. Updated ed. New York: Penguin Books.
2 Thaler, R.H., & Benartzi, S. (2004). Save more tomorrow™: Using behavioral economics to increase employee saving. *Journal of Political Economy, 112*(S1), S164–S187.
3 Peters, J., Beck, J., Lande, J., Pan, Z., Cardel, M., Ayoob, K., & Hill, J.O. (2016). Using healthy defaults in Walt Disney World restaurants to improve nutritional choices. *Journal of the Association for Consumer Research, 1*(1), 92–103.
4 Patel, M.S., Day, S.C., Halpern, S.D., Hanson, C.W., Martinez, J.R., Honeywell, S., & Volpp, K.G. (2016). Generic medication prescription rates after health system-wide redesign of default options within the electronic health record. *JAMA Internal Medicine, 176*(6), 847–8.
5 Sunstein, C.R. (2019). Sludge and ordeals. *Duke Law Journal, 68*, 1843–82. doi:10.2139/ssrn.3288192.
6 Haynes, L., Service, O., Goldacre, B., & Torgerson, D. (2012). Test, learn, adapt: Developing public policy with randomised controlled trials. London: Cabinet Office. Retrieved from: https://www.bi.team /publications/test-learn-adapt-developing-public-policy-with -randomised-controlled-trials/.
7 Organization for Economic Co-operation and Development. (2019). The BASIC manual. In OECDiLibrary, *Tools and ethics for applied behavioural insights: The BASIC toolkit*. Paris: OECD Publishing. doi. org/10.1787/0507cec0-en.
8 Government of Canada. (nd). Values and ethics of the public service. https://www.canada.ca/en/government/publicservice/values.html. Last accessed 17 January 2020.
9 Government of Ontario. (2016). Behavioural insights pilot project – organ donor registration. Retrieved from: https://www.ontario.ca/page /behavioural-insights-pilot-project-organ-donor-registration. Last accessed 12 December 2019.

10 Government of Canada. (2017). Increasing response rates to a Statistics
   Canada survey. Retrieved from: https://www.canada.ca/en/innovation
   -hub/services/reports-resources/increasing-response-rates-statistics
   -canada-survey-july-2017.html. Last accessed 16 December 2019.
11 Government of Canada. (2018). Increasing take-up of the Canada Learning
   Bond. Retrieved from: https://www.canada.ca/en/innovation-hub
   /services/reports-resources/behavioural-insights-project.html. Last
   accessed 16 December 2019.

CHAPTER TWELVE

Helping Low-Income Canadians to File Taxes and Access Benefits

Jennifer Robson

Sam and Tara are standing in line at a community income tax clinic. They have heard that someone might be able to help them file their taxes and apply for child benefits for their daughter. Sam recently lost his job, and Tara is not working either. When Sam was working, his employer just deducted the taxes, and he and Tara never figured there was any reason to file a tax return. They do not much like taking help from government, but things are bad with both of them out of work. The clerk who took Sam's claim for employment insurance told him to make sure his family is getting child benefits. So here they are to get help with that by first filing a bunch of tax returns. Sam and Tara do not qualify for the government tax-filing clinic, but the volunteer assures them they can get help from people in a different part of the community center. It takes a while, and the whole process is pretty confusing. A volunteer behind a desk asks them question after question and types their answers into a computer. They sign a form. After filing four years of returns, they learn they will be getting a check for just over $430 a month for their daughter, plus a retroactive payment of just under $4,600 for benefits they could have been receiving last year. They leave, grateful for the help, but also a little sad that no one had told them to do this sooner.

Sam and Tara are not alone. By best estimates, roughly one in ten working-age adults do not file a tax return in a given year.[1] These adults come from many different occupations, but when they have a low income or are living in poverty, not filing can have large consequences for their welfare. Many people may not need to file a return. If, like Sam, they know their employer remitted their taxes, they may be in full compliance with tax rules even if they do not file a personal income tax return.

While filing an income tax return may be about as enjoyable as getting a root-canal treatment, it is also the gateway to dozens of income-tested benefits from the federal and provincial governments, including child benefits, seniors' benefits, and refunds for sales and carbon taxes. Moreover, a tax return is often the preferred or even mandatory way for local and provincial governments to verify eligibility for drug insurance, subsidized housing, and childcare subsidies. When Canadians do not file a tax return, they may be missing out on thousands of dollars of benefits. Until recently, economists and policymakers had tended to assume that "if you build it, they will come." In the context of government benefits, a growing body of research is starting to show that tax filing can be an obstacle to benefit take-up and, in turn, the positive social-welfare effects that policymakers promise and expect from the programs they create and administer. However, community networks are starting to show some promising practices to facilitate access to benefits through the tax system. Taken together, this evidence suggests important lessons for increasing eligible participation in social programs using behaviorally informed interventions aimed at both individuals and institutions.

I draw on the academic research to first review the theory around tax compliance and participation in social benefits. I argue that the strongest models point to complex and behavioral explanations when people do not access the benefits that might help them. Here, the goal is to offer a starting set of principles for understanding what works in facilitating benefit take-up through tax filing. Next, I discuss examples of promising practices in community-based organizations working with individual clients, as well as system-level changes being made in Canada's national tax administrator, the Canada Revenue Agency. I conclude with some suggestions for advancing a behaviorally informed approach to benefit take-up through the tax system.

WHY WOULD YOU LEAVE MONEY ON THE TABLE?
MODELS OF TAX-FILING AND BENEFIT BEHAVIOR

Canada's income tax system relies heavily on voluntary compliance.[2] Since the 1940s, Canadians with standard employment have had their personal income tax deducted at source from their paycheck and remitted to the government by their employer. This pay-as-you-earn system was introduced with the promise that taxpayers would still file one return at the end of the year to make sure the right amounts had been paid and to reconcile any refunds they might be owed. This basic feature of the personal income tax system has largely remained the same ever since.

Early economic models of tax compliance have generally thought of the problem in terms of people who owe taxes and who must decide whether to disclose their income and pay what they owe. In this literature, economists have argued that unpaid taxes are like a bonus or asset for tax dodgers, but one that could be at risk (plus penalties) if they are caught cheating.[3] The extra income today has a value to the person, but so does the cost of being caught by tax authorities. Using this model, we could try to predict a person's behavior by figuring out how much the extra money (from the unpaid taxes) is worth to them relative to their sense of the costs of not following the rules and their feeling about the odds of being caught.

This model presumes that people make decisions in their own self-interest. We could also apply this approach to understand people's behavior regarding government benefits. The decision to file a return to get benefits could be modeled as a comparison between the full costs (including any taxes owed, professional fees, and costs to replace ID) of filing a return and completing benefit applications versus the expected value of government benefits. Sometimes this cost-benefit ratio does not make filing seem worthwhile.[4] But is this really all there is to explaining tax filing?

We need to think about what individual people *believe* about the costs of compliance and the value of extra money, as well as whether they believe the system is fair. This latter element includes whether they believe they will be caught and penalized for unpaid taxes or, conversely, granted a benefit when they apply. Sludge in the system – in the form of complex processes, attitudinal or communication barriers, and potential for stigma – can all shape people's beliefs about cost and benefits and about whether people think the system is fair (see chapter 5). Some benefits that are based on need can feel stigmatizing, increasing the cognitive and emotional costs of applying for them.[5] Recall in our opening vignette that Sam and Tara had never really seen themselves as people who need or want government help. Others have pointed out that the costs of applying for benefits also include the costs of time and attention to learn about the program, evaluate your odds of success, and fill out the application forms.[6] Unfamiliar programs (like tax and benefit rules) are hard to understand, particularly for nonspecialists; and when applying takes a lot time and effort, we should expect take-up to suffer. For example, in a recent pilot project to test the effects of a basic-income program, Ontario project administrators found it more difficult than expected to recruit eligible participants.[7] This might have been predictable from the forty-plus-page application that had to be completed to qualify to be entered in the lottery for the basic-income benefit.

Additional cognitive barriers arise as a result of competing demands on attention and inconsistent motivation.[8] People who are eligible for benefits suffer from the same human limitations that we all do – they procrastinate, they get distracted, or, very understandably, have to postpone taking some step (like booking an appointment to get help to file a return) because something more urgent (like work, illness, or even weather conditions) gets in the way. After a person learns about a benefit that could be accessed through the tax system, there will be several steps involved that will each require a decision and action on the part of the person. In turn, each decision point or action creates an opportunity to give up because it just does not seem worth it to keep trying. Those applicants who do persist and gain access to a new income benefit can face a whole new set of costs and barriers if well-intentioned program administrators review their file and ask for extra information to support their application. I will refer to these as process barriers. In table 12.1, I offer further examples of the various kinds of costs or barriers that low-income people seem to experience in filing a tax return and applying for benefits.

Table 12.1 I Am a Low-Income Person and Want to Apply for Benefits. What Costs or Barriers Might I Face?

Type of Barrier	Examples
Tangible costs	• Fees I'll pay to software providers or for-profit tax-filers • Fees I'll pay to get or replace required identification documents • Transportation costs to a government or community office • Wages I'll lose by taking time off work to attend an appointment • If I have kids, child-care expenses incurred to attend an appointment • Cost of using pre-paid minutes on my cell phone to call a busy government help line and wait on hold for a long time
Cognitive barriers	• Forms that are above my literacy level • Forms that aren't in my first language • Forms that demand calculations above my numeracy level • Expert calculations required to figure out effects on other benefits or programs I might be eligible for or already be using • Effort to learn about a program • Effort to guess about my own eligibility • Effort to keep track of my own file and follow up as needed • If I get new money, effort to decide how best to use it
Perceptual barriers	• Not knowing that a return is needed to get benefits • Expecting the benefits to be smaller than they are • Misunderstanding eligibility • Misunderstanding application rules • Feeling unwelcome in the government office • Feeling judged • Not trusting that my file will be treated fairly • Not feeling like "the kind of person" who gets this benefit • Worrying that I could be cut off from the benefit, even if I don't mean to break a rule
Process barriers	• Language from the tax agency that isn't clear on the need to file • Forms that take too long to fill out • Forms that ask for more information than is really needed • Forms that ask me to repeat the same information, over and over • Forms that can only be submitted one way • Delays in processing my application • Delays because more information is needed • Delays or cancelled payments because my file was picked for a review

CONNECTING PEOPLE TO THEIR BENEFITS THROUGH TAX FILING: EXAMPLES FROM CURRENT PRACTICE

While sludge exists, the good news is that there are organizations working to help people overcome these barriers and file a personal income-tax return when the return is the only gateway to several income-tested benefits. Several of these organizations are using interventions that are behaviorally informed and that address many of the barriers to tax filing identified in the academic literature. More specifically, organizations are working to:

- highlight the benefits of filing;
- overcome cognitive and other barriers to help reduce costs of filing;
- make institutional changes to eliminate process sludge.

Below, I briefly discuss examples of each of these approaches in action.

HIGHLIGHT THE BENEFITS

Behavioral researchers have shown that people consistently over-value losses (or costs) relative to gains (or benefits).[9] As applied to tax filing and access to benefits, this means that, all else being equal, people who don't file and don't claim their benefits are likely to overestimate the costs of filing and underestimate the value of the benefits they'll receive. One way to overcome this bias is to make the benefits highly salient and relevant to prospective clients as they decide whether to file a return and pursue benefits they are entitled to. Organizations can do this by making benefits more visible and emphasizing the dollar values involved.

For several years, in Manitoba and New Brunswick, community groups have been working to promote tax filing by reminding low-income clients of the benefits they can get. Both examples reframe tax filing as an exercise in claiming benefits. For example, in Manitoba, the initiative is called "Get Your Benefits!," and communications materials for potential clients describe, in plain language, several of the main federal and provincial cash transfers that depend on filing a return.[10] The initiative has also cleverly found ways to engage non-traditional but highly trusted intermediaries in promoting tax filing and benefit access. The Manitoba team develops and distributes tools to healthcare providers and patients, including posters and pamphlets that can remind them, while they are in a medical-care setting, of the income benefits they can access. In Ontario, in a similar vein, doctors at Toronto's St. Michael's Hospital have worked with partners to create, test, and field an online benefits screener to quickly give patients a sense of what benefits they may qualify for by undertaking the application process, including (for many) filing a tax return.[11] In both Manitoba and Toronto, doctors are encouraged to ask patients if they are having a hard time financially and, if yes, to provide a referral to community resources that can help them apply for benefits, including through tax filing. Now a patient may go to the doctor and get more than the usual medical tests or prescriptions. In addition to making benefits more salient, these initiatives are likely also addressing the stigma of claiming income-tested benefits by having a trusted care provider make the connection to their physical health and well-being.

HIGHLIGHT BENEFITS AND REDUCE BARRIERS TO FILING

In New Brunswick, the Economic and Social Inclusion Corporation (ESIC) runs several "super clinics" across the province to help low-income residents file returns, access benefits, and more. Working with the federal Community Volunteer Income Tax Program and the Canada Revenue Agency (discussed later in this chapter), ESIC's "Get Your Piece of the Money Pie" program very clearly and deliberately urges lower-income New Brunswickers to claim their "share" of benefits. The clinic provides free help to file tax returns and apply for benefits.[12] As with many other free income tax clinics, community volunteers are recruited and trained to prepare and file income tax returns for low-income clients at no cost to the client. But unlike many clinics that operate only during the usual income tax season (roughly January through to the end of April), the tax-filing service is offered year-round so that clients can catch up on missing returns and unclaimed benefits at any time in the year. According to an annual report, since the program launched in 2010, more than 22,600 residents in New Brunswick have filed a tax return through the program and, in the most recent year, have collectively claimed nearly $39 million in income-tested benefits because of those returns.[13] This means an average of $1,725 in additional income for filers using the program in New Brunswick.[14]

As a key plank of the province's poverty-reduction plan, "Get Your Piece of the Money Pie" is working to increase the incomes of New Brunswickers by connecting them to federal and provincial benefits they are eligible for. However, interestingly, the "super clinics" have also found ways to add on yet more benefits for clients who come and file a return. By partnering with federal and provincial government departments, the "super clinics" now also offer additional services like helping clients apply for or replace identification documents (such as social insurance numbers) and providing personalized help with applications for benefits that aren't directly tied to a tax return (such as the federal Canada Learning Bond, an income-tested contribution to education savings for low-income children). By co-locating these additional services, the "super clinics" are tackling multiple tangible cognitive and procedural barriers to filing and claiming benefits. For example, clients who are missing identification do not have to leave and come back another day when they can move to a different desk and get help confirming or replacing their social insurance number. Co-locating multiple and interrelated services that can be delivered in person means that clients' costs in time, transportation, and more are significantly reduced. But beyond just reducing costs, ESIC has also worked to increase the number of government programs and benefits that are represented in the "super clinics." This has meant significant investment in mapping out the various programs and benefits that low-income tax-filing clients might also be eligible for and then partnering with the administering departments. The end result for clients is an increase in the all-in dollar value of the benefits they can receive after one visit to a "super clinic."

In the United States, a community-based organization has used a different approach to address the barriers to tax filing and access to benefits. Like the Community Volunteer Income Tax Program in Canada, the Internal Revenue Service's Volunteer Income Tax Assistance (VITA) Program connects trained volunteers to low-income clients who need help to file a return. In New York City, Single Stop has been leading innovative approaches to increase the accessibility and reach of the VITA model. Like Sam and Tara in the opening vignette, users of volunteer income tax clinics can face long wait times. In traditional tax-filing clinics, a volunteer meets face to face with each new client, completing and filing the return before the client leaves. Even when returns are reasonably simple, this can take a significant amount of time.

To start to reduce wait times and other procedural barriers, Single Stop has started to triage their clients while they wait in line and encourage interested clients to use self-serve kiosks available on site.[15] Those clients with adequate literacy and capability can use, free of charge, secure software to complete and file their own return, generally with much shorter wait times than those for the traditional in-person service. Volunteers are still available to help these clients with questions or to trouble-shoot as needed; using an assisted self-help approach allows clients to feel supported but also empowered to complete the task themselves. Triaging clients toward the assisted self-help option significantly reduces overall wait times, even for those clients who still need the traditional one-on-one help with a tax preparer. In another innovation, Single Stop has started to de-link the locations for client intake and the actual work of preparing and filing returns. In a relatively new "virtual" clinic, clients can come to a location in their neighborhood and drop off all the information needed to prepare and file their return and to access key benefits tied to tax filing. These forms are then collected and brought, by Single Stop, to a centralized office where volunteer tax preparers complete the rest of the process. Afterwards, clients receive a copy of their return as confirmation that the filing was completed. Like the assisted self-help model, this "virtual" clinic significantly reduces wait times, as well as out-of-pocket costs related to transportation and time away from work, by separating the intake and tax-filing portions of the service. While nearly 80 percent of the tax returns prepared by Single Stop are still completed through the traditional one-on-one in-person service, the assisted self-help and "virtual" clinics are growing faster because they are easier to scale up. In 2012, just 73 returns were completed using the "virtual" clinic, a number that had grown exponentially to more than 11,000 in 2016.[16]

THE CRITICAL ROLE OF INTERDEPARTMENT COLLABORATIONS AND INSTITUTIONAL CHANGES

So far, this chapter has discussed promising practices in community settings that help make it easier and more rewarding for low-income people to file a return and access associated cash transfers. However, the role of institutions should already be apparent. Chapter 11 suggests that, for behavioral-science practitioners in the government, getting executive buy-in is an important step to help support project success; indeed, in our case, it is important because executive buy-in facilitates interdepartment collaborations and institutional changes. The work of ESIC in New Brunswick is only possible through inter-departmental and intergovernmental collaboration. Likewise, the innovations in tax-filing clinics in New Brunswick and New York all rely on underlying institutional supports for volunteer income tax preparation programs such as VITA in the United States and the Community Volunteer Income Tax Program (CVITP) in Canada. Both programs rely on technical and technological services from tax administrators (such as software and systems to permit volunteer tax preparers to submit a return for a client). Moreover, both programs rely on some standardized training materials so that all volunteers have a basic level of knowledge and competence to serve their clients.

In late 2015 and early 2016, the Canada Revenue Agency (CRA) was asked to change its focus on the dozens of income benefits it administers to treat access to benefits as a key part of its institutional mandate. This meant that, beyond its role in diligently processing the benefit claims the agency received from tax filers, it was now charged with helping "Canadians obtain the support and information they need to know about what benefits they may be eligible to receive."[17] This new priority required a significant shift in posture for an agency that had been focusing on the enforcement of tax collection. It has required, and will continue to require, some behaviorally informed shifts in the conduct of the institution itself. Below, I describe three such changes.

One small way in which a tax-collection and benefits-administration agency like the CRA can change its own conduct in relation to access to benefits is to make better use of its own internal records and proactively contact eligible nonparticipants. In other words, if you know who isn't getting their benefits because they have not filed, maybe proactively inviting them to file and collect those benefits might spur some nonfilers to respond by filing a return and claiming the benefits they are eligible for. In 2017–2018, the agency reports that it sent out letters to 300,000 lower-income Canadians who had not yet filed a personal income tax return for the year. The CRA would have been able to identify these persons based on previous years' returns or from other administrative records filed by third parties, such as T-4 reports from employers on employment income or T-5 reports from provincial governments on social-assistance income. According to the agency's annual report, this relatively modest initiative had a 12.6 percent response rate, measured as the number of returns received following the nonfiler benefit letters, and it triggered the payment of $32.4 million in benefits to the new filers, or an average of $854 per person.[18]

Potentially more transformative changes in the behavior of the CRA have been in the move toward better processes for Canadians with regard to tax filing and access to benefits. Even though the response rate for the modest letter campaign was respectable, it still meant that some 87 percent of lower-income Canadians contacted by letter did not respond. In other words, the barriers to filing and claiming their benefits were likely still too high for most people, even when they were actively invited to file a return.

Starting in 2017, the CRA also introduced a new program called "File My Return." Aimed again at lower-income Canadians with uncomplicated returns and those whose incomes had not changed substantially from one year to the next, this program goes one step further than earlier initiatives by providing invited users the opportunity to file a tax return over the phone. Rather than asking taxpayers to complete forms, with or without community assistance, in the "File My Return" program, the CRA completes the return for the taxpayer. Using an automated phone system with voice recognition, a taxpayer can file their return by verbally confirming the information the agency already has on file. Like the "virtual" tax-filing clinics in New York, this approach substantially reduces the tangible costs of filing a return, making it something that can be done in minutes by phone in the privacy of your own home. Moreover, it goes a long way toward addressing some of the cognitive and procedural barriers that can otherwise discourage filers.

However, not all low-income Canadians are eligible for the program. Users must still be identified by the agency and receive a letter inviting them to use the "File My Return" service. This is almost certainly maintaining both perceptual as well as procedural obstacles to tax filing and access to benefits for many nonfilers who may be similar to "File My Return" target clients but who aren't invited by the agency. Still, this incremental move toward pre-filled forms should be a welcome change. It recognizes that the work of collecting and completing often complex tax forms that has been expected of tax filers is something that can, and maybe should, be done by the agency itself. In fact, pre-filled forms are often the norm for tax administration in other countries, where officials have recognized that compliance behavior is stronger when it is as effortless as possible for individuals. It is an approach that largely reverses the onus for tax filing, placing it on the institutional tax administrator rather than the individual – an approach that, when combined with an institutional change toward automatic evaluation and enrolment in benefits – could have large and positive effects on access to benefits for lower-income Canadians.

In terms of automatic evaluation and enrolment in benefits, there has been a major change to one important benefit that is tied to tax filing. The Canada Workers Benefit (formerly the Working Income Tax Benefit) is an income-tested refundable credit that is payable to persons with some working income but low total income.[19] This benefit is similar to the more generous Earned Income Tax Credit in the United States, and is intended to encourage labour-market participation by topping up wages and self-employment earnings. For some time, policymakers had known that an important segment of tax filers were eligible for but not claiming the benefit. In other words, these tax filers had not completed and included the separate schedule to their personal income tax return that is treated as the application for the benefit, although their overall personal income tax information showed they were otherwise eligible. The problem of nonparticipation by eligible persons was particularly pronounced among tax filers using paper forms to complete their returns.[20] This is perhaps unsurprising given that the form required forty-two different responses and calculations to determine whether the respondent was likely eligible. Starting in 2019, the CRA will instead automatically review income tax returns for eligibility for the Canada Workers Benefit. This means no separate forms for low-income individuals to fill out with their return, so that, as long as a return is filed, eligible low-income workers will get the benefit they are entitled to. This change sets something of a precedent for thinking about the administration of other cash benefits through the income tax system.[21] If the CRA has been able to find a feasible way to collect the information it needs to assess eligibility, what other changes might be possible that would permit automatic assessment and enrolment for other important benefits – for example, child benefits?

PULLING IT ALL TOGETHER

Connecting Canadians to their benefits has not traditionally been a top priority for the Canada Revenue Agency or policymakers in charge of Canada's personal income tax system. As a country, we have relied and continue to rely on individuals to voluntarily disclose information through an income tax return and to proactively signal their interest in receiving cash benefits that are administered through the same tax system. The net result has been a system in which a significant number of Canadians lose out on benefits because they don't file a return, and some miss out on benefits even when they do file.

Getting individuals to change their behavior can be hard; changing long-standing institutional practices can be even harder. However, in a variety of ways, behaviorally informed approaches are starting to have positive effects in Canadian communities and among policymakers.

NOTES

1 Robson, J., & Schwartz, S. (2019, 4 December). Hidden inequalities. *Maclean's Magazine.*
2 Brooks, N., & Doob, A. (1990). Tax evasion: Searching for a theory of compliant behaviour. In M. Friedland (Ed.), *Securing compliance: Seven case studies*, 129–73. Toronto: University of Toronto Press.
3 Andreoni, J., Errard, B., & Feinsten, J. (1998). Tax compliance. *Journal of Economic Literature, 36*(2): 818–60; and Kleven, H., Knudsen, M., Kreiner, C., Pedersen, S., & Saez, E. (2010). Unwilling or unable to cheat? Evidence from a randomized tax audit experiment in Denmark. Working paper 15769. *National Bureau of Economic Research.*
4 Robson, J., & Schwartz, S. (2020). Who doesn't file a tax return?: A portrait of non-filers. *Canadian Public Policy.* doi:10.3138/cpp.2019-063
5 Moffitt, R. (1983). An economic model of welfare stigma. *American Economic Review, 73*(5): 1023–35.
6 Currie, J. (2004). The take-up of social benefits. Working paper 10488. *National Bureau of Economic Research*; and Varatharasan, N., Raphael, P., & Umme-Jihad, A. (2019). Tax time insights: Experiences of people living on low income in Canada. Toronto: Prosper Canada.
7 Mason, G. (2018, 9 August). It was time to walk away from Ontario's flawed basic income project. *The Conversation.* https://theconversation. com/it-was-time-to-walk-away-from-ontarios-flawed-basic-income -project-101217.
8 Anzelone, C., Yu, J., & Subedi, P. (2018). Using behavioral insights to increase participation in social services programs: A case study. OPRE Report 2018-73. Washington, DC: Office of Planning, Research, and Evaluation, Administration for Children and Families, U.S. Department of Health and Human Services.
9 Kahneman, D., Knetsch, J., & Thaler, R. (1991). The endowment effect, loss aversion and status quo bias. *Journal of Economic Perspectives, 5*(1), 193–206.
10 University of Manitoba, Rady Faculty of Health Sciences. (2018). Get your benefits. Retrieved from http://umanitoba.ca/faculties/health_sciences /medicine/units/chs/benefits/.

11 Prosper Canada. (2016). Benefits screening tool project: Phase 1 report. Toronto: Prosper Canada.

12 Arsenault, A. (2019, 7 February). Get your piece of the money pie. Presentation at Research Symposium on Overcoming Barriers to Tax Filing for People with Low Incomes, hosted by Prosper Canada and Intuit, Ottawa. Retrieved from https://learninghub.prospercanada.org /knowledge/research-symposium-overcoming-barriers-to-tax-filing/.

13 Economic and Social Inclusion Corporation. (2018). Overcoming poverty together: 2014–2019 progress report. Fredericton: Government of New Brunswick.

14 Author's calculation based on information in the ESIC report cited at note 14.

15 Tejeda, G. (2019, 7 February). Innovative use of technology for VITA. Presentation at Research Symposium on Overcoming Barriers to Tax Filing for People with Low Incomes, hosted by Prosper Canada and Intuit, Ottawa. Retrieved from https://learninghub.prospercanada.org /knowledge/research-symposium-overcoming-barriers-to-tax-filing/.

16 Ibid.

17 Canada Revenue Agency. (2018). Departmental results report: 2017–2018, 43. Ottawa: Government of Canada.

18 Author's calculations based on information in the CRA report cited at note 19.

19 Canada Revenue Agency. (2019). Canada workers benefit. Retrieved from https://www.canada.ca/en/revenue-agency/programs/about-canada -revenue-agency-cra/federal-government-budgets/budget-2018-equality -growth-strong-middle-class/canada-workers-benefit.html.

20 Ibid. See also Finance Canada. (2016). Report on tax expenditures and evaluations. Ottawa: Government of Canada.

21 Some important advances have also been made toward automatically assessing low-income seniors and enrolling them in the Guaranteed Income Supplement program when they complete an application for the quasi-universal Old Age Security benefit.

CHAPTER THIRTEEN

Online Privacy

Melanie Kim, Kim Ly, and Dilip Soman

In recent years, a number of high-profile cases involving the violation of online customer privacy have raised public alarm. For example, hotel group Marriott made headlines in 2018 when a massive theft of its guest database exposed the personal information of up to 500 million customers.[1] In 2012, Target was in the spotlight for a newsworthy privacy violation: the company's data-driven algorithm had correctly identified a customer's pregnancy and proceeded to send the teenage girl coupons for baby gear – even before her father knew about the pregnancy.[2]

Perhaps the most controversial scandal surrounds social-media giant Facebook, which was fined an unprecedented $5 billion penalty in 2019 for mishandling users' personal information.[3] Facebook had allowed harvesting of vast numbers of user profiles – largely without users' knowledge – which were then sold to a political-analysis firm that used the information to micro-target voters ahead of the 2016 US presidential election.[4]

Why are we seeing such an increase in high-profile violations? We believe that two forces have fueled this trend.

First, companies now have greater incentives to collect and share data about their customers. Since a growing amount of customer activity – from information search to browsing to actual transactions – now occurs online, it is both easy and inexpensive to collect and build large customer-behavior datasets.

Having all these data at its fingertips enables a company to build rich customer profiles, and this in turn enables it to narrowly target its marketing to specific customers. As the Target example highlights, almost every major retailer now has a "predictive analytics" department that uses data to understand customers' shopping and personal habits. For the streaming service Netflix, its recommendation algorithm drives more than 80 percent of user activity on the platform.[5] Other companies known as data brokers have even built entire business models around buying, curating, and selling customer data to third parties.[6] The bottom line is, the more information a company can get about you, the greater the revenue potential.

The second force behind the increase in privacy violations is that, from a consumer perspective, the risks of sharing personal information online have increased exponentially – but this is not widely recognized by consumers. The ease with which companies can collect and share consumers' personal data – coupled with technological advances that improve the ability to analyze and draw deep insights – increases the potential for misuse that includes identity fraud, manipulation, and social and economic discrimination. For instance, marketers may use ethnicity information to keep attractive offers out of reach of the least-profitable and most-costly-to-serve population segments;[7] or, knowing that particular demographics are likely to use social media more effectively than others, businesses may reward them with better service and shorter wait times.[8] And, as illustrated in the Facebook scandal, the consequences of misuse are far-reaching in ways we could not have imagined even a few years ago.

Despite the growing risks, it is not clear that consumers typically think about the sharing of data online as risky. From posting suggestive photos on social networking sites, to navigating streets with geotracking systems turned on, to installing smart devices throughout their homes, consumers appear to have become increasingly disposed to share data with companies. We believe that a large percentage of online consumers do not even think about the risks of sharing information, and the ones who do probably do not have the right information to be able to make an accurate assessment of risk levels.

In this chapter, we take a look at the challenge of online privacy from a behavioral lens. While the broader societal challenge is to safeguard consumer interests in a rapidly evolving digital environment, we believe that a key element of this challenge is the individual – and lies in the millions of decisions consumers are making each and every day.

We start by unpacking the assumptions about how consumers should make privacy-related decisions, and how they actually do it. We then draw on insights from behavioral sciences to explain behavioral puzzles in privacy decisions. For instance, why is it that even the most deeply privacy-concerned individuals readily trade off sensitive information online for trivial rewards, like the chance to win a prize? We examine these behaviors in the current context of privacy decision making online.

Finally, we identify ways to help consumers make more informed and safer choices online. In the discussion that follows, managers in business and policy will learn to think differently about how to help consumers manage their online privacy. In particular, by acknowledging the not-entirely-rational tendencies of their end-users, managers can contribute to designing the appropriate decision-making environment for them.

A BEHAVIORAL LENS ON ONLINE PRIVACY

As they go about their online activities, consumers are faced with an increasing number of privacy decisions – from configuring visibility on social-media platforms, to deciding whether to connect to public Wi-Fi hotspots, to determining whether to trust an app or a website. Millions of privacy-related decisions are made by consumers on a daily basis.

From a behavioral-sciences perspective, we believe that the root of the online privacy challenge is, at least partly, a decision-making problem on the part of consumers. To appreciate the decision-making hurdles consumers face, we examine what is required in order to make a fully informed privacy decision.

To make a fully informed decision about what information should be shared online on any given occasion, the fully rational consumer needs to go through three important decision-making steps. First, they need to employ the appropriate mental model to think about "information sharing" itself as a risky prospect – similar to the risks of contracting disease on exposure to contaminated food, the risk of a side-effect after consuming medication, or the risk of losing money when trading in risky assets.

Second, they need to use available information to quantify the risk and identify the possible outcomes. Information in disclosures and privacy policies exists that would allow them to identify harmful outcomes. Finally, consumers would need to integrate the "identified risk level" with the "outcome information" to arrive at a judgment as to whether the benefits of sharing their information exceed the potential harm.

Unfortunately, as shown by decades of research in the behavioral sciences, most humans lack both the cognitive apparatus and the motivation to go through these three steps. A further complication is that consumers display highly inconsistent attitudes and behaviors in the domain of online privacy. This is commonly referred to as the "privacy paradox," the phenomenon whereby people say they care a lot about privacy yet their behavior online indicates the complete opposite.[9] Many who express shock and outrage at data breaches – or even changes to Facebook's privacy policy – are the very same people who seemingly recklessly posted details of their vacations, purchases, and geographic locations on various social-media sites.

We believe the field of behavioral sciences can shed some light on everyday privacy behaviors. Following are five explanations for why we observe these dramatic inconsistencies.

Consumers Are Limited Processors of Information

While it might be tempting to suggest that providing more information to consumers will help them evaluate costs and benefits and make better decisions, evidence from behavioral sciences indicates otherwise. Most consumers make decisions using heuristics, or mental shortcuts, rather than processing information fully, and as a result, they are often susceptible to suboptimal decisions.[10] For instance, the mere presence of privacy policies on websites can lead consumers to believe that websites protect their information.[11] Or, they may rely on contextual cues, such as the look-and-feel of a website or the manner in which personal information is solicited, to gauge the appropriate level of privacy concern and determine their level of divulgence.[12]

Consequently, the details of what happens to one's personal information in the cloud – the specific ways it is being sold, traded, shared, and used – is a mystery to most people. For instance, individuals who send a vial of saliva to 23andme know they're sharing their DNA with a genomics company, but they may not realize that it will be resold to pharmaceutical companies.[13] And lengthy privacy-disclosure statements on websites written in legal jargon are not the answer; we are all too familiar with – and likely guilty of – the action of hastily scrolling through a detailed disclosure to click the "I agree" button and proceed with a desired download or purchase.

Cognitive Laziness Is a Hallmark of Human Behavior

One hallmark of human behavior is cognitive laziness or inertia. Consequently, consumers may avoid the effort involved in actively seeking alternatives to address their privacy concerns. In study after study, people prefer to stay with the default option, whatever it might be – and in the context of online privacy, the default orientation is most likely "being tracked" and "surrendering data." In a study of online social networks, Carnegie Mellon professor Alessandro Acquisti and researcher Ralph Gross found that the vast majority of users had not changed their default privacy settings.[14]

While online sites may have dozens of privacy settings that are supposedly meant to give users control over every aspect of their experience, the cognitive effort needed to evaluate trade-offs leads most people to stick with the status quo. And despite the recent announcement from Google that it will let users automatically delete their history after three or eighteen months, the burden is still on the users to know the option exists, navigate through the settings, and make the changes.[15] Furthermore, the "experience effect" may lead consumers to develop an actual preference for the default option, after spending some time enjoying the convenience it offers.[16]

It Is Difficult for Consumers to Anticipate the Ways in Which Their Information Might Be Made Vulnerable

Perhaps one of the biggest challenges to an accurate assessment of risk on the part of the consumer arises from the dynamic nature of the online environment caused by rapid technological advances. A few years ago, the ability to control one's refrigerator through a mobile device from another country using the Internet would have been unimaginable; yet today, it is a reality. Similarly, the idea of self-driving cars would have seemed like science fiction; yet testing programs for self-driving cars are currently underway, thanks to developments in artificial intelligence and other technologies.[17]

As technologies and capabilities change, data-sharing practices that were once considered safe might not be safe anymore. In the past, Facebook users could post pictures and avoid being identified in those pictures by not "tagging" themselves. But with developments in facial-recognition technology, it is possible for social media websites to recognize your face in photographs posted online, even when you are not tagged in them.[18] This serves as a warning for those who sometimes post questionable – but untagged – photos of themselves. Insofar as consumers have difficulty anticipating changes in the environment, their vulnerabilities will increase as technological advances expand the boundaries of potential privacy risks.

Consumers Struggle with Abstract Concepts like Privacy

Consumers' behaviors are most strongly affected by concrete and certain outcomes.[19] Privacy, on the other hand, is an abstract concept, where the costs of giving up privacy are often amorphous. Like, how much privacy have you lost if someone gains access to your Amazon purchase history? Or if your private conversations have been overheard? Moreover, the risks associated with any one instance of surrendering data are hard to assess individually, since it is the collective pattern emerging from one's digital trail that has meaning, and that can make one vulnerable to significant harm.

Research in behavioral sciences shows that when something is intangible and hard to quantify – like the potential risks related to privacy – decisions are disproportionately influenced by seemingly irrelevant variables in the context.[20] In recent research, Harvard professor Leslie John and Carnegie Mellon professors Alessandro Acquisti and George Loewenstein showed that the value that consumers assign to privacy – and indeed, whether privacy is a relevant concern for them at all – is highly dependent upon the context in which the value is elicited.[21] Results showed that individuals value privacy more when they stand to lose it (i.e., when asked how much they would *accept* to disclose otherwise private information) compared to when they stand to gain it (i.e., when asked how much they would *pay* to protect otherwise public information). This context dependence was significantly greater for privacy than it was for other products and services, suggesting that consumers lack an internal "meter" for valuing privacy.

The Digital Context Is Designed in a Way That Motivates People to Share Data

With the fast and instant nature of online transactions, consumers are increasingly displaying impulsive behavior online – without necessarily considering privacy implications. Many websites are laden with features that seem designed to motivate such behavior, including special promotions, discounts, and chances to win prizes in exchange for personal information.

Another feature of the digital context is that consumers have instant access to the preferences and behaviors of others. It has been widely demonstrated that consumers care about social norms, and often infer those norms by observing what other people are doing.[22] To the extent that consumers can easily observe the personal information other people are sharing, we can expect them to look to peers' choices to inform their own sharing behavior. This tendency can be problematic in the domain of privacy decision making, however, where social-media sites create the impression that sharing is the norm, while the consequences of over-sharing are hidden.[23]

Finally, we argue that the existing tools and policies meant to help end-users make informed privacy decisions online are designed more for "econs" than for "humans." Take privacy-disclosure statements for instance. If everyone followed the decision-making steps of fully rational consumers – people who read disclosure statements and understand the trade-offs they are making by disclosing information online – it is likely that some would have raised concerns early on about questionable practices by companies, and even shown hesitation in participating in aspects of the digital market. But in the world of "humans," that doesn't happen, because nobody reads disclosure statements.

Taken together, these findings provide insights into why consumers make inconsistent and seemingly illogical decisions with respect to their online privacy. A central tenet of behavioral sciences is that behavior is heavily influenced by the context – that the little things in the environment become variables that influence behavior in systematic ways.[24] While a traditional economist may look to consumers' revealed preferences to conclude that our society doesn't place much value on privacy, we instead highlight the importance of examining the choice architecture – the features of the choice environment – to understand why we observe the behaviors we do.

Any choice architecture, whether it was intentionally designed to affect users' behavior or not, will impact how users interact with a system. If we, as a system, start thinking about end-users as humans rather than fully rational agents, then we can focus on creating a digital environment that is more human-friendly, with tools and controls designed with human tendencies in mind. In this new approach, we should expect most consumers not to read lengthy disclosure statements, to stick with the default privacy setting, to display impulsive behaviors, and so on.

In the next section, we draw from these insights to inform interventions designed to help consumers better assess risks and make safer choices.

BEHAVIORALLY INFORMED APPROACHES TO HELP MANAGE ONLINE PRIVACY

Traditional interventions in public policy have taken the form of regulations or incentives. For example, a regulatory body can enforce a law banning the processing of customer data without consent and impose a large penalty on companies that do not comply; and the government can provide monetary incentives for companies to invest in more secure technology to safeguard customer data. Another approach – and the one we recommend – is to recognize the limitations of the human mind and design behaviorally informed solutions that can lead to better choices.

Many of the human tendencies described herein can be thought of as "cognitive gaps," and a simple way to think about these gaps is to treat them like physical deficiencies – say, for instance, a broken ankle. In such a scenario, once corrective surgery has been performed, two sets of things need to be done: first, you must provide the now handicapped individual with a mobility device and have them work with a physiotherapist to strengthen the injured area; and second, you must make sure the patient is in a safe environment to minimize further injuries.

These same concepts can be applied to "cognitively handicapped" consumers who are over-sharing personal data online with minimal thinking. First, we can equip them to better assess the risks of sharing data online, and second, we can make the environment safer, so that they don't get badly "hurt" when they stumble. We have also developed a third set of solutions that addresses the role of businesses from a behavioral perspective (see figure 13.1). Below we review each solution set in turn.

Solution 1: Equip the Consumer

The first step in equipping consumers to better assess risks is to sensitize them to the notion that information shared online constitutes a potential risk. This could take the form of educational programs on privacy literacy that include awareness campaigns and curricula in schools and colleges. Once that goal has been achieved,

Figure 13.1 Three sets of behaviorally informed solutions

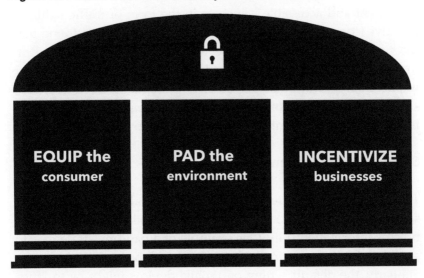

the appropriate use of disclosure can further educate the consumer about the level of risk.

The food industry, for example, has done a good job of sensitizing consumers to risk. Health risks are similar to privacy risks in that they are difficult to quantify, hard to assess individually, and delayed in time. A particular feature of the food industry's success is nutrition labelling. In part to address low literacy rates, nutrition labelling was designed to simplify information as much as possible for consumers and provide a common terminology for talking about nutrition and health risks.[25] The use of standardized labels across food items enables consumers to quickly find what information they are looking for on any label and easily compare products. A similarly standardized privacy label could serve as a useful tool to help consumers assess and compare risks in the digital space. (See chapter 15 for a discussion of the role of guidelines and tools in helping consumers navigate decisions in complex information environments.)

Importantly, empirical studies have shown that the "how" and "when" matter a lot for the effectiveness of privacy labels or other forms of disclosure. A recent laboratory experiment showed that consumers are willing to pay a premium to purchase from privacy protective websites, but only when privacy information is made prominent and accessible – such as in the form of traffic lights or intuitive icons denoting a privacy meter.[26] Other studies found that the timing of the privacy notice was important; privacy indicators that were in place before users visited a website had a greater impact than indicators displayed after users had arrived at a website.[27] These are all important areas for consideration when developing and testing interventions designed to equip the consumer.

Solution 2: Pad the Environment

This approach simply refers to actions that make the environment safe for consumers who might not have the ability or motivation to process information fully. One example of a padding strategy is to set the defaults on online websites to the highest level of privacy. Similarly, the default setting on mobile devices might be to "turn location devices off." Given consumers' tendency to stick with the default, it is imperative for system designers to consider users' cognitive gaps and ensure that defaults align with users' privacy preferences and expectations. A second, simpler tactic might include the use of reminders or decision points to nudge users about the potential risk associated with sharing information online.

Another way to pad the environment is to make it easier for consumers to control privacy settings and opt out of unwanted default settings. Recognizing the substantial cognitive effort required by consumers to make choices on the dozens of dimensions of privacy, we propose an avatar-based approach. In this approach, the consumer can identify an avatar – a role model or a similar other – retrieve their choices, and use those choices as an anchor and adjust for personal circumstances. For instance, rather than wading through each decision in one's privacy settings, consumers can have the system generate a list of choices that others like themselves (e.g., people with similar level of online activity and number of social-media accounts) have made, and use these as a starting point for their own decisions. With recent findings that people worldwide are now increasingly reliant on "a person like me" for advice,[28] this approach is promising in that it is familiar, trustworthy, and relatively easy to act on.

Solution 3: Incentivize Businesses Suitably

Every business operating on the cloud needs to think about managing customer privacy. The series of high-profile scandals in recent years has put a spotlight on irresponsible business practices, from underinvesting in privacy and security protections to misrepresenting the use made of customer data. In our opinion, it is important to focus privacy efforts not just on consumers but also on the providers of online content.

As many online companies have strong interests in collecting and sharing customer data, it has not been easy to incentivize them to invest appropriately in privacy. Like individuals, businesses also suffer from short-sightedness: investing in privacy-protective technologies costs money now, whereas the consequences of potentially losing customer trust are delayed and probabilistic.[29] Furthermore, the immediate benefits of gaining access to customer data for targeted marketing and perhaps sale to third parties appear too good to forgo.

Yet, with each new data breach on the news, the false sense of security – or the optimism that our *own* data are safe – is being challenged. In our view, this creates an opportunity for businesses to get ahead by getting privacy right. For example, firms could offer products or services that *explicitly* make consumer privacy a central part of their value proposition. If consumers start recognizing the importance of privacy and have the ability to measure the privacy quality of a given website or company, there would be increased demand for higher levels of security, which in turn might make privacy a central value proposition for all online businesses.

How might businesses be nudged into improving consumer privacy? Restaurant-hygiene grade cards are a good example of how this could work. When Los Angeles County introduced these grade cards, to be displayed in restaurant windows, its health-inspection scores increased, consumers became more sensitive to restaurant hygiene, and the number of hospitalizations due to food-borne illnesses dropped by 13 percent.[30] These grade cards, which provided consumers with a simple way of evaluating and comparing a complex variable like hygiene, were successful in convincing restaurants to incorporate hygiene as an important value proposition in their business. Likewise, we believe that the use of "privacy badges" or a rating system that evaluates the privacy policies of a given business would nudge businesses into creating a safer environment for their customers.

So far, we have discussed how choice-architecture interventions can address the negative effects of decision-making hurdles. The recommendations made in this section aim to incorporate our understanding of behavioral science to help managers in business and policy better assist consumers in navigating the complex online space. To result in better privacy outcomes, privacy initiatives must be designed for real humans – those who are limited processors of information, susceptible to cognitive biases, and prone to displaying impulsive behavior online.

WHAT'S NEXT?

While the data revolution has opened up countless opportunities for global businesses, it has also created new challenges for consumers. As we indicate here, at the heart of the problem are the actions of consumers themselves in sharing too much of their private information online, thereby exposing themselves to harm.

Needless to say, traditional approaches to safeguarding online customer privacy face several challenges. Online businesses have strong financial interests in amassing customer data and making the data easily accessible; hence, they are not motivated to change their practices unless consumers demand it or it is required by law. As discussed earlier, however, because of the decision-making hurdles they face, consumers have not been rewarding firms for getting it right, nor have they been properly punishing firms for getting it wrong. And when it comes to regulatory approaches, these technological innovations are largely taking place beyond the purview of governments. The rate of innovation is outpacing governments' ability to keep abreast of the latest developments and their potential societal impacts. For example, both Amazon and Google have filed patent applications for "voice sniffer algorithms" that could analyze conversations heard by their smart speakers.[31] Policy to manage these effects will inevitably be lagging, and the global reach of many emerging technologies and their impacts will add another layer of complexity for regulators. What that means is that consumers will be exposed to greater potential privacy harm, long before appropriate regulation is introduced.

It would be easy to passively accept that, in our interconnected age, "privacy is dead." However, it doesn't have to be that way. Given that consumers possess cognitive handicaps, the responsibility for ensuring public welfare lies equally with businesses and government agencies. And that begins with understanding how consumers think about their privacy online – which isn't entirely rationally. Research in behavioral sciences has demonstrated how small variables in the context – like the timing of disclosure or the manner in which privacy preferences are elicited – significantly influence decision making. If managers in business and policy started considering end-users as human, and designed the digital environment for humans, then we could expect to see privacy behaviors that are more in line with human preferences. Moreover, we believe that if consumer groups work with governments and businesses to build up the three pillars described herein – equipping consumers, padding the environment, and making privacy a core value of business – the data revolution can deliver on all of its promises without compromising the safety of the consumers who are enabling it.

NOTES

1 O'Flaherty, K. (2019, 9 July). Marriott faces $123 million fine for 2018 mega-breach. *Forbes*. Retrieved from https://www.forbes.com/sites/kateoflahertyuk/2019/07/09/marriott-faces-gdpr-fine-of-123-million/#e406ca245253.

2 Duhigg, C. (2012, 16 February). How companies learn your secrets. *The New York Times Magazine*. Retrieved from https://www.nytimes.com/2012/02/19/magazine/shoppinghabits.html?_r=0.

3 Kang, C. (2019, 12 July). F.T.C. approves Facebook fine of about $5 billion. *The New York Times*. Retrieved from https://www.nytimes.com/2019/07/12/technology/facebook-ftc-fine.html.

4 Naughton, J. (2019, 17 March). How Cambridge Analytica sparked the great privacy awakening. *Wired*. Retrieved from https://www.wired.com /story/cambridge-analytica-facebook-privacy-awakening/.

5 Plummer, L. (2017, 22 August). This is how Netflix's top-secret recommendation system works. *Wired*. Retrieved from https://www .wired.co.uk/article/how-do-netflixs-algorithms-work-machine-learning -helps-to-predict-what-viewers-will-like.

6 Melendez, S., & Pasternack, A. (2018, 2 March). Here are the data brokers quietly buying and selling your personal information. *Fast Company*. Retrieved from https://www.fastcompany.com/90310803/here-are-the -data-brokers-quietly-buying-and-selling-your-personal-information.

7 Noyes, K. (2015, 15 January). Will big data help end discrimination – or make it worse? *Fortune*. Retrieved from https://fortune.com/2015/01/15 /will-bigdata-help-end-discrimination-or-make-it-worse/.

8 Schrage, M. (2014, 29 January). Big data's dangerous new era of discrimination. *Harvard Business Review*. Retrieved from https://hbr .org/2014/01/big-datas-dangerous-new-era-ofdiscrimination/.

9 Norberg, P.A., Horne, D.R., & Horne, D.A. (2007). The privacy paradox: Personal information disclosure intentions versus behaviors. *Journal of Consumer Affaris, 41*(1), 100–26.

10 Kahneman, D. (2011). *Thinking, fast and slow*. London: Penguin Books Ltd.

11 Turow, J., Feldman, L., & Meltzer, K. (2005). Open to exploitation: American shoppers online and offline. *A Report from the Annenberg Public Policy Center of the University of Pennsylvania*. Retrieved from http:// repository.upenn.edu/asc_papers/35.

12 John, L.K., Acquisti, A., & Loewenstein, G. (2009). Strangers on a plane: Context dependent willingness to divulge personal information. *Journal of Consumer Research, 37*, 858–73.

13 Chin, C. (2018). 23andMe's pharma deals have been the plan all along. *Wired*. Retrieved from https://www.wired.com/story/23andme -glaxosmithkline-pharma-deal/.

14 Gross, R., & Acquisti, A. (2005). Information revelation and privacy in online social networks (The Facebook Case). ACM Workshop on Privacy in the Electronic Society, Virginia. Retrieved from https://www.heinz.cmu .edu/~acquisti/papers/privacy-facebook-gross-acquisti.pdf.

15 Aten, J. (2019, 22 May). 4 things Facebook and Google don't want you know about privacy, and what you should do. *Inc.* Retrieved from https:// www.inc.com/jason-aten/4-things-facebook-google-dont-want-you -know-about-privacy-what-you-should-do.html.

16 Kahneman, D., Knetsch, J., & Thaler, R.H. (1991). The endowment effect, loss aversion, and status quo bias. *The Journal of Economic Perspectives, 5*(1), 193–206.

17 Spence, R. (2019, 11 July). Everything you need to know about the future of self-driving cars. *Maclean's*. Retrieved from https://www.macleans.ca /society/technology/the-future-of-self-driving-cars/.

18 Dean, J. (2015, 24 June). Facebook can identify its faceless users. *The Times.* Retrieved from http://www.thetimes.co.uk/tto/technology/internet/article4478251.ece.

19 Nisbett, R.E., & Ross, L. (1980). *Human inference: Strategies and shortcomings of social judgment.* Englewood Cliffs, NJ: Prentice-Hall.

20 Acquisti, A., Brandimarte, L., & Loewenstein, G. (2015). Privacy and human behavior in the age of information. *Science, 347*(6221), 509–14.

21 Acquisti, A., John, L.K., & Loewenstein, G. (2013). What is privacy worth? *Journal of Legal Studies, 42*(2), 249–74.

22 Asch, S.E. (1956). Studies of independence and conformity: I. A minority of one against a unanimous majority. *Psychological Monographs: General and Applied, 70*(9), 1–70.

23 John, L.K. (2015). The consumer psychology of online privacy: Insights and opportunities from behavioral decision theory. In M. Norton, D. Rucker, & C. Lamberton (Eds.), *The Cambridge Handbook of Consumer Psychology.* Cambridge Handbooks in Psychology, 619–46. Cambridge: Cambridge University Press. doi:10.1017/CBO9781107706552.023.

24 Tversky, A., & Simonson, I. (1993). Context-dependent preferences. *Management Science, 39*(10), 1179–89.

25 Kelley, P.G., Bresee, J., Cranor, L.F., & Reeder, R.W. (2009). A "nutrition label" for privacy. In *Proceedings of the 5th Symposium on Usable Privacy and Security (SOUPS'09).* ACM, New York, Article 4, 1–12. doi: 10.1145/1572532.1572538.

26 Tsai, J.Y., Egelman, S., Cranor, L.F., & Acquisti, A. (2011). The effect of online privacy information on purchasing behavior: An experimental study. *Information Systems Research, 22*(2), 254– 68.

27 Egelman, S., Tsai, J., Cranor, L.F., & Acquisti, A. (2009). Timing is everything?: The effects of timing and placement of online privacy indicators. In *Proceedings of the 27th International Conference on Human Factors in Computing Systems (CHI'09).* ACM, New York, 319–28.

28 Bush, M. (2016). 2016 Edelman Trust barometer finds global trust inequality is growing. *Edelman.* Retrieved from https://www.edelman.com/news/2016-edelman-trust-barometer-release/.

29 Harvard Business Review Staff. (2014, November). With big data comes big responsibility. *Harvard Business Review.* Retrieved from https://hbr.org/2014/11/with-big-data-comes-big-responsibility.

30 Simon, P.A., Leslie, P., Run, G., Jin, G.Z., Reporter, R., Aguirre, A., & Fielding, J.E. (2005). Impact of restaurant hygiene grade cards on foodborne-disease hospitalizations in Los Angeles County. *Journal of Environmental Health, 67,* 32–6.

31 Miller, A. (2018, 3 April). Amazon patent reveals "voice sniffer algorithm" that could analyze conversations. *ABC News.* Retrieved from https://abcnews.go.com/Business/amazon-patent-reveals-voice-sniffer-algorithm-analyze-conversations/story?id=54175793.

CHAPTER FOURTEEN

Behavioral Science for International Development

Abigail Dalton, Varun Gauri, and Renos Vakis

Behavioral-science enthusiasts know the power of the field for improving how policies and programs are designed, implemented, and received; that by taking into account the "predictable irrationality" – as Dan Ariely would say – of human behavior, we can improve how governments function, how services are delivered, and the well-being of citizens.[1] People are better off when we redesign policy architecture to encourage better decision making and reduce biases. Globally, policymakers are increasingly turning to the behavioral sciences to tackle intractable policy challenges, including the need to increase student learning, raise savings rates, promote energy and resource conservation, increase productivity, improve sanitation practices, strengthen institutions, and reduce corruption. For those who work in international development, including staff at the World Bank, the potential for behavioral science to help solve intractable policy challenges is enormous.

Behaviorally informed policy emphasizes the importance of context for decision making and behavior. It examines a wide set of influences, paying attention to the social, psychological, and economic factors that affect what people think and do. It addresses details in bureaucracies, technologies, and service delivery that are often overlooked in standard policy design but that dramatically influence the effectiveness of development programs and projects, especially in low-income contexts. Behaviorally informed policy can provide creative solutions to difficult challenges, often at low cost. Finally, it helps policymakers themselves avoid some of the decision traps and biases that affect all individuals.

Behavioral-science applications to policy had impressive early successes with simple tweaks that resulted in big payoffs for governments. Think of the Behavioural Insights Team, whose early tax work – increasing compliance by leveraging social norms in communications from Her Majesty's Revenue and Customs – was an elegant exercise in showing the power of behavioral science for easy tweaking and significant monetary returns. How do we manage this in settings where the infrastructure of governments and policies is unpredictable, under-resourced, or occupied with overwhelming structural challenges?

In international-development settings, the challenges faced by behavioral scientists can be daunting. Behavioral-science teams based in single countries – whether at the federal or the local level – face challenges around implementation and buy-in. But what's a practitioner to do when faced with dozens of governments, each dealing with a unique set of challenges as wide ranging as a lack of infrastructure for data collection or communication, political instability and quickly changing governments, scarcity of resources (of both time and money), and a daunting list of urgent needs to ensure a safe society? The issues are even greater when dealing with countries that are experiencing or have recently been through conflict. The innovative techniques that behavioral and social scientists have applied – including disseminating new teaching techniques, improving delivery through technology, and more – remain challenging in settings where technologies are incipient, bureaucracies are decentralized or in flux, and capacity is limited.[2] In such situations, the standard infrastructure, rules, and bureaucratic norms that behavioral scientists rely on to deliver choice-architecture interventions are not in place, adding an extra layer of complexity in designing behavioral solutions.

BEHAVIORAL SCIENCE AT THE WORLD BANK

The World Bank has been mired in these challenges since its founding in 1944. Established with the goal of helping countries that had been devastated by World War II to rebuild, the bank's mandate has evolved over time to offer not only monetary loans to countries but also knowledge and advice.[3] As the bank has emerged as a knowledge hub, it has begun incorporating the innovative and effective tools of its day – including behavioral science. Staff at the bank have been incorporating behavioral science – in the form of designing projects that incorporate an understanding of how program design might affect human behavior – since the focus on anthropology appeared at the bank in the 1990s. Indeed, development economists had been applying the lessons of behavioral science to field contexts for some time (including the recently Nobel-awarded work of Abhijit Banerjee and Esther Duflo). However, the publication of the *2015 World Development Report* (WDR) – one of the bank's annual flagship reports – on *Mind, Society, and Behavior*, solidified the bank's commitment to incorporating behavioral science into its operations. As then-president Jim Young Kim wrote in the report's foreword, the report's message was that, "when it comes to understanding and changing human behavior, we can do better. Many development economists and practitioners believe that the 'irrational' elements of human decision making are inscrutable or that they cancel each other out when large numbers of people interact, as in markets. Yet, we now know this is not the case. Recent research has advanced our understanding of the psychological, social, and cultural influences on decision-making and human behavior and has demonstrated that they have a significant impact on development outcomes."[4]

The WDR posited three principles of human decision making:

1. **People think automatically**. Much of our thinking is automatic and based on what comes to mind effortlessly. Deliberative thinking, in which we weigh the value of all available choices, is less common. We use mental shortcuts much of the time. Thus, minor changes in the immediate context in which decisions are made can have disproportionate effects on behavior. This means

that policies are often more effective when they make it easy to enroll in programs, for example, by making good options the default.

2. **People think socially**. Human beings are deeply social. We like to cooperate – as long as others are doing their fair share. We tend to follow descriptive and proscriptive norms. We tend to be most persuaded by information when it comes from a trusted social contact. Institutions and interventions can be designed to support cooperative behavior. Social networks and social norms can make policies and interventions more effective.

3. **People think with mental models**. When people think, they generally do not invent concepts. Instead, they use mental models drawn from their societies and their shared histories. Societies provide people with multiple and often conflicting mental models; which one is invoked depends on contextual cues. Policies and interventions to activate empowering mental models can make people more productive and effective at achieving their goals.[5]

By considering new policy and program design with these three things in mind, the report suggested, development practitioners and the governments with which they partner can dramatically improve services and outcomes for beneficiaries. Not only that, but when applied to the policymakers themselves – recognizing that even those individuals who are creating and administering these policies, whether in governments, at the World Bank, or elsewhere, are subject to making biased and predictable errors – a behavioral approach can reduce biases and create a more equitable, effective society, no matter what the context or region.

EMBEDDING BEHAVIORAL SCIENCE AT THE WORLD BANK

The World Bank's Mind, Behavior, and Development Unit (eMBeD) was formed from teams in Development Economics Vice-Presidency (DEC) and the Poverty and Equity Global Practice in 2017 to operationalize the learnings and outcomes from the WDR with bank projects and teams. The unit does not have the only staff members at the bank engaged in applying behavioral science for policy – across the bank, there are numerous entities also applying behavioral science to projects, including the Africa Gender Innovation Lab (and other regional Gender Innovation Labs), Development Impact Evaluation (DIME) in DEC, and many Global Practices including Education, Social Protection and Jobs, Energy, Governance, and the Independent Evaluation Group (IEG). However, eMBeD aims to collaborate across the bank, and to highlight the work being done by other units and teams. The eMBeD unit also acts as the central point for developing new behaviorally informed solutions in frontier topics and areas, and for building behavioral capacity at the bank through workshops, training, public events, and more.

Figure 14.1 shows an overview of eMBeD's approach. It begins with careful diagnostics with bank and partner countries. People can be quick to make assumptions about the problem or even solutions early on, and by using desk research, fieldwork, and qualitative and quantitative research to identify behavioral bottlenecks, we ensure that assumptions are validated or updated. A core part of eMBeD's process is to start with comprehensive diagnostics based on literature reviews of existing programming, as well as the collection of original qualitative and quantitative data. Because context is so important – in general, but particularly in development settings – we end up spending a lot of time on diagnostics. This process has also helped our partners – from bank staff to government counterparts – better understand the behavioral bottlenecks inherent in various systems and processes. After all, what may make sense on paper may prove challenging for a beneficiary in practice, and looking in depth at the journey of our target beneficiaries gives everyone involved a better understanding of how to develop effective interventions.

Figure 14.2 is an example from Haiti of what may come up during the diagnostic phase. It summarizes findings of the journey of a Haitian during a natural disaster. With this, we can help our counterparts understand the various steps each beneficiary encounters, and where we can potentially work to change behaviors. After this, eMBeD identifies the key bottlenecks to behavior change and develops specific,

Figure 14.1 eMBeD's approach to behaviorally informed policy

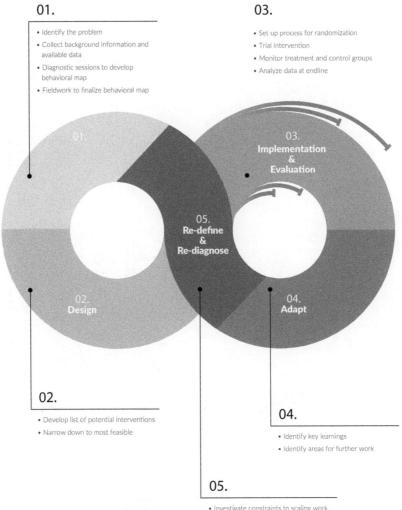

01.
• Identify the problem
• Collect background information and available data
• Diagnostic sessions to develop behavioral map
• Fieldwork to finalize behavioral map

03.
• Set up process for randomization
• Trial intervention
• Monitor treatment and control groups
• Analyze data at endline

02.
• Develop list of potential interventions
• Narrow down to most feasible

04.
• Identify key learnings
• Identify areas for further work

05.
• Investigate constraints to scaling work
• Identify furtherbehavioral challenges

01.

03.
Implementation
&
Evaluation

05.
Re-define
&
Re-diagnose

02.
Design

04.
Adapt

Source: Courtesy of Lorena Guedes.

feasible, and essential behavior changes. Throughout, we work closely with project partners. We learn from existing programming (including programming that integrates behavioral design), review existing literature, and connect with colleagues working globally to

Figure 14.2 Nudging to save lives

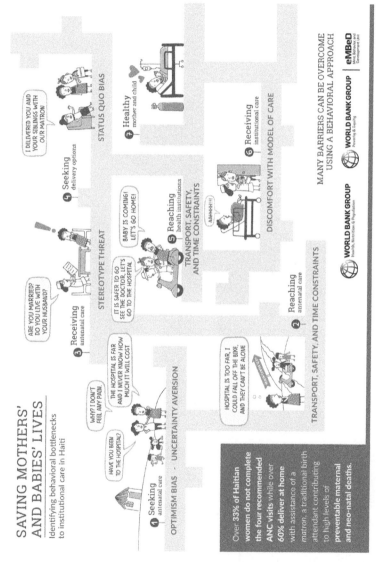

Source: Courtesy of Lorena Guedes.

implement behaviorally informed interventions and human-centered design to learn from ongoing efforts and inform our diagnosis accordingly. We then work with the teams to identify viable entry points. Are there existing programs in which we can embed? Are there upcoming components where we can inform design? The goal is to ensure that we are providing a value-added and innovative solution to scalable work, rather than creating a new, likely expensive program or solution that will be challenging for a government to later take to scale. We also always look for cost-effective methods of measuring our impact. Can we use existing administrative data? What about already-planned evaluation tools to determine if the intervention worked? At every step, co-creation and capacity building with our partners is an essential part of the process.

Of course, this is the ideal scenario of the eMBeD approach; in practice, reality can get in the way. Sometimes we – and our partners – face enormous structural challenges that may need to be addressed to make real progress. Sometimes, we might be tasked with increasing program take-up – only to determine that the program itself is not particularly effective. The joy and frustration of working with partners in the field is the reality of public policy, including varied opinions on what works and does not, what is most important, and how to improve it.

CONTEXT MATTERS – LEARNING FROM REPLICATIONS

Improving Tax Revenues

The challenges of the World Bank and eMBeD staff include not only navigating the complexities of developing countries but also the challenges of adapting to multiple contexts. Earlier, we pointed to the success of the Behavioural Insights Team's work on tax compliance as a straightforward example of a high-impact, low-cost intervention using a simple social-norm intervention. But how does something like a behavioral intervention for tax compliance look in the setting of a different country? Will the same intervention work in a different context? In multiple contexts?

eMBeD applies across every region and theme of the bank's work. However, perhaps the most illustrative case for the challenges and promise of contextual complexity is the way in which the bank has applied behavioral science to tax compliance in a variety of different settings. Take the early work of increasing tax compliance in Guatemala, a partnership between the World Bank, the Behavioural Insights Team, and the Guatemala Superintendency of the Tax Administration. In contrast to the case in the United Kingdom, tax-compliance rates in Guatemala were low, with only 64.5 percent of citizens declaring their income tax for 2019 on time. Together with government partners, who believed that social norms, reminders, deterrence, and active choice might motivate tax compliance in Guatemala, the team interviewed and consulted tax officials, citizens, and academics in order to develop its approach. In this setting, would a social-norm message have the same impact as it had in the United Kingdom, where compliance rates were much higher? To find out, the team conducted a randomized controlled trial across a targeted 43,387 individuals and firms who had failed to pay their income taxes in 2013. Delinquent taxpayers were randomly assigned to receive no letter or a letter with one of five messages:

- **Simple Reminder**: A simple reminder to declare taxes, with no information on how to do so.
- **Behaviorally Informed Design (Deterrence Message)**: Information on where to declare, the possibility of paying in installments, and the deterrence message: "If you do not declare, you may be audited and face the procedure established by law."
- **Behaviorally Informed Design (Social Norm)**: "According to our records, 64.5 percent of Guatemalans declared their income tax for the year 2013 on time. You are part of the minority of Guatemalans who are yet to declare for this tax."
- **Behaviorally Informed Design (Deliberate Choice)**: "Previously, we have considered your failure to declare an oversight. However, if you don't declare now, we will consider it an active choice, and you may, therefore, be audited and could face the procedure established by law."

- **Behaviorally Informed Design (National Pride)**: "You are a Guatemalan citizen, and Guatemala needs you. Be a good citizen and submit the 2013 annual return of income tax. Are you going to support your country?"

We found that all behaviorally informed letters increased tax declarations despite the dramatically different compliance context in Guatemala, replicating the basic findings from the field. In addition, a closer investigation revealed that the deterrence message and the social-norms message increased not only tax declarations but also the number of people who paid and the average amounts paid. In addition, the deliberate-choice message helped raise the average amount paid per taxpayer by \$17.95, or 269 percent.[6]

We have also examined the impact of cultural context on the potential for behavioral messages to increase compliance. In Poland, the bank ran a randomized controlled trial with 149,925 taxpayers from both urban and rural areas, who were randomly assigned to receive either a default reminder letter (known as a "dunning" letter) or one of nine behaviorally informed letters. The letters were sent to individuals who had declared their taxes for the 2015 fiscal year but had failed to pay what they owed by the deadline. The behaviorally informed letters included different introductory paragraphs and varied in tone, as follows:

- **Soft-Tone Messages**: These messages highlight social incentives. This included reinforcing social norms by informing taxpayers about the high percentage of residents who had paid their taxes on time. Positive framing was used to explain how taxes finance schools, roads, and safety, and negative framing outlined how those services cannot be provided without taxes.
- **Hard-Tone Messages:** These deterrent messages highlight sanctions for noncompliance or frame nonpayment as an intentional, deliberate choice.
- Some letters used a **blend** of these techniques.

Here again, the behaviorally informed messages worked. However, crucially, different messages had different impacts; women had a higher repayment rate overall and responded best to the hard-toned message. Letters with public goods messages were not as effective among people between fifty and sixty-four years old but increased compliance among younger people and rural taxpayers. Why? It is possible that youth and rural taxpayers see themselves as more likely to benefit from the public goods listed in the letter.[7] Ultimately, a key lesson here is that iteration and evaluation are essential for determining the most effective behavioral intervention for your desired outcome. This resonates well with the BI approach's emphasis on iteration and experimentation in different contexts, as pointed out by other partners (see chapters 11 and 16).

Student Learning and Beliefs

Another area in which the bank and eMBeD have explored replication in different contexts is education. Inspired by Stanford University professor Carol Dweck, the team posited that Growth Mindset – a belief about one's ability that runs in a continuum from believing you are born with certain abilities and cannot change them (Fixed Mindset), to believing you can develop your abilities through effort and hard work (Growth Mindset) – could improve student outcomes in development settings. The theory posits that once a student's mindset changes from a Fixed Mindset to a Growth Mindset, the student is motivated to engage in positive learning behaviors (studying more, asking for help, persisting longer in the face of setbacks, etc.), driven by the belief that one can always do better with persistent effort and hard work. This, in turn, may result in improved academic outcomes.

In Peru, the eMBeD and Education teams partnered with the University of Oxford and the Group for the Analysis of Development (GRADE) to create "Expand Your Mind," an intervention that focused on developing motivation and perseverance. Through this Growth Mindset intervention, students and teachers in 800 selected public schools and high schools were asked to read an essay titled "Did You Know You Can Grow Your Intelligence?" and to do a series of activities to demonstrate that they understood the content of that essay. The intervention reached more than 50,000 students in only a few months and was implemented at a cost of only twenty cents per student. An impact evaluation of the project showed an effect of 0.14 standard deviation (hereafter, sd) increase in math test scores (a 0.1 sd is equivalent to one school month of catchup in terms of test performance). Results to adjust for lower than expected take-up challenges during implementation suggest an effect up to 0.35 sd increase in math test scores and up to 0.23 sd in language, equivalent to catching up four months of schooling, with the effects focused in two of the regions where the project was implemented. This compares favorably to expensive remedial education programs that have not been shown to be as effective. Importantly, the results persisted over time – preliminary results show continued improvement in students fourteen months later, suggesting that the intervention targeted at changing mindsets has sustainable effects on learning. These latter results were found in eighth-grade students who received the intervention in seventh grade. As a result of the success of the intervention, the eMBeD team supported a second year of additional interventions to scale, expand, and refine the intervention, reaching another 200,000 students. The government plans to scale the intervention nationally.

With success in Peru, the World Bank partnered with the Western Cape Government of South Africa to develop a series of sessions and videos that would help primary and high school students develop a Growth Mindset. Eight high schools and twelve primary schools were recruited for the study; 578 high school students from the eighth and ninth grades and 558 primary students from the third and fourth grades were randomized to either a treatment group (which received the program) or a control group. It should be noted that our experience with the Peru intervention suggested that 30 percent of the packets containing the Growth Mindset materials were never received by schools (perhaps due to errors with addresses or other infrastructure challenges). In anticipation of this challenge in the South Africa program, we identified new modalities to deliver the materials. In the initial three sessions, students watched, on individual computers, five three-minute videos created by Class Dojo, an eMBeD partner, during their after-school program. After each video, students participated in reflection questions; high school students interacted with these questions individually through the online interface, while primary students participated in group discussions guided by fieldworkers. In the high schools, fieldworkers were available to help students if needed.

Students also completed reinforcement activities in the months following the sessions, in which they consolidated the knowledge learned in the video sessions. High school students were first reminded of the five videos they had previously watched; then they were presented with a new video that restated the idea of a Growth Mindset, and finally, they were asked to respond to a few questions related to the content.

Math tests and school grades were used to measure improved academic outcomes. The intervention dramatically improved school math grades: among the learners who attended the three intervention days, their attitudes toward learning improved by 13 percent, and math scores improved by 4.36 points (out of 100) in their 2017 final math grade, a result that was further sustained and improved to a 6.76-point increase in their next math grade. This is equivalent to an 11 percent and 17 percent increase in grades, respectively, showing a persistent and increasing effect. Ultimately, the average student in the treatment achieved a math grade of 45.76 (out of 100) compared to the average control student, who achieved a math grade of 39 – a very large result in the world of low-cost educational improvements. Both treatment and control groups were fully comparable across age, grade, school, math, and other tests. Additionally, we saw an improvement in student attitudes toward learning with a higher Growth Mindset using self-report scales testing Growth Mindset beliefs. All these improvements were achieved by investing fifty cents per student to implement this intervention.[8]

The eMBeD team also looked at possibilities in a different global region. In Indonesia, student learning outcomes have remained lower than those of their regional neighbors and other middle-income countries, as suggested by the results of the Program for International Student Assessment (PISA 2015). Aside from socioeconomic conditions and access to educational resources, student motivation may be another relevant reason behind the lag, particularly among poor students.[9] Data from PISA 2015 indicate that poor fif-teen-year-old students exhibit lower reading and mathematics pro-ficiency than their nonpoor peers.[10]

In Indonesia, eMBeD together with the World Bank Indonesia Poverty team utilized comic books to make Growth Mindset mes-sages as simple and attractive as possible. The "Semua Bisa Suk-ses!" (Everyone Can Get Smarter!) intervention was developed with the intention to expand our results in Peru. The design features largely the same key messages about Growth Mindset, self-belief, and perseverance as in Peru, but repackaged in a way that could be more easily absorbed by students. Four comic books used several behavioral principles and relatable characters designed in the style of modern-day cartoons to convince students of the key messages. The redesign also included a reworking of the classroom discus-sions to emphasize key messages, simplify delivery for teachers, and make the activities more interactive and engaging. The instruc-tion manuals were designed to allow teachers to deliver the sessions with minimal preparation, including multiple behavioral insights to guarantee maximum comprehension.

Working in 2,404 schools with approximately 200,000 students, we sampled across four categories of schools according to their academic performance as established by the official standard-ized tests: low-performance schools with homogeneous scores among students; low performance with heterogeneous scores; high performance with homogeneous scores; and high perfor-mance with heterogeneous scores. The results were promising. Overwhelmingly, schools complied with the treatment. From the 1,202 schools selected to receive the program materials, only 198 (16.5 percent) did not send a message confirming that they effectively delivered the sessions. Additionally, we verified that these noncomplying schools did not have different performance characteristics than the rest of participating schools before the application of the program.

Again, the intervention contributed to an overall increase in test scores. Schools that were selected to receive the intervention showed an increase of 0.06 sd on the aggregate score of the national standardized exam and of 0.08 sd on the math score, conducted at the end of the academic year. Furthermore, schools that effectively complied with the activities of the intervention presented slightly larger impacts on science and English scores, 1 to 2 percentage points higher.

The program was implemented in the two main islands of Indonesia, Java and Sumatra, which together represent 72 percent of the population of the country. In the past, the provinces from Java had tended to present higher scores on the national exam than the ones from Sumatra. However, with this intervention, the impact on student performance was higher in the schools of Sumatra, where test scores increased for all subjects covered by the national exam. In schools from Sumatra that effectively implemented the sessions, test scores increased by 0.08 sd for language and 0.18 sd for math, while scores in English and science increased by 0.14 sd. These effects represent between four and nine additional months of learning across subjects for students from Sumatra. In addition, we found high impact with low cost. As with the experience from Peru, the "Semua Bisa Pintar!" program was highly cost-effective, providing substantial impacts on academic performance at an average cost of twenty-five cents (in US dollars) per student, at the moment of implementation. Crucially, the results from Indonesia also corroborate the important takeaway that we have seen in other country contexts: while Growth Mindset can have an impact on all students, it seems particularly impactful for students from distinctive backgrounds. In the case of Indonesia, students from schools in Sumatra, with lower average test scores than those from Java, experienced more substantial impacts, suggesting that the intervention shifted beliefs about learning and helped even those who might otherwise be "left behind."[11]

Each of these interventions demonstrates the promising impact of teaching Growth Mindset to students to improve effort and, subsequently, test scores and student performance over time, and in a cost-effective manner. The results also emphasize the importance of adaptation to local contexts. In both South Africa and Indonesia, by adapting to local needs and simplifying the materials for students and instructions for teachers, providing humorous content, and introducing novel, country-specific visuals, the team was able to modify what has worked elsewhere for maximum impact. This demonstrates that successful interventions need not use a "one-size-fits-all" approach but rather can be adapted and contextualized.

EXCITING CHALLENGES AHEAD

Social Norms and Behavioral Change around the World

With success in both adapting to context and replication (of a kind), behavioral scientists at the World Bank are in the fortunate position of taking on increasingly complex challenges. One of these areas is social norms – examining how individual and societal beliefs affect behaviors and outcomes. The motivating factor behind this work is that by understanding the norms that impact behavior (the "thinking socially" aspect of the WDR), we can implement communications campaigns and other behavioral interventions – from the individual level all the way up to policymakers – that can change those societal norms and, consequently, behavior. One such project looked at the social norms around open defecation (OD) in India. The team developed a framework to measure social norms related to latrine use in Uttar Pradesh, a state in northern India, focusing on beliefs about what others do and beliefs about what others believe. The framework on barriers to latrine use was informed by focus-group discussions with latrine owners and a baseline survey that included questions about latrine access and use, structural barriers, beliefs and social norms regarding OD, and the social-reference network of respondents in each village. The team found that, while latrine use is common, and most respondents agree that OD is mostly harmful or shameful, both men and women think that it is acceptable to engage in the practice under various extenuating circumstances and expect others to have similar beliefs, as well.

The results also confirm that whether someone uses a latrine depends, in large part, on whether they think their peers use latrines and to what extent they believe that others think OD is acceptable. Initial findings also suggested a strong association of the word "*ganda*" (unclean) with latrines, with individuals generally perceiving latrines as unclean.

Armed with this knowledge, the eMBeD team set out to update pro-latrine social norms and rebrand latrines through a communication campaign. Three types of messages were delivered; the first informed people about how commonly their peers use latrines, and the second and third challenged the association of latrines with uncleanliness (*ganda*) by highlighting that latrines are cleaner and safer than OD through direct associations of latrine use with cleanliness and other clean practices.

These messages were delivered over a period of one week to five villages. For two villages, key individuals, or norm entrepreneurs (NEs), who are well connected or highly central to the village's social network, personally delivered pamphlets to households. For the remaining three villages, in addition to NEs-disseminated pamphlets, a communication campaign was also implemented to disseminate messages through community events and posters at key locations around the village. The control group, comprising about 10 percent of the households in the first two villages, received no interventions. A follow-up survey was conducted to evaluate the impact of the interventions and identify changes in individual behaviors and beliefs about latrines.

What did we find? First, "marketing" social norms can be an effective and low-cost way to raise awareness of the number of people engaging in OD. The results show relatively large changes in both behavior and attitudes related to latrines when compared to the start of the study.

Second, personalized delivery of messages allows for quick internalization of new ideas – villagers who received pamphlets from NEs demonstrated large changes in their personal beliefs about latrines. However, those who were *also* exposed to the communication campaign demonstrated large changes in their beliefs about what others do and consider acceptable, suggesting that targeting entire communities through communication campaigns may be more likely to change not only personal beliefs but also common knowledge of these beliefs.[12]

Ultimately, the project shows that social norms are malleable and, when challenged, can lead to behavior change. We are applying this work to other realms, including several projects on examining norms around female labor-force participation.[13]

Tackling Policy Practitioners' and Policymakers' Biases

Another exciting challenge that eMBeD pursues is in the area of biases that plague everyone, including those in positions of influence – from teachers to policymakers. Behavioral science teaches us that even those well informed about the research on judgmental and cognitive biases are not immune to their effects, including policy professionals. Cognitive biases of policy professionals – which may be influenced by social environment, mental models, or limited cognitive bandwidth – can thus have a significant impact on key policies and decisions. Biases can compromise work effectiveness and, subsequently, efforts toward poverty reduction. Working together with the Department for International Development (DFID), we conducted a study designed to identify decision-making biases within a sample of our own colleagues, using a series of experiments adapted to the development context to test for several decision-making areas and biases that loom in development policymaking. Crucially, we found that various biases – from confirmation bias to sunk-cost bias – could affect the decisions policymakers make.[14]

In another project, we examined how teachers' biases toward students might impact their assessment of students from different backgrounds. Teachers watched a video – where a student, "Diego," is shown in either a middle- or a low-income background; to assess the extent to which teachers use social background as a shortcut to assess aptitude and behavior, teachers were presented with one of two variants of the video in which Diego takes an exam. In the first version, Diego's performance is ambiguous. He correctly answers some difficult questions but also incorrectly answers easy questions. Sometimes he is paying attention; sometimes he is distracted. In the second version, Diego's performance is less ambiguous. He correctly answers most questions and behaves like a model student.

The team found that when Diego's performance was ambiguous, unconscious bias influenced how teachers perceived Diego: "Poor" Diego was 22 percent more likely to be rated as performing below grade level than "nonpoor" Diego, a difference equivalent to two months of school delays. By contrast, when performance was clearly positive (i.e., unambiguous), teachers assessed "poor" Diego's performance as better than that of "nonpoor" Diego. Apparently, these effects, known as assimilation and contrast effects, were partly driven by the teachers' *a priori* expectation that "poor" Diego would not perform well. Indeed, when the teachers were asked to indicate their expectations for Diego's final educational attainment, regardless of which variant was used, teachers had lower expectations for Diego's final educational attainment when they were primed to think that he was poor.[15]

What do these projects teach us about improving outcomes? Ultimately, we know we can use behavioral science to counteract biases. Interventions that encourage deliberation, demonstrate positive role models, or promote empathy can all work to reduce biases. The main goal is to inform development policy moving forward based on what we know about these behavioral biases.

LOOKING FORWARD

The power of behavioral science to dramatically improve the way we undertake policies and programs is unprecedented. By considering context, adapting to often resource-constrained environments, and thinking about impacting upstream – including counteracting the biases we all experience – development professionals have extraordinary scope to improve outcomes for society, often in meaningful, sustainable ways. In some ways, the eMBeD experience has taught us that the application of behavioral science has a way to go and great potential to complement existing policies around the world to improve development outcomes, eliminate poverty, and improve equity. This is just the beginning.

NOTES

1 Ariely, D. (2010). *Predictably irrational: The hidden forces that shape our decisions*. New York: Harper Perennial.

2 Gauri, V. (2018). EMBeDding for impact and scale in developing contexts. *Behavioural Public Policy*, 2(2), 256–62. doi:10.1017/bpp.2018.11.

3 World Bank. (2019). *Who we are: History*. Retrieved from https://www .worldbank.org/en/about/history.

4 World Bank. (2015). *World development report 2015: Mind, society, and behavior*. Washington, DC: World Bank, xi. doi: 10.1596/978-1-4648-0342-0.

5 Ibid.

6 Kettle, S., Hernandez, M.A., Ruda, S., & Sanders, M. (2016). Behavioral interventions in tax compliance: Evidence from Guatemala (English). *Policy Research Working Paper* no. WPS 7690; Impact Evaluation series. Washington, DC: World Bank Group.

7 World Bank. (2018). When context matters: Increasing tax payments in Poland (English). eMBeD Brief. Washington, DC: World Bank Group. http://documents1.worldbank.org/curated/en/472181576511865338 /pdf/Behavioral-Insights-for-Tax-Compliance.pdf.

8 World Bank. (2018). Instilling a growth mindset in South Africa (English). eMBeD Brief. Washington, DC : World Bank Group. https:// documents.worldbank.org/en/publication/documents-reports/ documentdetail/731961542391505661/instilling-a-growth-mindset-in -south-africa.

9 See Blackwell, L.S., Trzesniewski, K.H., & Dweck, C.S. (2007). Implicit theories of intelligence predict achievement across an adolescent transition: A longitudinal study and an intervention. *Child Development*, 78, 246–63. doi:10.1111/j.1467-8624.2007.00995.x; Paunesku, D., Walton, G.M., Romero, C., Smith, E.N., Yeager, D.S., & Dweck, C.S. (2015). Mind-set interventions are a scalable treatment for academic underachievement. *Psychological Science*, 26(6), 784–93. https://doi.org/10.1177/0956797615571017; and Yeager, D.S., Johnson, R., Spitzer, B.J., Trzesniewski, K.H., Powers, J., & Dweck, C.S. (2014). The far-reaching effects of believing people can change: Implicit theories of personality shape stress, health, and achievement during adolescence. *Journal of Personality and Social Psychology, 106*(6), 867–84. https://doi.org/10.1037/a0036335.

10 As part of the Agenda for Sustainable Development, the National Development Planning Agency (BAPENAS) and UNICEF have prepared a comprehensive assessment of the quality of education in Indonesia. See https://www.unicef.org/indonesia/sites/unicef.org.indonesia /files/2019-05/SDG%20Baseline%20Full%20Report.pdf.

11 World Bank. (2019). Instilling a growth mindset in Indonesia (English). eMBeD Brief. Washington, DC : World Bank Group. https://documents

.worldbank.org/en/publication/documents-reports/documentdetail
/331271576268298373/instilling-a-growth-mindset-in-indonesia.

12 Gauri, V., Rahman, T., & Sen, I.K. (2018). Shifting social norms to reduce
   open defecation in rural India (English). *Policy Research Working Paper* no.
   WPS 8684. Washington, DC: World Bank Group.

13 Gauri, V., Rahman, T., & Sen, I.K. (2019). Measuring social norms about
   female labor force participation in Jordan (English). *Policy Research Working
   Paper* no. WPS 8916. Washington, DC: World Bank Group.

14 World Bank. (2018). Policy professionals can't defeat their own biases
   (English). eMBeD Brief. Washington, DC: World Bank Group. http://
   documents.worldbank.org/curated/en/800491522426233987/Policy
   -Professionals-Cant-Defeat-Their-Own-Biases.

15 World Bank. (2018). Even teachers are bested by their biases (English).
   eMBeD Brief. Washington, DC: World Bank Group. http://documents1
   .worldbank.org/curated/en/976931525330213869/pdf/125908-eMBeD
   -Teacher-Bias-Brief.pdf.

PART FOUR

Making It Work

CHAPTER FIFTEEN

Building Partnerships for Behavioral-Science Initiatives in the Public Sector

Mathieu Audet, Emilie Eve Gravel, Rebecca Friesdorf, and Hasti Rahbar

Imagine going on a blind date. You have a rough idea of what to expect, but as the night goes on, you begin to get a better sense of this person's values, interests, and life goals. You will then ask yourself whether you two are compatible enough to have a successful relationship. What are the key characteristics that define whether the fit will be right for both of you?

In behavioral-insights (BI) collaborations, a behavioral unit will meet a variety of partners. Some are genuinely interested and invested in improving their current practices and culture. As a BI practitioner, these are the partners with whom you can build a strong and trusting relationship, allowing BI to showcase its value to the organization and generate maximum impact. There is also a type of partner that wants to "pepper" behavioral insights into a project to meet an organizational-innovation requirement. In our experience, tell-tale signs of this type of partner include short deadlines with little or no rationale (e.g., "We need this in three weeks"), a shallow level of imagined BI inputs (e.g., "We were hoping you could look over our materials and provide behavioral framing suggestions"), and persistent resistance to any changes. These behaviors are in contrast with the features of a good BI partner, one that is open to change, flexible, and eager to learn what works and what does not. This chapter will explore the establishment and maintenance of partnerships in the context of BI projects, including potential challenges and advice for setting yourself up for success.

OUR CONTEXT

Before we begin, a bit about the organizational context that framed our thinking is helpful. We are a team of four behavioral scientists working for Employment and Social Development Canada's (ESDC) Innovation Lab. ESDC is the fourth-largest federal government department, responsible for improving the standard of living and quality of life for all Canadians through social and labor-market policy, programs, and services, such as the Child Care Benefit, Employment Insurance, pensions, student loans, and Passport Services. With more than 25,000 employees, ESDC has a large, complex organizational structure with a strong regional presence from coast to coast to coast. As with many large government organizations, the need to continually innovate, change, and be responsive to the emerging needs and priorities of government and clients is paramount. At the same time, behavioral-science research methods and data literacy are not yet common skill sets across the whole organization. That said, the experiences we share in this chapter reflect the realities of our context and may not readily generalize to all types of organizations. However, much of our advice can still apply to a variety of groups wanting to conduct BI research in organizations.

The Innovation Lab was established as an internal multidisciplinary consulting team to work within ESDC and with external stakeholders to tackle difficult challenges related to policy, program, and service delivery using design thinking, systems thinking, qualitative research, and behavioral insights. We work with department experts in policy, program, and service delivery to engage with Canadians at the outset of policy, program, or service design, rather than adopting a more traditional process whereby clients are consulted *after* these have already been designed. Although some of our projects originate from decisions of senior management, the Innovation Lab also has a high degree of autonomy in terms of choosing projects and partners. For these projects, we begin by engaging with potential partners through an intake process to determine whether they are a good fit for a BI project. We do this prior to undertaking any phases of a BI project (e.g., exploration, literature review, intervention design, etc.). This careful selection process is critical to the success of incorporating BI into an organization. This means working with partners who have an experimental mindset – that is, an openness and willingness to innovate and use rigorous research methods. Such partners will give BI a real chance to demonstrate its value at the outset and leave the organization wanting more.

A FULFILLING RELATIONSHIP

What are the characteristics of a fulfilling relationship? How do you find someone with whom to thrive, and how is that connection maintained over the long term? Regardless of whether you are thinking about romantic or professional relationships, the factors that lead to success can be similar. Compatibility, effective communication skills, and commitment to a shared goal are key. Of course, just as some individuals are fundamentally incompatible, a BI approach is not suited to every problem, group, or organization. In this chapter, we discuss our experiences as BI practitioners in building successful relationships and embedding behavioral insights in policy, program, and service projects within the context of a federal government department. To make our discussion both more accessible and more engaging, we used the stages of a romantic relationship as a metaphor: getting noticed, the first dates, making a commitment, moving in together, keeping the spark alive, and moving on.

GETTING NOTICED

First impressions count, so we recommend that BI practitioners take time to develop a pitch for maximum impact because you often have only one chance.

Be Relatable

Researchers love to discuss theory, but grounding behavioral-science theories in real-life practical examples is a great way to garner interest from potential partners. Describe how others have used BI to improve their organization, balance their books, and improve outcomes for citizens. Even better, have your audience reflect on how their own behavioral biases manifest in their everyday lives. For example, why do we continue to delete unwanted e-mails from online retailers instead of taking a few seconds to unsubscribe from the mailing list? Tailoring examples to the potential partner's background is always beneficial. Talking to economists? Highlight how the 2017 Nobel Prize in Economics went to Dr. Richard Thaler, a pioneer of BI. One convincing argument is how the subtle changes advocated by the BI approach can have significant impacts on behavior and can be incorporated within existing policies and programs without the need to amend rules or regulations – and, importantly, at low or even no cost.

Be Honest

BI can be misunderstood. Many wonder whether using BI is ethical, given that it can be such a powerful tool. Does BI manipulate citizens without their awareness? It is important to address these concerns at the outset. Cass Sunstein's[1] analysis (see also the Foreword) can help to build your case. Sunstein's central arguments are that (a) objecting to nudges and choice architecture is futile because they are an inevitable feature of our social world and all governments, even the most libertarian, need to nudge citizens, and (b) some forms of nudging and choice architecture are necessary based on ethical grounds, notably those aimed at improving social welfare.

What has helped us in our BI work is to emphasize the rigor of behavioral-science research and experimentation as an approach for public-sector policy, program, and service decision making. Highlighting the inherent risks associated with the approach and demonstrating how rigorous testing is applied before scaling BI interventions can mitigate partner concerns about ethics and acceptability. To push the conversation further and ensure checks and balances, our team has recently developed an ethics framework based on the Canadian research-ethics guidelines[2] to evaluate our projects. Although this does not replace an independent review by a research-ethics board, it does allow us to better protect citizens as well as build confidence in our approach with partners. Should there be no ethics framework, our advice is to seek out someone with a background in research ethics for a project proposal review.

Not Everything Is Fifty/Fifty

Organizations often have the basic ingredients needed to integrate BI and experimentation into their work, but they may not have the skills necessary to do so. These skills include a solid understanding of BI, statistics, and research methods. You can fill the gap between desire to experiment and ability to apply BI by bringing your expertise to the table. Having the BI expertise also means that the behavioral unit must bear the responsibilities associated with the technical facets of the project while partners provide policy, program, and service expertise, and support coordination and logistics. We make a point of reassuring partners that they do not need to worry about much of the legwork. For example, the random selection of participants into groups and the subsequent analysis of the data are our responsibility.

THE FIRST DATES

Getting to know a new partner takes time and an investment of energy by all. It is important to talk about the motivations for wanting to experiment, and to know both partners' intentions, biases, hopes, and challenges in order to determine whether you share a common understanding and goals. It is also important to consider whether the organization can support testing. This section will shed some light on how we evaluate whether a potential partner is a good fit for us, and vice versa, before making a commitment.

Building on a Solid Foundation

Your early discussions should surface the elephant in the room: no BI without experimentation. Think of this as the "Do you want children?" conversation. It is best to get it out of the way before any commitments are made.

When doing BI experiments, there are unique, higher levels of initial scoping required compared to other approaches. They mainly include mindsets and access to high-quality data. Let us start with mindsets.

Partners willing to try something new will often embrace the idea of testing alternative approaches or nudges against how they had done things previously. The process of building new content is always best done collaboratively with the partner and is often an exciting part of a project. Partners bring their institutional knowledge and their program and/or service expertise, while BI practitioners bring their behavioral-science and methodological expertise. As with any relationship, both parties try to bring their best selves, but inevitably everyone brings their own biases and personal preferences. This can lead to "sparks flying" in both the good and the bad sense of the term. When things go well, the partner may be so enamored of one of the new alternatives that they start to question whether there is a need to conduct testing at all. "This one is clearly the best!" We would also be lying if we did not admit to having a favorite nudge. In other cases, BI practitioners might be underwhelmed and demotivated by the limited changes a partner is willing to test. Both scenarios jeopardize what matters most: the experiment itself.

As social scientists, we recognize that we do not walk in the shoes of those we are looking to serve. We must all be humble and approach experiments with a desire to find out what works by observing behaviors through rigorous testing. In our experience, favorite nudges are often not the top performers, and very subtle changes do not always make a measurable difference. In both of these cases, experimentation provides us with the ability to put multiple options to the test and identify the top performers or insights that enable us to move forward and continue iterating.

We also take the time to set realistic expectations on the impacts of BI interventions and emphasize the need for iteration. Some risk taking is necessary for achieving a bigger reward. Starting small is often necessary to build up comfort with the BI approach.

Project timeframes also need to be realistic to allow the experiment to bear fruit. In some instances, a waiting period may be necessary for the intervention to take effect before we measure any impact (e.g., differences in benefit or service take-up may only emerge after some months have passed).

Cultivating Mindsets with Empathy

In BI, we embrace the skills to empathize with citizens. It is also important to extend that empathy to our project partners. Specifically, we empathize with the fact that adoption of an experimentation mindset requires partners to have the confidence to admit that they may not have the answers to some of their problems. Experimentation demands that we admit to not knowing all of the answers, an approach that may not seem conducive to sound decision making. In addition, it can be unsettling for some to adopt a methodology without knowing what it may reveal about the net impact of existing processes. When the net impact is unknown, sometimes the assumption is that the status quo is "working optimally." Using the BI experimental approach to discover the net impact is an opportunity to enrich the evidence base for organizational decision making.

In other cases, partners have come to us because they know that there could be improvements, having observed repeatedly and over time that the usual "tried-and-true" approaches have not generated the desired results or impact. This willingness to come at an age-old challenge from a new perspective is a powerful impetus for change. It also aligns very well with the public-service mindset of wanting to improve the lives of our fellow citizens. This mindset is strong at ESDC, as we serve many of the most vulnerable in society. This common foundation between BI practitioners (and others) in the Innovation Lab and our partners has often served us well on our projects; we are all public servants.

Show Me the Data

Beyond mindsets, our second foundational point is about data. Many partners have an idea of the behaviors they want to impact but are uncertain about how to track behavior in a meaningful way. To conduct any BI trial, having access to adequate data is paramount. Some good conversation starters include questions about the need to observe the targeted behavior, and if so, how best to do so (e.g., using administrative data, web analytics, surveys).

One caveat is that simply having data is sometimes insufficient because of how data are stored and linked. Data in many large government organizations often serve a singular purpose (e.g., delivery of a specific service) and tend to be fragmented. For example, web analytics tracks end-users' behavior but may not be linked to rich user-level data housed elsewhere, and thus may tell an incomplete and superficial story. Some good prompting questions around data are needed to uncover potential positive interlinkages. We typically ask about the available data sources on the target population and whether they can be linked together. Then we ask about who owns the data and whether they are accessible for research purposes; additional partnerships may also be required.

Lastly, we explore whether the ecosystem supports testing. Outside of an online environment, randomized controlled trials (RCT) are not always feasible. Expertise in research design is useful to find an appropriate but rigorous approach that fits such organizational constraints.

When Do You Need to Meet the Parents?

Many government organizations new to BI and experimentation can be heterogeneous in their support for BI. It is important to understand their operational environment: Who or what else could impede the trial? For example, is there a third party involved in the project that could jeopardize the validity of the experimental design and hence any conclusion? Having a good understanding of the various stakeholders in and outside of the organization who could have an impact on the research and its implementation is always beneficial.

SHOWING THEM YOU'RE READY FOR A COMMITMENT

Integrating BI into an organization is rewarding, but it is not easy. Our partners responsible for policy, program, and services have an existing way of operating – an operational and organizational culture. The introduction of BI and experimental approaches can be uncomfortable as it introduces unfamiliar concepts and often requires adaptations to systems that were often not designed for BI research purposes. It can be challenging sometimes for partners to imagine how existing systems and resources could be used differently.

It is not uncommon to hear, "Our systems can't do that," "That can't be done," "We don't have the resources to do that," "The legislation doesn't allow us to change anything." Such comments can be disappointing for a BI researcher to hear – but do not lose hope. In most cases, these statements mean, "I don't know how to do that." This is where building a strong relationship of trust and support can make the difference between whether a project goes forward or not. Consider asking your partners to clarify the issue or offering to help clarify the issue by looking at their data. Go through the legislation with them; sometimes, this level of detail is actually absent from legislation. Offer your support to do the legwork, such as randomization. Take on as many aspects of the change as possible to support your partners.

MAKING A COMMITMENT

Once you and your partner have a shared vision, objectives, and timelines, it is time for deeper discussions about concrete expectations. These expectations need to be explicitly negotiated prior to moving forward with a project. Think of this as getting a "prenuptial" agreement that protects both partners and specifies agreed-upon courses of action should challenges arise down the line. At the Innovation Lab, we use both informal and formal approaches to support this process for all of our projects, including BI-specific projects.

The informal process has the advantage of allowing increased flexibility. You can easily adjust timelines, pivot on objectives, and adjust project scope. These adjustments can be difficult to implement with rigid project timelines and goals. The informal process can also feel more collaborative. For example, informal expectations may be enough with a partner you have successfully worked with in the past. Other characteristics of partners better suited for an informal approach include having realistic expectations about the impact of BI interventions; a desire to learn what works and what does not; and comfort with research methods, statistics, and evidence-based decision making.

A possible disadvantage of the informal process is increased risk. In our experience, it is typically not suitable for partners who are new to BI experimentation or who are significantly risk-averse. In these cases, we have found that a formal project charter signed by both partners and senior management supporting the project is helpful. The charter clarifies and solidifies the project objectives, goals, milestones, and scope. It details key processes and resources that both partners commit to contributing, such as access to data or staff knowledge and expertise. In addition, a step-by-step plan can reassure a partner that has difficulty imagining the road ahead. The charter also identifies additional parties outside the core project team who would be needed to implement the interventions (e.g., functional teams such as information technology, legal, evaluation, etc.). A charter can also prevent project failure when there is high turnover or a change in management, because it holds both parties accountable for project completion. The explicit expression of project goals and tasks mitigates risks related to misunderstandings and communication problems. However, an overly rigid charter may lead to missed opportunities and reduce your ability to encourage your partner toward more ambitious objectives when they arise.

MOVING IN TOGETHER

You have made a commitment and you are ready to start the project. What should the everyday operations of the partnership look like to achieve your milestones? What types of challenges and rewards can you anticipate with a BI project? What types of conflicts might you need to resolve? How do you quell concerns? Moreover, how do you learn from both successes and failures?

It will come as no surprise to anyone that cultivating positive relationships is hard work. In our experience, the bulk of our project work is devoted to logistics and change management as opposed to the research itself. Logistics often involve background research and meetings to understand the operational context, including data technology systems and their flexibility or rigidity, and the groups responsible for these systems, including their ability and willingness to accept the additional workload required to implement changes. For example, interventions that seem relatively easy to implement (e.g., an RCT with promotional letters) can require a set of system changes that touch a variety of groups in the organization (e.g., printing services, database administrators, processing centers). Depending on the relationships between the groups, different levels of effort may be required to convince them of the value of the additional work and testing. Another tricky situation arises when, upon closer examination of a seemingly simple problem, we see "sludge," or an excessive paperwork burden, the resolution of which requires coordination among a number of teams in the organization (see Soman and colleagues in chapter 5 for a detailed discussion of "sludge"). This type of sludge is hard to fix because teams often work in silos, and it is not acceptable in the organization's culture to interfere with other teams' affairs. However, as Soman and colleagues point out, while this can be a delicate situation to handle, it can also be an excellent opportunity for us to contribute to a positive relationship – our independence from any of the teams often puts us in the best position to generate "sludge-busting" solutions.

Just as meeting and spending time with family members of a new partner often reveal their idiosyncrasies, in a large organization there are typically existing dynamics between groups that reveal themselves throughout the course of a project. History, goal alignment, and communication abilities all influence the ability of the ecosystem to implement the BI intervention successfully. Identify your project champions: partners who are excited about BI and the value of evidence-based approaches. They can often be recognized by their enthusiasm and readiness to take action, and their comfort with describing BI and its benefits at a high level to others after the initial conversations. Leverage their insider knowledge of the organization, get them involved in planning and implementation, and get their feedback on strategic decisions to maximize project success. Conversely, identify those with apprehensions and take great care in addressing their concerns. Spend additional time explaining the methodology and expected results to reassure them about the value of BI and testing.

Because a BI approach is often novel, simply signing a charter may not be enough to give your partner the assurance they need. Your partner will need ongoing socialization about the BI research processes throughout the entire project. This means regular (e.g., weekly, bi-monthly) meetings with updates. Do not assume that your partner accepts each part of the process only to later discover that the two of you do not share the same understanding of the purpose and values of some steps. For example, the concept of continuous testing is not always intuitive (e.g., doing a second and third trial with a control group).

Because ups and downs are part of every relationship, prepare your partner for the possibility of an unsuccessful intervention or unintended effects. Ideally, you can mitigate feelings of disappointment by highlighting the benefits of learning what works and what does not. We also emphasize that because the BI approach allows you to measure an intervention's impact before it is scaled, we do not run the risk of implementing a change that, although well intentioned, may be ineffective or have unintended effects. The bottom line is that measuring the exact impact of an activity in and of itself is invaluable.

Thus far, we have focused on some of the challenges to anticipate, but the process of integrating behavioral insights into an organization's activities is also rewarding. We have found that once you have a successful trial under your belt, partners' appetite for change usually grows. When the mechanisms to implement a trial are in place, the effort required to conduct a subsequent trial substantially decreases. In addition, being able to draw causal relationships when using RCTs and quantifying the impact of change is powerful. Once partners know they can design interventions that increase effectiveness and demonstrate concrete outcomes, they will want to keep experimenting and improving.

KEEPING THE SPARK ALIVE

You have now completed a first trial with your partner. Perhaps your BI intervention showed improved performance and is now adopted as standard practice. However, there is a good chance that no significant difference was found in the trial. Now what? How can you sustain your partner's appetite for BI? Beyond emphasizing the value of iteration and experimentation, as we discussed above, we share two takeaways for keeping the spark alive with your partner: harnessing the power of mixed methods, and inspiring your partner to dream beyond nudges.

A BI intervention may not bear fruit in the first trial. Moreover, even when results are statistically significant, their impacts are often modest. This is in part because the generalizability of the evidence we use to design BI interventions is limited. BI findings have been demonstrated under the more sterile conditions of a university laboratory, often with a student population. When taken out of the laboratory, the intervention's effectiveness becomes diluted by the complexity of real-life settings. When we started conducting BI experiments, many of our trial results were underwhelming, and some interventions backfired – even though they were evidenced-based. Our experiences were by no means unusual, as Yeung and Tham discuss in chapter 16. To address this issue, we decided to get a taste of our own innovation medicine by harnessing the power of mixed methods.[3]

A mixed-methods approach combines quantitative and qualitative research. Many behavioral-science practitioners, such as ideas42, use a diagnosis step involving both qualitative and quantitative analysis prior to designing interventions. For instance, you could begin your project with in-person interviews to understand citizens' own experiences. Then, you could follow with a classic RCT testing a BI intervention informed by these lived experiences. Using mixed methods, we have gained invaluable insights about our users that would have been difficult to obtain with literature reviews. This was a game changer for us, given that our department serves many groups of vulnerable and underrepresented populations. Our interventions often target groups with urgent socioeconomic needs and challenges (e.g., poverty, disability, isolation). For instance, using our Innovation Lab team's additional expertise in human-centered design, we created a hybrid approach combining design thinking with ethnography. In one project using this approach, we discovered that the language used in a program's outreach material did not resonate with our target population's experiences and created a barrier to program uptake. Using these insights, we adapted the language of our BI intervention, a change that doubled its effectiveness in a subsequent trial. Although qualitative research is more resource intensive upfront in both time and funding, it is a worthy investment. By increasing your understanding of and empathy for users' needs, you can design a more effective BI intervention. Ultimately, you will save resources down the line because you will reduce both guesswork about your target populations and an accumulation of trials with underwhelming results.

Many of our partners who are not behavioral scientists think of BI strictly in terms of nudges. Keep the spark alive by inspiring your partners to dream beyond nudging. Chapter 2 of this book provides a framework for the different (non-nudging) roles that BI can play in an organization. Nudging is just the tip of the iceberg of what BI offers – think for example of a resilience tool to help unemployed job seekers better cope with rejection.[4] This kind of BI intervention requires inspiring your partner to think past optimizing their current processes to consider how BI can be leveraged to create new products, processes, and services. This can be a daunting task because these types of interventions often involve larger resource investments and deeper organizational changes. Socializing the value of prototyping comes into play here. Framing bolder interventions in terms of noncommittal, low-risk, and low-cost beta version prototypes to be explored, tested, and implemented in a phased approach – where applicable – can appease apprehensions.

Timing, organizational readiness, and formal support from senior management are also instrumental in helping to motivate the partner to take on more ambitious goals and follow through with their implementation. Overall, we recommend starting small and patiently accumulating evidence to advocate for more innovative BI interventions. Even though success stories abound in the BI literature, partners often understandably need to see success stories unfold incrementally in their *own* organization before they take a deeper dive. Finally, setting those ambitious goals requires cultivating trust and a solid understanding of your partner's organizational culture. This requires time, so empathy and patience are key. If your resources allow, it can be useful to spend time as an observer in your partner's group to get a more concrete understanding of their organizational culture.

MOVING ON

The end of a project is a time for evaluation and reflection on lessons learned, not only scientifically but also in terms of the partnership. Conduct a postmortem with your partner. Together, identify discrepancies between estimated and actual resource investments, team-related processes, and the quality of the deliverables. Ideally, include an independent moderator to ensure neutrality and promote a growth mindset, and hold the postmortem shortly after the project ends so that memories and impressions are at their most vivid.

Negotiate a dissemination plan. In some situations, dissemination is understandably limited (e.g., industrial secrets). When possible, though, encourage dissemination to a wide variety of channels and audiences. Stress the value of dissemination as an opportunity to gain new insights for future projects and to find new collaborators. Dissemination also fosters the growth of the BI literature; we are still doing science, after all, and we have the responsibility to share our findings, when appropriate, with the scientific community. Organizational contexts are settings in which BI principles developed under laboratory conditions are put through the toughest test of all: reality. Academic researchers need to know our results in order to calibrate or review theories and conceptual models.

You and your partner have invested precious resources in developing and testing your intervention. Therefore, you want to make sure that the findings, when meaningful, are scaled as a standard practice. This is why we do the heavy lifting during the design of the experiments in order to set up the structures necessary to run it in the real world, as opposed to testing in simulated conditions. This upfront cost can translate to seamless scaling of the best intervention. If this is not possible, then support your partner in developing the structures that will allow them to scale up the intervention. For example, provide recommendations on the technological requirements to send automated texts to users.

Make sure you put in place ongoing performance-measurement structures so your partner can monitor the effectiveness of their intervention over time once the trial is over. Take time to help them understand how the effects of an intervention may change over time because of a variety of factors (e.g., maturation, historical effects, and design contamination). Additionally, encourage your partner to think beyond outputs (e.g., number of applications sent out, number of calls answered) and to develop a multidimensional suite of metrics that includes outcomes (e.g., access to a benefit), experiences (e.g., user satisfaction), and financial impacts (e.g., savings).

Performance measurement brings us to capacity building. Indeed, there needs to be someone with adequate statistical skills on your partner's team to effectively measure performance. In some cases, partners might have the skill sets required to continue without your support. If this is not the case, teach them the basics, and direct them to resources for upgrading their skills in behavioral science, research methods, and statistics. Alternatively, connect them with talent in your networks or offer advice on how to hire for these skills. Empowering your partner to continue experimenting with BI once the project is over is key to the sustainability of this approach. If their capacity is not strong enough to pursue BI work once you leave, then your collaboration will have turned into a one-time "experimentation" with BI, and this defeats one fundamental goal of embedding BI in organizations. This is one of the biggest organizational challenges our team faces. Because we are only a handful of BI practitioners serving a large organization, we cannot remain in a collaboration with a particular group indefinitely. Otherwise, we limit our own capacity to support other groups, and embedding BI across the organization becomes an issue. To offset these challenges, we often remain in an advisory role in the weeks and months following a project.

Currently, a considerable amount of our reflection time is devoted to understanding how to encourage the organization to hire BI (and others such as design-thinking) practitioners. In the Canadian public sector, this remains a challenge because managers may not know where to start, since both BI as an approach and BI practitioners as a workforce are still relatively "new" concepts. To address these challenges, one of our next steps as BI practitioners at ESDC is to develop a framework to provide concrete guidance on how to recruit, integrate, retain, and evaluate BI practitioners in the public sector. Therefore, for each project, we also take care to document our lessons learned from each partnership to demonstrate the individual, social, and economic value of BI. With each new success story, we hope to move BI one step closer to becoming a standard approach in the public service.

NOTES

1 Sunstein, C. (2015). The ethics of nudging. *Yale Journal on Regulation, 32*, 413–50.
2 Government of Canada. (2018). Tri-council policy statement: Ethical conduct for research involving humans. Retrieved from https://ethics .gc.ca/eng/policy-politique_tcps2-eptc2_2018.html.
3 Creswell, J.W., & Plano Clark, V.L. (2017). *Designing and conducting mixed methods research* (2nd ed). Washington, DC: Sage Publications.
4 Briscese, G., & Tan, C. (2018). Applying behavioural insights to labour markets: How behavioural insights can improve employment policies and programmes. Research report prepared for the Behavioural Insights Team. Retrieved from https://www.bi.team/publications/applying -behavioural-insights-to-labour-markets/.

CHAPTER SIXTEEN

Behavioral Science in Policy and Government: A Roadmap

Catherine Yeung and Sharon Tham

Behavioral science has provided solutions to many business and policy problems. Indeed, this book is replete with success stories from for-profit and government and welfare organizations alike. In chapter 1, however, Soman cautions readers against believing that the application of BI is straightforward. Behind many of the success stories are struggles, and significant effort has been needed to overcome challenges in bringing behavioral-science projects to fruition. In this chapter, we look past the success and zoom in on these challenges.

Our partners have shared stories of obstacles faced and lessons learnt. Some of them went through a long process to get to the root cause of a problem, while others expended tremendous effort to understand how behavioral principles could be contextualized. For example, in an initiative to increase tax-filing among low-income Canadians, it was unclear why low-income citizens were not filing tax returns despite the fact that many income-tested benefits are tied to tax returns. Only after extensive research did community groups in charge of the initiative realize that low-income citizens wanted to avoid being stigmatized as being in need of government support (see chapter 12). Identifying this cause was a breakthrough, because designing interventions to address the stigma issue was key to truly helping the low-income group. If the community groups had not dug deep into understanding the root cause but had used a standard, off-the-shelf solution that had been shown to work elsewhere (e.g., a social-norm message), the initiative would have been much less successful.

The stories of eMBeD illustrate the team's daunting challenges of contextualizing and adapting behavioral-science principles in different countries (see chapter 14). The team could not implement the same interventions in countries where people and their behaviors differed, and where infrastructures, political landscapes, and resource constraints of the countries were also different. An education program that worked in the United States needed to be modified before it could be conducted in Peru, and modified yet again for Indonesia. Each adaptation was a brand-new project with its very own behavioral issues to tackle and constraints to overcome.

In this chapter, we build on our partners' experiences and insights to propose four key points that can guide policymakers and practitioners through their challenges and help them discover the best way of using behavioral insights for their own policymaking. Although we focus on the applications of behavioral science to policy and governments, we note that the insights apply to organizations more generally.

We start by first digging deeper into the fundamental differences between BI scientists and policymakers that were first identified in chapter 1. This will help us better understand the chasm between research-based knowledge and policy practice and will inform us on how to bridge it and work toward building coherence in designing behaviorally compatible public policy.

THE IMPERFECT MATCH

The two major players in the ecosystem of behavioral public policy are academic scientists and policymakers. Scientists are producers of knowledge, and policymakers consume this knowledge and embed it into policies and programs. Ideally, the two parties pursue the common goal of using behavioral insights to benefit society and build on one another's expertise by focusing on what they are best at. Scientists design and test intervention ideas, often in small-scale, "proof-of-concept" studies; policymakers make use of the research findings and decide on adoption and adaptation based on their domain knowledge and frontline experience.

However, the incentives of both players are not aligned. Scientists' careers are predominantly advanced through publications. Papers that show large effects for solving important policy problems are more likely to be published than non-novel results or small-effect sizes.[1] Therefore, in conducting a proof-of-concept study, scientists are motivated to give an intervention idea the best shot at success by selecting a sample or situation that might yield a large treatment effect. In reporting the findings, scientists tend to leave out details that expose the limitations of the applicability and generalizability of their findings. Scientists may further be tempted to position an intervention as capable of solving a grand policy problem when in reality it might only tackle the problem in some very specific contexts. Therefore, academic research findings are often "premature" – not ready to be embedded into policies *in full scale* – until they have been tested or replicated in field studies representative of a specific context.

Unfortunately, policymakers could easily accept a premature evaluation of a solution because of pressure to reach a solution to a problem. Solution-minded policymakers may be inclined to seize on a seemingly adequate "off-the-shelf" solution[2] before achieving a sufficient understanding of the true nature of the problem and the suitability of the proposed solution. They may read results reported in the academic literature without attending to research details that are consequential to implementation success. If BI is presented as a powerful tool to design public policy, behavioral scientists could be likened to passionate salespersons who promote the tool as powerful, economical, and user-friendly, while policymakers are the excited and enthusiastic consumers who begin to use the tool without going through the details of the user manual. Indeed, the seemingly good match between solution-hungry policymakers and scientists offering attractive solutions can create blind spots that lead to frustrations and ineffective use of BI, from the beginning of a BI project when a policy problem is defined all the way through to the later stages when contextualization and adaptation of BI principles take place.

THE PROBLEM WITH PROBLEMS

"If I had an hour to solve a problem, I'd spend 55 minutes thinking about the problem and 5 minutes thinking about solutions." This famous quotation, attributed to Albert Einstein, underlines that accurate problem definition is critical to finding an appropriate solution. While there is no way for us to verify whether the quotation actually comes from Einstein, we do know that many behavioral-science practitioners – ideas42, eMBeD, BEworks, to name a few – stick to the discipline of starting BI projects with a comprehensive diagnosis of a problem based on fieldwork and qualitative and quantitative research. By sticking to this discipline, BI practitioners guard against the tendency to make assumptions about a problem and propose a solution early on (see chapter 14, for example, for eMBeD's approach). We believe this insight is of particular relevance to policymakers who solve complex problems – what at first seems to be the problem is often a symptom of a deeper problem. When a problem is complex, finding an effective solution entails breaking it up into smaller problems and tackling each (or part) of them in targeted ways. This is the fundamental idea of problem definition; while the idea is deceptively simple, it is often quite challenging in practice.

Imagine a supervisor who gives their team a problem to solve. What would happen if the team tells the supervisor that there are actually five problems in it? It is not inconceivable for the supervisor to lament that the team is creating more problems rather than solving the one pressing problem. Unfortunately, teams will learn from such a pushback that they need to find quick fixes to problems. In a nutshell, the challenge of putting problem definition into practice is that there is a psychological force that sets us in motion toward solving the problem at hand; breaking it up into several problems slows things down and sends the signal that we are not making progress toward finding a solution. This tendency, known as solution-mindedness,[3] stimulates the eagerness to reach a solution to a problem "as given" without due diligence being done to uncover the true character of the problem. Solution-mindedness can be further entrenched by scientists who supply policymakers with

Figure 16.1 Behavioral science and public policy: A nudge-centric view

the quick solutions they ask for. We illustrate how this happens using one of the most widely adopted nudges – the use of reminders.

Reminders have been used in various behavioral domains across different countries. In the United Kingdom, sending text messages that remind patients of their upcoming medical appointments, the phone number to call for cancellation and appointment rearrangement, and the cost of missing appointments ("Not attending costs NHS £160 approx.") was found to reduce the incidence of missed appointments from 11.1 percent to 8.4 percent.[4] In Singapore, reminding patients that "missed appointments keep others waiting" reduced the incidence of missed appointments by 6.9 percent.[5] In medical care, reminders have also been found to improve disease-combating behaviors. A number of studies have shown that reminders (through SMS messages or other electronic reminder devices) improve patients' adherence to medication among patients with chronic diseases such as HIV, hypertension, asthma, and glaucoma.[6]

Now imagine that a member of a diabetes care team is identifying ways to improve medication adherence among patients. After surveying the literature on the positive effects of reminders (and knowing that it is inexpensive to do so), they might start thinking about nudging medication adherence by sending patients text messages three times a day to remind them to take their medicines. This sounds like a reasonable judgment that leads to the decision to nudge medication adherence using reminders, as depicted in figure 16.1.

However, a missing step in this process is an analysis of the factors that contribute to medication nonadherence. A closer look at these contributing factors reveals that while some people simply mindlessly forget to take their medicines, others might skip doses deliberatively – for example, diabetic patients may think it is fine to skip when they do not "feel" sick. For patients who hold this belief, the inconvenience and discomfort of taking medicine might outweigh the small perceived benefits of taking the medicine, and so

Figure 16.2 Behavioral science and public policy: A problem-centric view

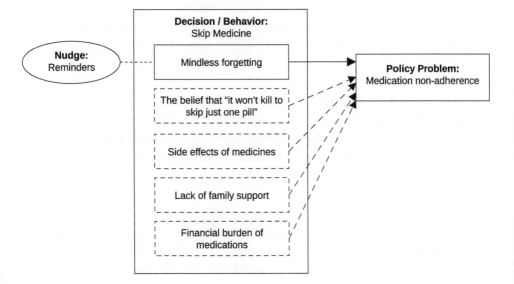

they intentionally skip some doses.[7] Reminders can reduce mindless nonadherence but not deliberative nonadherence. The adoption of this problem-centric view of medication nonadherence shows clearly that the use of reminders could at best solve part of the problem (figure 16.2). So, back to a healthcare provider's question of whether reminders can solve the medication (non)adherence problem – the answer is "yes" only if the problem is primarily one of mindless nonadherence (i.e., when a significant number of the patients know the importance of taking medicines and intend to take the medicine as prescribed but simply forget to do so).

Taking a problem-centric view of a policy problem from the outset allows the true nature of the problem to show, thereby resulting in a more robust process of finding a truly effective solution. Healthcare providers will come to realize that they must find out which type of patient (the mindless or the deliberative) is more representative of their nonadherent patient population. If a significant number of patients know the importance of taking medicines as prescribed but simply forget to do so, reminders will work very well. But if a significant number of patients hold wrong beliefs about how diabetic medicines work, an informational approach that aims at changing beliefs and raising awareness of the benefits of adherence would be more suitable (see chapter 1 for a discussion of the cocktail of approaches that could be used to solve different shades of problems).

There are hurdles that policymakers must overcome before they gain access to the problem-centric view. Their solution-mindedness is a major hurdle, but the publication strategy adopted by many scientists could aggravate the problem. As we have mentioned, scientists who publish their proof-of-concept studies might position their nudge ideas almost as a silver bullet to a grand policy problem. A meta-analysis that examined thirteen studies on the topic of electronic medication reminders found that none of the studies differentiated between mindless and deliberative nonadherence, despite the theoretical and practical relevance of doing so.[8] If scientists do not tie an intervention idea to a specific contributing factor but instead frame it as a solution to a general policy problem, we can imagine how tempting it is for a solution-minded policymaker to adopt the intervention without going through a thorough problem-definition process.

Our suggestion to policymakers is therefore to resist this temptation, accept that a given intervention can at best address only part of the broader policy problem, and commit to a thorough problem-definition stage of a BI project, one that deconstructs every policy problem in order to drill down to the very specific behavioral issue that needs to be tackled. Although a solution sounds narrow when it can only address part of a problem, policymakers must learn to embrace the "narrowness" of a behavioral solution, because specificity is the key to unlocking the full potential of behavioral public policy.

SAMPLE REPRESENTATIVENESS: DEMOGRAPHICS AND BEYOND

One of the most common questions policymakers ask when they attempt to use BI research findings for policymaking is, "Can the research participants be considered representative of my audience?" Indeed, humans can potentially vary along many different dimensions, and a policymaker's audience may not react the same way to a nudge as those in the original study. It is rare for a nudge to have the same effect on every type of person. Chapter 7 illustrates that some people are more rational than others; some are more nudgeable; while the rest are not ready to change. As many of our partners have pointed out, there is no hard-and-fast rule to finding out whether the participants in one trial are comparable to the targeted population of another; the key is to estimate and manage the uncertainties.

Unfortunately, policymakers may start off assuming that findings are generalizable at some level and that the participants are representative of the population unless they see obvious signs that suggest otherwise. As a result, policymakers incur substantial costs in implementing policies with little prospect of success. For example, after iron-fortified salt was found to reduce anemia among adolescents in several trials, India's National Institute of Nutrition and the Indian government granted licenses to produce iron-fortified salt and issued a policy to encourage broad public adoption of iron-fortified salt. Back then, the assumption underlying this policy was that iron-fortified salt is effective in reducing anemia in all sectors of the population. However, a large-scale experiment[9] subsequently found an increase in hemoglobin only among adolescents but not in any other age groups, so the fortified salt had no effect on the policy goal of reducing anemia in the general public. This finding was very disappointing, considering that vast amounts of money and resources had been allocated to the formulation, production, and public-wide distribution of iron-fortified salt.

In the fortified-salt case, the policy did not consider the representativeness of the research sample in relation to the broader population. Sample unrepresentativeness is one of the major causes of the problem of "voltage drop" – the phenomenon that when a treatment is implemented at scale in a community, the size of the measured treatment effect diminishes significantly relative to that found in the original research study, greatly undermining policy success.[10]

There are two major factors that contribute to sample unrepresentativeness. The first is the scientist's biased choice of subject samples. Scientists might seek out a specific research sample that will benefit significantly from an intervention in order to yield a more promising treatment effect (the "let's give the idea its best shot of working" approach).[11] The reason, as we discussed, is that findings showing large treatment effects often increase publication success. The bias could also be a consequence of constraints on the ability to access representative samples. For example, in Volpp and colleagues' (2008)[12] ground-breaking study examining the use of financial incentives to promote weight loss, 94.7 percent of the participants were males, because the study was conducted at a veterans' affairs medical center. Yet another example comes from the domain of pharmaceutical testing; women of child-bearing potential are often excluded from participation because of concerns about potential adverse reproductive effects. Therefore, historically, women's involvement in clinical trials for prescription drugs has been limited, and prescription drugs have been mostly tested on males. Not until recently have pharmaceutical scientists pointed out systematic gender differences in drug response, and hence the importance of accounting for gender differences in pharmaceutical research.[13] Whether the selection of a subject sample is driven by convenience or interest in securing a promising result, this selection bias may yield a particular group of subjects with different characteristics from the policy-relevant population.

The second contributing factor to sample unrepresentativeness is known as "volunteer bias." People are fundamentally not interested in participating in scientific research unless they can derive meaningful benefit from their participation – the benefit could be money (in the form of a participation fee), but more often it is the expected positive outcomes of the treatment. Therefore, people who volunteer to participate in a research project could be more concerned with the issue being studied than the rest of the population.[14] For example, people who volunteer to sign up for a randomized controlled trial (RCT) that tests the effect of incentives on exercise are likely to be already convinced of the benefits of exercise but need help to get started; they represent only a subset of the wider population that also includes people who think "exercise is not for me."

What can policymakers do to ensure sample representativeness? Currently, the CONSORT (Consolidated Standards of Reporting Trials) guidelines require scientists to report subject characteristics in their research papers, including information on gender, age, income, race, and other socioeconomic information about the sample. It is also mandatory for scientists to provide a detailed diagram showing the number of participants who received and declined the invitation to join a study, and the number of those who quit mid-way, thereby providing policymakers with some (very) basic information with regard to the unrepresentativeness bias.

However, even with such information at hand, it would be challenging for policymakers to determine the nature and extent of sample unrepresentativeness. Consider again the example from the pharmaceutical domain. For a long time, knowing that participants in pharmaceutical trials are predominately males has not led practitioners to question the generalizability of the findings to females, except when there has been broad awareness of the possible connection between gender and medication effects. In addition, several other individual characteristics – such as age, ethnicity, family orientation, culture, and worldview – might also play a role.

To truly tackle the issue, economists and public-policy experts strongly encourage policymakers to subject a behavioral-intervention idea to a "stage-two trial" – a trial conducted by the organization in the community that is representative of where an intervention would eventually be implemented. The aim of conducting this trial is to confront the problems that an intervention would have met with when implemented at scale. Many of the studies conducted at the Privy Council Office of Canada, the ESDC Innovation Lab, eMBeD, and Ontario BIU serve this purpose, at least in part. Also, machine-learning techniques could allow us to identify heterogeneity in response to interventions and hence allow the practitioner to customize interventions as a function of observable features of the respondent.[15]

THE TRICKY SITUATION OF SITUATION REPRESENTATIVENESS

The features of a situation in which an intervention is launched have an effect on intervention effectiveness. A situation encapsulates a collection of variables, so it is challenging for policymakers to anticipate whether any of those variables will interfere with an intervention.

We draw on an example[16] to illustrate the role of situation change on the efficacy of an intervention. The intervention was a pedagogical approach known as "Teaching at the Right Level" (TaRL) designed by Pratham (a nongovernmental organization in India). The basic idea was to organize children by their level of knowledge (but not according to their age) and match the teaching to the knowledge level of the students. In the proof-of-concept study, students identified as "lagging behind" were withdrawn from regular classes for two hours every day and were instead taught by paid community members trained by Pratham. The pedagogical approach was simple and the result promising. However, when TaRL was integrated with the government school system, its overall effect size was much smaller. One interesting observation was that it did not work when it was made part of the in-school effort but did work well when implemented *outside* school hours (e.g., in summer camp). It turns out that in the regular school year, there was strong resistance against TaRL from teachers and parents because of their emphasis on covering the grade-level curriculum during formal school hours. Teachers and parents were, however, more receptive to the idea in summer camps, when there was no formal curriculum to follow.

In the TaRL example, the results differed dramatically when the situation changed from the regular school term to summer camp, even though the same students were involved. Given the complexity of real-life settings, it is almost impossible to fully anticipate the influence of situation characteristics. In academia, scientists are advised to handle this uncertainty by replicating findings in different situations, so that they can explore how treatment effects vary across those situations.[17] Similarly, we encourage policymakers to adopt this strategy in experimentation.

The value of replicating an experiment is evident at the Civil Service College (hereafter, CSC) Singapore, which has been experimenting with blended learning (blending online content with in-class training) to deliver its training programs. Blending has the benefit of letting course participants cover some online reading assignments prior to the course so that the in-class sessions are used more productively to answer questions and facilitate discussion. The challenge, however, is to help participants overcome procrastination and complete the pre-course assignments prior to the in-class sessions. The completion rate was as low as 11–13 percent. This meant that a large majority of the participants would not be ready to dive into deeper discussions in class as intended.

In 2019, a team at CSC redesigned the pre-course e-mail notification to include a nudge with two key features.[18] First, the team made it salient that each reading assignment was bite-sized – they indicated the time required to complete each reading item (e.g., five minutes for Article 1; seven minutes for Article 2). This was designed to make the pre-course reading seem less daunting and hence to reduce procrastination. The CSC team also set the deadline for the online reading assignment to be on the Friday of the same week as the notification was sent out. Prior research has shown that people tend to procrastinate less when the deadline is in the same time period (e.g., the same week) than when it is in a later time period (e.g., next week).[19] Nevertheless, the decision to use the "this-week intervention" was not taken trivially, because the task and situation studied in the original article were clearly different from the blended learning task. So the CSC conducted a small trial to test the idea; the "this-week intervention" group was tested against a control group, which was given two weeks to complete the same assignment. The initial results showed that 50 percent of the "this-week intervention" group completed the online reading assignment by the suggested deadline, compared to only 12.5 percent in the control group, even though the latter had more time to finish the assignment.

In the second step of putting the idea of replication into practice, the CSC team sought to find out whether the same nudge would work as effectively in a course covering different content or one with heavier content. While the trial is still ongoing, initial findings already show differences in the effectiveness of the "same-week intervention" among courses of similar duration but different content, even though the broad objective of improving the completion of the reading assignment has still been met. The findings of these replication efforts will direct the team to the best use of the "this-week intervention." This is where and how replicating the same intervention is key to understanding the generalizability of the nudge.

FORMING AN ECOSYSTEM OF LEARNING

Making BI work in solving various policy problems is almost a moving target in the complex and fast-changing environment we operate in. There is a plethora of target groups and contexts such that interventions that work in one context may not in others, or even if they did, could evolve over time. Therefore, in our last point, we want to emphasize the importance of having a platform for sharing and learning in order to save resources and promote the generation of new ideas.

As mentioned in chapter 15, often there are only a handful of BI experts serving an organization. Therefore, the capacity for BI experts to support "non-BI" colleagues is often limited, and collaborations on BI projects may only last for a limited time. To keep the BI momentum going after a project is over, it is important for organizations to build organization-wide BI capacity. Having access to resources for upgrading BI sciences will facilitate learning and keep people engaged. A platform for people to learn about one another's BI initiatives will serve this purpose.

The Ecosystem of Learning: Aspirations of the Singapore BI Community. In Singapore, BI application to public policies is decentralized across ministries and statutory boards, with the Innovation Lab housed in the Public Service Division (PSD) working with agencies through an innovation process that incorporates BI (among other tools) in interagency projects.[20] In such a landscape, the Civil Service College (CSC) plays a unique role in curating and facilitating an ecosystem of learning opportunities across the public service. This ecosystem goes beyond large-scale conferences and workshops to include more informal settings such as the BI and Design Community of Practice within the government, where agencies get to share their projects and to hear from others in the community. The next phase of work aims to increase the vibrancy of the ecosystem by boosting learning opportunities via "LEARN," an online learning platform and an internal repository of BI projects aimed at more organic sharing and at forming networks across the public service more nimbly.

However, it is not just the platforms for learning that matter but also the nature of the content that is shared. It is easy to celebrate successes (experiments that yield positive and statistically significant results) but much harder to be open about what can be learnt from experiments with nil or negative results. This is because, in the policymaking environment, the actions of bureaucrats and politicians are greatly affected by the need both to claim credit and to avoid blame. Often, policymakers will prefer inaction (i.e., status-quo bias) because of the fear of making mistakes and attracting blame.[21] Frequently, not making mistakes (rather than gaining praise for policies done right) is sufficient for career progression.

Bearing this in mind, experimentation that includes creating a fail-safe environment is crucial to the successful integration of BI in organizations,[22] because not all interventions will be spot-on no matter how well they have been designed or how much deliberation has gone into the process. In other words, learning to using BI effectively in policy design involves learning from experiments that yield both positive and negative results. In an RCT that the Singapore Ministry of Manpower ran to test messaging that reminded self-employed people to make mandatory Medisave (health insurance) contributions, the use of infographics (in the form of cartoons) was found to reduce contributions.[23] What was thought to be an effective way to explain difficult government policies in public communications did not work in this context. The team hypothesized that using cartoons may have trivialized the subject rather than encouraging compliance.

Experiments like this that yield nil or negative results could have been readily seen as a failure, not to be shared or mentioned further. However, it is possible to frame such findings as ways to prevent potentially large investments in programs that would not have succeeded, or worse, that would have produced unintended negative results. Sharing and learning from such experiments is thus just as valuable as building on those that yield positive results, because they help policymakers to avoid making mistakes on a larger scale. Therefore, a repository of results (or a "what-works" database, as

Feng, Kim, and Soman call it in chapter 2) is actually an excellent way to bring down the costs of experimentation and to increase the chances of success.

In short, to create and facilitate an ecosystem of learning opportunities to make BI work effectively in public policies, attention needs to be paid to what is being shared (both successes and failures), as much as to the availability of channels and platforms for such sharing and learning.

MAKING IT WORK

"Making it work" is the theme of the last two chapters of this book. Interestingly, we often talk about "making it work" when "it" is something challenging. Indeed, the implementation of BI in policies can be challenging. But these challenges can be overcome. In this chapter, we discuss a sequence of things to think about that could guide policymakers through a more fruitful implementation of BI. The sequence is summarized in figure 16.3. We have gone beyond discussing the importance of making the right choice of intervention (something that our readers are well aware of) to explain how the other steps – problem definition, assessment of sample and situation representativeness, and experimentations and iterations – determine the success (or failure) of the intervention.

A roadmap of how to make things work often entails not only "what to do" but also "when to do it." Healthcare providers may order a CT scan of the brain for people who have head injuries (what to do), but most of the time CT scans are ordered only when specific signs are observed, such as reduced vision, repeated vomiting, tenderness over the skull, and so on (when to do). This is so because unnecessary tests and scans use up scarce resources. In an ideal world, more testing – assuming that the testing has high validity and reliability – can only be a good thing. However, too much testing comes at a cost. Hence, it would be helpful for practitioners to have a checklist to help them assess when in-situ testing (step 4, figure 16.3) is relatively more valuable, and when it might be skipped in the face of cost and other constraints.

Figure 16.3 Our roadmap

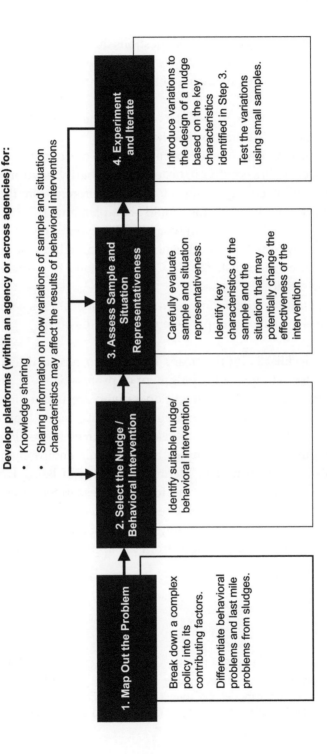

Develop platforms (within an agency or across agencies) for:

- Knowledge sharing
- Sharing information on how variations of sample and situation characteristics may affect the results of behavioral interventions

1. Map Out the Problem

Break down a complex policy into its contributing factors.

Differentiate behavioral problems and last mile problems from sludges.

2. Select the Nudge / Behavioral Intervention

Identify suitable nudge/ behavioral intervention.

3. Assess Sample and Situation Representativeness

Carefully evaluate sample and situation representativeness.

Identify key characteristics of the sample and the situation that may potentially change the effectiveness of the intervention.

4. Experiment and Iterate

Introduce variations to the design of a nudge based on the key characteristics identified in Step 3.

Test the variations using small samples.

Here, we put together a list of questions that practitioners can ask. The greater the number of *Yes* responses, the higher the marginal value of running in-situ testing of an intervention:

- Does past evidence of the intervention come primarily from laboratory studies rather than field studies?
- Does past evidence come from a discipline or domain (finance, health, education, tax payment, charity, environment conservation, energy saving, etc.) that is different from the one in which your intervention would be implemented?
- Compared with the RCT in which the intervention was previously tested, is the audience significantly different in terms of the dimensions listed in the CONSORT table of participant characteristics?
- Would intervention failure harm your audience? (Yes = there will be harm; No = simply no effects or status quo).

This checklist is by no means intended to replace in-situ testing, nor does it replace the judgment of professionals. It provides preliminary guidance for practitioners who are under significant resource constraints for running in-situ testing, face a high cost of experimentation, or need to conserve resources for testing interventions in other more complex and dynamic environments (see Soman's discussion under "Identify the Value of Being Evidence Based"in chapter 1, and the call for future research on this topic). Use of these pragmatic guidelines will increase the feasibility of using BI in policymaking, thereby facilitating a positive impact on the public and in organizations from the application of behavioral science.

NOTES

1 Al-Ubaydli, O., Lee, M.S., List, J.A., Mackevicius, C., & Suskind, D. (2019). How can experiments play a greater role in public policy? 12 proposals from an economic model of scaling. *University of Chicago, Becker Friedman Institute for Economics Working Paper* (2019-131); Al-Ubaydli, O., List,

J.A., & Suskind, D. (2019). The science of using science: Towards an understanding of the threats to scaling experiments. *University of Chicago, Becker Friedman Institute for Economics Working Paper* (2019-73); National Academies of Sciences, Engineering, and Medicine. (2019). *Reproducibility and replicability in science*. Washington, DC: The National Academies Press.

2 Soman, D., & Hossain, T. (2020). Successfully scaled interventions need not be homogeneous. *Behavioral Public Policy*. In press.

3 Solem, A.R. (1958). An evaluation of two attitudinal approaches to delegation. *Journal of Applied Psychology, 42*(1), 36–9; Maier, N.R., & Solem, A.R. (1962). Improving solutions by turning choice situations into problems. *Personnel Psychology, 15*(2), 151–7.

4 Hallsworth, M., Berry, D., Sanders, M., Sallis, A., King, D., Vlaev, I., et al. (2015). Stating appointment costs in SMS reminders reduces missed hospital appointments: Findings from two randomised controlled trials. *PLOS One, 10*(9), e0137306.

5 Chen, L. (2017). Using behavioral insights to improve service delivery. *Ethos, 17*, 17–24. Civil Service College Singapore.

6 Vervloet, M., Linn, A.J., van Weert, J.C., De Bakker, D.H., Bouvy, M.L., & Van Dijk, L. (2012). The effectiveness of interventions using electronic reminders to improve adherence to chronic medication: A systematic review of the literature. *Journal of the American Medical Informatics Association, 19*(5), 696–704.

7 Wroe, A. (2002). Intentional and unintentional nonadherence: A study of decision making. *Journal of Behavioral Medicine, 25*(4), 355–72.

8 Vervloet, M., Linn, A.J., van Weert, J.C., De Bakker, D.H., Bouvy, M.L., & Van Dijk, L. (2012). The effectiveness of interventions using electronic reminders to improve adherence to chronic medication: A systematic review of the literature. *Journal of the American Medical Informatics Association, 19*(5), 696–704.

9 Banerjee, A., Barnhardt, S., & Duflo, E. (2018). Can iron-fortified salt control anemia? Evidence from two experiments in rural Bihar. *Journal of Development Economics, 133*, 127–46.

10 Al-Ubaydli, O., Lee, M.S., List, J.A., Mackevicius, C., & Suskind, D. (2019). How can experiments play a greater role in public policy? 12 proposals from an economic model of scaling. *University of Chicago, Becker Friedman Institute for Economics Working Paper* (2019-131); Al-Ubaydli, O., List, J.A., & Suskind, D. (2019). The science of using science: Towards an understanding of the threats to scaling experiments. *University of Chicago, Becker Friedman Institute for Economics Working Paper* (2019-73); Banerjee, A., Barnhardt, S., & Duflo, E. (2018). Can iron-fortified salt control anemia? Evidence from two experiments in rural Bihar. *Journal of Development Economics, 133*, 127–46. Banerjee, A., Banerji, R., Berry, J., Duflo, E., Kannan, H., Mukerji, S., et al. (2017). From proof of concept to scalable

policies: Challenges and solutions, with an application. *Journal of Economic Perspectives, 31*(4), 73–102.

11 Ibid.

12 Volpp, K., John, L., Troxel, A., Norton, L., Fassbender, J., & Loewenstein, G. (2008). Financial incentive-based approaches for weight loss: A randomized trial. *JAMA, 300*(22), 2631–7.

13 Liu, K.A., & Dipietro Mager, N.A. (2016). Women's involvement in clinical trials: Historical perspective and future implications. *Pharmacy Practice (Granada), 14*(1), 1–9.

14 National Research Council. (2013). *Nonresponse in social science surveys: A research agenda*. Washington, DC: National Academies Press.

15 Shah, A., Osborne, M., Lefkowitz, J., Fishbane, A., & Soman, D. (2019, 25 September). Can making family salient increase financial savings? Quantifying heterogeneous treatment effects in voluntary retirement contributions using a field experiment in Mexico. http://dx.doi .org/10.2139/ssrn.3460722.

16 Banerjee, A., Banerji, R., Berry, J., Duflo, E., Kannan, H., Mukerji, S., et al. (2017). From proof of concept to scalable policies: Challenges and solutions, with an application. *Journal of Economic Perspectives, 31*(4): 73–102.

17 Al-Ubaydli, O., Lee, M.S., List, J.A., Mackevicius, C., & Suskind, D. (2019). How can experiments play a greater role in public policy? 12 proposals from an economic model of scaling. *University of Chicago, Becker Friedman Institute for Economics Working Paper* (2019-131)

18 Lim, C. (2020). Nudging a higher completion of pre-course online assignments for blended learning. *Institute of Governance and Policy, Civil Service College*. Ongoing work.

19 Tu, Y., & Soman, D. (2014). The categorization of time and its impact on task initiation. *Journal of Consumer Research, 41*(3), 810–22. doi:10.1086/677840.

20 Afif, Z., Islan, W.W., Calvo-Gonzalez, O., & Dalton, A.G. (2018). *Behavioral Science around the World: Profiles of 10 Countries* (English). eMBeD brief. Washington, DC: World Bank Group.

21 Ho, T-H., Leong, C., & Yeung C. (2020). Success at scale: Six suggestions from implementation and policy sciences. *Behavioral Public Policy*. In press.

22 Kok, P-S. (2017). Nudges: Why, how and what next. *Ethos, 17*. Civil Service College, Singapore.

23 Ibid.

Contributors

Mathieu Audet is an economist and the lead of the Behavioural Insights Research and Design (BIRD) team at Employment and Social Development Canada's Innovation Lab. Mathieu and his team have completed more than thirty behavioral-insights trials in the areas of pensions, student loans, job search, and education savings, among others.

Shirley Chen (PhD University of Alberta) is an assistant professor of marketing at the Lazaridis School of Business and Economics, Wilfrid Laurier University. Her research examines consumer judgment and decision making in the digital context and how we consume technology. In her spare time, Shirley enjoys reading and travel.

Lauryn Conway is a behavioral scientist and Impact Canada fellow at the Impact and Innovation Unit (IIU), Privy Council Office. Prior to joining the Government of Canada, Lauryn worked as a researcher at the Hospital for Sick Children (SickKids) where she examined quality of life in children with neurodevelopmental disorders. She holds a PhD in psychology from the University of Toronto, and a master's degree in educational psychology from McGill University.

Daniel Cowen leads evaluation and resource development for the Build from Within Alliance, a cohort of entrepreneurship programs that aim to help marginalized individuals and neighborhoods revitalize their own communities. He has degrees in both business administration and policy studies. Daniel is interested in developing interventions that get organizations to act more socially and environmentally consciously, building upon an in-depth understanding of psychological and behavioral-science principles that impact business decision making. He loves activities that give him an excuse to be outdoors.

Abigail Dalton is the operations officer for the World Bank's Mind, Behavior, and Development Unit (eMBeD) within the Poverty and Equity Global Practice, where she manages team operations, fundraising, communications, and strategy. Previously, she was the assistant director of the Behavioral Insights Group (BIG) at the Harvard Kennedy School, a university-wide initiative engaging faculty, students, and international organizations applying behavioral science for the public good. She holds a BA from Wellesley College, and an EdM in higher education from the Harvard Graduate School of Education.

Sophie Duncan has degrees in business administration and history. Her work focuses on food systems, social and environmental justice, and rural community development. Her previous research has been focused on Canada's Food Guide and ideas about innovation and authenticity in traditional Moroccan food. Sophie enjoys cooking, reading, and spending time canoeing, gardening, and skiing.

Bing Feng is the research associate and coordinator at Behavioural Economics in Action at Rotman (BEAR), where her work focuses on helping organizations find the best way to embed and harness behavioral insights in their everyday processes. Bing holds an MBA degree from the University of Toronto and a BA in economics from Western University. She is interested in applying behavioral economics to help organizations accomplish the desired behavioral change in their stakeholders. In her spare time, Bing enjoys travelling, calligraphy, skiing, and photography.

Rebecca Friesdorf is a behavioral scientist at the Behavioural Insights Research and Design (BIRD) team at Employment and Social Development Canada's Innovation Lab. She uses behavioral insights and qualitative-data-analysis approaches to better understand, design, and test solutions to service, program, and policy challenges in domains such as education, employment, and pensions. She holds a PhD in social psychology, with research areas focusing on planning and prediction, as well as moral psychology. She has a passion for using evidence-based practices, including experimentation, to find and implement solutions to social issues.

Varun Gauri is visiting lecturer at Princeton University and non-resident senior fellow at the Brookings Institution. Previously, he was senior economist at the World Bank, where he co-headed the Mind, Behavior, and Development Unit (eMBeD). He co-directed the *World Development Report 2015: Mind, Society, and Behavior*. He has served on the editorial boards of the journals *Behavioral Public Policy* and *Health and Human Rights*, and has been a member of the World Economic Forum Council on Behavior and the Board of the Behavioural Economics Action Research Centre at the University of Toronto. He holds a BA from the University of Chicago and a PhD from Princeton University.

Emilie Eve Gravel is an experimental psychologist working with the Research, Experimentation, and Innovation team at Employment and Social Development Canada's (ESDC) Program Operations Branch. She is also a collaborator with ESDC's Behavioural Insights Research and Design (BIRD) team. At night, she dreams of a day when evidenced-based research will be an integral part of decision making in the public sector. During the day, she works to makes this happen. When she is not doing that, she is cooking for those she loves, revelling in the beauty of arts and nature, and being deeply grateful that cats exist.

Elizabeth Hardy is the senior director of research and experimentation at the Treasury Board Secretariat (TBS), Government of Canada. Prior to joining TBS, she founded and led the Behavioural Insights team for Impact Canada, Privy Council Office, overseeing the application of behavioral science to public-policy challenges. Previously, she led the Behavioural Insights Unit in the Government of Ontario, where she was instrumental in creating and building Canada's first behavioral-science team in government. Elizabeth founded the Behavioural Insights Community of Practice in the Government of Canada and chairs the pan-Canadian Behavioural Insights Network (BIN).

Alex Henderson is a senior consultant in Monitor Deloitte's Customer Strategy team. Alex uses social-science research methods and business strategy to help organizations build products, services, and experiences that resonate with their customers. Alex co-leads Deloitte Canada's Behavioural Insights and Design Team, which seeks to elevate the application of behavioral science across the firm's diverse offerings. He has worked with clients in the financial services, retail, government, and technology sectors and holds an MSc in management from the Smith School of Business at Queen's University and a BA in government and philosophy from Georgetown University.

Matthew Hilchey is a cognitive psychologist at Behavioural Economics in Action at Rotman (BEAR). He has broad interest in applying experimental methods to understand how our environments, goals, and experience jointly determine what information is most likely to attract our attention and influence decision making. Before joining BEAR, Matt served as a post-doctoral research fellow in the visual-cognition lab at the University of Toronto, conducting laboratory experiments on attention and memory while lecturing on attention and human performance. Before that, Matt earned a PhD in experimental psychology from Dalhousie University. Outside the office, you'll find Matt playing strategy games, golf, and anything on ice.

Jane Howe is a senior manager at Deloitte, focused on helping her clients innovate and experiment. She has a master's degree in behavioural science from the London School of Economics. She works with clients to stand up innovation programs, design and scale new products and services, and measure outcomes through testing and evaluation. She recently helped clients complete behavior-change experiments in the areas of sustainability, health, and financial services.

Derek Ireland (PhD Carleton University) has been a policy analyst, senior economist, and manager in the Canadian public and private sectors for better than five decades, and is currently operating his own policy consulting firm. His research and consulting work for Canadian and international clients over the last two decades has focused on law and economics, with emphasis on competition policy and law; consumer policy and consumer protection law; regulatory reform and impact analysis; and how the insights from behavioral economics can be applied to these and other policy and regulatory issues and regimes.

Niketana Kannan is a recent graduate of the University of Toronto's Rotman Commerce program, with a specialization in finance and economics. She is interested in the application of behavioral insights and interventions in socioeconomic policy. In her spare time, Niketana enjoys taking photos, travelling, cooking, and watching basketball.

Haris Khan is an economic policy specialist at Deloitte Canada. Prior to joining Deloitte, Haris worked as a behavioral-insights adviser at the Impact and Innovation Unit at the Government of Canada's Privy Council Office, where he applied the principles of behavioral science and experimentation to a wide range of policies and programs. He holds a master of public policy degree and an undergraduate degree in economics, both from the University of Toronto.

Melanie Kim is a behavioural-insights consultant at the World Health Organization. Previously, she was an associate director at Behavioural Economics in Action at Rotman (BEAR), where she helped organizations apply insights from the field of behavioral economics to tackle business and public-policy challenges. She has co-authored white paper reports that look at consumer privacy and online financial behavior through a behavioral lens. She also taught marketing and behavioural economics at the University of Toronto. She has a joint MBA/master of global affairs degree at the University of Toronto, and a BA in international development from McGill University.

Kim Ly is a research fellow at Behavioural Economics in Action at Rotman (BEAR). She has degrees in electrical engineering and an MBA from the Rotman School of Management. She is particularly interested in understanding how behavioral economics can be applied to new product development and financial decision making and its intersection with new and emerging technologies. In her spare time, she enjoys travelling, photography, and coffee.

Kyle Murray (PhD University of Alberta) is the vice-dean at the Alberta School of Business and a professor of marketing. Dr. Murray studies human judgment and decision making. His work uses the tools of experimental psychology and behavioral economics to better understand the choices that people make. Based on his research, Dr. Murray has advised several different organizations, including the Competition Bureau of Canada, General Motors, Industry Canada, Johnson and Johnson, LoyaltyOne, and Microsoft. His two books are *The Retail Value Proposition* and *Consumer Behaviour*. When not working, Kyle enjoys opera, travel, reading, and spending time with family.

Jennifer Nachshen (PhD Queen's University; MBA Rotman School of Management) is a manager in Doblin, Deloitte's design-led innovation consultancy. Jennifer specializes in behavioral design, merging behavioral science, human-centred design, and business strategy to solve wicked challenges for businesses and public-sector clients. Jennifer has two decades of experience in applying findings from psychological research to practical challenges facing businesses and other organizations. Since joining the firm, Jennifer has worked with financial, government and retail clients, helping them to harness the power of human-centered design (HCD) and behavioral science to understand their users and to design products and services that meet them where they are.

Shannon O'Malley is a senior associate at BEworks. She earned her PhD in cognitive psychology at the University of Waterloo where she studied the role of attention and visual processing. She has held two post-doctoral positions, one at the University of Montreal and one at McMaster University, and has published her academic work in several top-tier scientific journals. At BEworks, Shannon applies her expertise in experiment design and advanced statistical analysis to evaluate solutions to various client challenges in financial services, retail, and transit.

Kelly Peters is the CEO and co-founder of BEworks, the world's leading behavioral-economics firm and one of the largest employers of psychologists in the private sector. She believes that, when applied properly, scientific thinking has the power to transform society. Kelly developed the BEworks Method, a proprietary framework that fuses behavioral insights with scientific method. Throughout her career, Kelly has overseen the launch of hundreds of field experiments and uncovered pioneering research on the factors influencing decision making, helping to close the gap between academic research and real-world applications. She has led complex innovation projects and commercialized new ideas and concepts to disrupt traditional models.

Hasti Rahbar is a senior research adviser with the Behavioural Insights Research and Design (BIRD) team at Employment and Social Development Canada's Innovation Lab. She enjoys taking a multidisciplinary approach to problem solving, combining human-centered design disciplines like BI and design thinking with systems thinking to tackle socioeconomic challenges. Her academic background is in psychology and public administration.

Sarah Reid (PhD University of Toronto), leads Doblin Canada, Deloitte's design-led innovation consultancy. She fuses sociology, behavior design, and innovation tradecraft to help clients imagine and bring to market products, services, and experiences that matter to people. Recent projects include standing up a behavioral-insights function in one of Canada's largest regulators, prototyping new ways to help Canadians get employment insurance, and standing up new business offerings in the green energy space. Her work on how to combine behavioral insights and innovation can be found in the *Harvard Business Review*, *Rotman Magazine*, and the *Behavioral Scientist*.

Jennifer Robson is an associate professor of political management at Kroeger College, Carleton University, where she teaches courses in public policy and research methods. Her research on Canadian social policy has included studies of family benefits, education savings, poverty in Canada, wealth inequality, tax policy, and the financial lives of low- and modest-income persons.

Dilip Soman is a Canada Research Chair in behavioural science and economics, and the project leader of the "Behaviorally Informed Organizations" project at the Rotman School of Management, University of Toronto. He has degrees in behavioral science, management, and engineering, and is interested in the applications of behavioral science to welfare and policy. He is the author of five books (including *The Last Mile*: University of Toronto Press, 2015). His nonacademic interests include procrastination, cricket, travel, and taking weekends seriously.

J. Eric T. Taylor studies artificial cognition – the science of decision making in artificial-intelligence systems – at the Vector Institute for Artificial Intelligence in Toronto. Previously, he worked as a management consultant in behavioral economics designing experiments for major corporations and nonprofit institutions. Eric has completed research fellowships and lectured extensively at the University of Toronto and the Brain and Mind Institute at Western University. He earned his PhD in cognitive psychology from Purdue University, studying perceptual decision making and attention. In his spare time, Eric plays board games and guitars, and likes climbing and hiking.

Sharon Tham is principal researcher at the Institute of Governance and Policy, Civil Service College, Singapore (CSC). She has led several project collaborations on applying evidence-based policy tools, including using behavioral insights, surveys, and randomized controlled trials to gain greater insights into effective policy interventions. In 2017, she was the guest editor for a special issue of *Ethos*, a journal published by CSC, on the use of behavioral insights in Singapore public policies. Prior to joining CSC, she was an assistant director at the Ministry of Education and the Public Service Commission Secretariat. Sharon graduated with a double major in geography and economics, and a BA (Hon.) in geography from the National University of Singapore.

Renos Vakis is a lead economist with the Poverty and Equity Global Practice where he heads the Mind, Behavior, and Development Unit (eMBeD). The unit integrates behavioral science in the design of anti-poverty policies related to a wide range of issues such as financial inclusion, early childhood development, social protection, health, and education. As a member of the Living Standards Measurement Study (LSMS) team in the Development Data Group of the World Bank, he also conducts experiments to improve household-survey measures of behavioral dimensions of well-being. He has written extensively on issues related to poverty dynamics and mobility, risk management, social protection, market failures, and rural development, especially in Latin America and South Asia, and has led the design of impact evaluation of anti-poverty interventions in various settings. Most recently, he has completed a book on chronic poverty in Latin America and the Caribbean. Renos has also taught economics at Johns Hopkins University (SAIS). He holds a PhD from the University of California, Berkeley.

Melaina Vinski is a behavioral-science and behavior-change specialist in Pricewaterhouse Cooper's (PwC's) Advisory practice. She has more than a decade of experience in the experimental study of cognitive science and human behavior, and seven years of experience in crafting evidence-based solutions for global companies on stakeholder engagement, reputation risk, issues management, operational model design, and behavior change. As the behavioral insights lead for PwC Canada and co-lead of the Global Community of Practice for the firm, Melaina is recognized as the firm's leading expert in weaving behavioral science within traditional problem-solving paradigms to tackle some of the toughest challenges facing business and society. She holds a degree in cognitive neuropsychology and business from the University of Guelph, and both an MSc and a PhD in cognitive neuropsychology from McMaster University.

Catherine Yeung is an associate professor of marketing at the Chinese University of Hong Kong. Prior to that, she was an associate professor at the National University of Singapore. Catherine holds a PhD in marketing. Her main research areas are behavioral decision making and consumer psychology. She conducts both academic and community-based research on the design and testing of interventions that aim at improving individual and community well-being. Her research cuts across multiple domains, including weight loss, diabetes prevention, medication adherence, transportation, and workforce development. Her research has been published in leading academic journals, including *Management Science*, *Journal of Marketing Research*, and *Journal of Consumer Research*.

Milton Keynes UK
Ingram Content Group UK Ltd.
UKHW011255210424
441408UK00003B/79/J